THE PEACE CORPS EXPERIENCE

THE PEACE CORPS EXPERIENCE

Challenge and Change
1969-1976

P. DAVID SEARLES

THE UNIVERSITY PRESS OF KENTUCKY

Publication of this volume was made possible in part by a grant from the National Endowment for the Humanities.

Scholarly publisher for the Commonwealth,
serving Bellarmine College, Berea College, Centre
College of Kentucky, Eastern Kentucky University,
The Filson Club Historical Society, Georgetown College,
Kentucky Historical Society, Kentucky State University,
Morehead State University, Murray State University,
Northern Kentucky University, Transylvania University,
University of Kentucky, University of Louisville,
and Western Kentucky University.

Editorial and Sales Offices: The University Press of Kentucky
663 South Limestone Street, Lexington, Kentucky 40508-4008

01 00 99 98 97   5 4 3 2 1

Library of Congress Cataloging-in-Publication Data

Searles, P. David, 1933-
   The Peace Corps experience : challenge and change, 1969-1976 / P.
David Searles.
      p. cm.
   Includes bibliographical references and index.
   ISBN 0-8131-2009-8 (alk. paper)
   1. Peace Corps (U.S.)—History.   I. Title
HC60.5.S4   1997
361.6—dc20   96-38656

This book is printed on acid-free recycled paper meeting
the requirements of the American National Standard
for Permanence of Paper for Printed Library Materials.

Manufactured in the United States of America

Contents

Preface

In 1996 the Peace Corps celebrated thirty-five years of work helping the peoples of the Third World build a better life. During those
years 150,000 Americans served as volunteers and staff members in
well over one hundred countries. They participated in an experience
that was demanding, often frustrating, but in the end richly rewarding—an experience unlike that found anywhere else. Remarkably,
however, there has been only a limited interest in exploring the
organization's history. Except for a dozen or more books devoted
to its early years, neither the academic community nor the writers
who serve broader markets have paid much attention to the extensive body of research material that now exists. Virtually no comprehensive effort has been made to understand the nature of the
Peace Corps, the impact it has had on the Third World, the way it
has changed those who served in it, and the effect it has had on the
United States.

The serious reader who wants to understand the organization
has few choices. In 1986, on the occasion of the agency's twenty-fifth
anniversary, Peace Corps veterans published a collection of remi-
niscences, but these were only enough to whet the appetite for deeper
analysis. A few former volunteers have written memoirs, some of
which are very good, but these concentrate on personal experiences
and provide little insight into the larger issues that have faced the
institution. Fewer than a half dozen other studies exist. Only one
of these, Karen Schwarz's *What You Can Do for Your Country*, attempts both to cover the post-1960s and to examine how the agency
has changed. Her book is a start, but only a start, in telling one of the
great American stories of the second half of the twentieth century.

This work, then, is an effort to begin filling the gap. It examines
primarily the late sixties through the mid-seventies, a period of
much greater importance in making the agency what it is today than
is generally acknowledged, even by those who consider themselves

well informed about Peace Corps matters. The strategic decisions made during those years in large measure shaped the Peace Corps that followed. Yet they were so badly misinterpreted that what was actually key to the agency's survival was labeled a threat to its well-being.

By the end of the sixties, the Peace Corps had reached the point where it needed to change in some important respects or to accept the likelihood that it would disappear. The initial idea was conceptually brilliant, but it suffered from a lack of specifics. No one really knew how to place thousands of young Americans in Third World settings and make them productive. During its early years the Peace Corps was driven by sheer enthusiasm alone. Any failures or shortcomings were obscured by a genuine and heartfelt assurance that its mission was so right and so reflective of America at its best that success was inevitable. Unfortunately, all of this had changed by the time the 1960s—begun with such confidence—stumbled to a close.

The glory days of Camelot were long gone by then. The Peace Corps was spending large amounts of its institutional energy on internal problems dealing with anti–Vietnam War sentiment among volunteers, as well as inappropriate conduct—volunteers had discovered sex, drugs, and rock 'n' roll, as had many of their generation; host country officials and volunteers alike were demanding jobs that would require them to *do something* as well as to *be somewhere;* and, ominously, a growing segment of the Congress and the public at large had begun to question the agency's reason for existence.

In late 1969, President Richard Nixon's first Peace Corps director, Joseph H. Blatchford, announced a set of policies, which he labeled New Directions, that changed its nature and ensured its survival. These policies were designed to, and in fact did, make the Peace Corps a stronger, more relevant, and better managed organization. They included a fundamental rethinking of the way the organization accomplished its mission, a greater emphasis on developing volunteer jobs more directly related to the real needs of host countries, an explicit recognition that host countries were equal partners in the work, delegation of far greater decision-making authority to the field, and the recognition that volunteers were adults deserving to be supported and treated as such. All this was accomplished without diluting the Peace Corps's wholehearted commitment to living simply, to participating in the life of the local communities, and to representing the United States in a warmer and more humane manner than the official diplomatic and military establishments could. Without these changes its tenth anniversary would have been a wake mourning the death of the last legacy of the Kennedy era rather than a proud observance of an important milestone. Far from being a period of retrenchment and discord under a hostile administration, as many believed then and others continue to believe now, the Peace Corps was renewed and reaffirmed.

Before leaving the subject of the main message of this book, it might be helpful to offer an explanation of why the others got it wrong. The most important reason is that the sense of disgrace which permeates the Nixon presidency is so deeply rooted that it affects every analysis of the period. People simply cannot believe that something good happened in so wretched an administration. Shortly after Nixon's death in 1994, it appeared that many people were willing to set aside the persistent knee-jerk reaction that caused them to condemn his administration and everything it did. But then came *The Haldeman Diaries* with its devastating portrait of the demon-afflicted president, and the moment passed. Perhaps this work will in some small way encourage others to give those years the objective look they deserve.

A second reason is that many observers relied too heavily on Washington-based sources. One cannot judge the Peace Corps from a study of its headquarters alone. Unlike most other federal agencies where the important actions do take place in Washington, the reverse is true in the Peace Corps. The real work is in the field. What matters most is the agency's activities in the countries abroad, not the often purposeless jockeying for position, the self-serving declarations, personality clashes, and rumor-mongering of the capital. The Peace Corps headquarters was in turmoil after 1972. Directors came and went with great frequency. A fierce struggle was under way to protect Peace Corps autonomy after it had been absorbed into the larger federal bureaucracy of ACTION. And there was a clash of egos between those who had won their spurs in overseas posts and those for whom the possession of a passport was a newfound thrill. Given this situation, it may be hard to accept that the organization not only survived but prospered. Yet this did happen—because the Peace Corps's vitality, or lack thereof, is determined far from the banks of the Potomac. It is important to establish this point because much of what was written at the time and virtually all of what has been written since fails to grasp this point. The situation in Washington is assumed to represent the whole. With respect to the Peace Corps, nothing could be further from the truth.

I do not mean to give credit to President Nixon personally or to his close associates for the progress that was made in the Peace

Corps—that would be neither desired by them nor warranted by the facts. But this work does contend that it is simplistic in the extreme to assume that everything that happened during their time was tainted. The apparatus of the U.S. government is so large and complex that determined administrators, especially in the smaller agencies, have far greater freedom than most realize. That freedom was put to good use in the case of the Peace Corps.

My interpretation of these events is a departure, a radical departure perhaps, from the conventional reading of the organization's history. The traditional accounts indicate that the Peace Corps was a cherished remnant of a better time under assault from the forces of evil. I was astonished at how different that reading of the period was from my own recollection. And because mine was based on experience between 1971 and 1976 as a country director in the Philippines and as a ranking Peace Corps official in Washington, I came to realize that the other side of the story needed to be told. There followed an extensive period of research and reflection that, in turn, led me to visit the Peace Corps Archives, to contact scores of former volunteers and staff members, and finally to write this book.

About half of what follows took place in the Philippines. My close association with the program there has allowed me to use examples from that country to illustrate my larger points. In addition, since the strategic changes included in New Directions were introduced in the Philippines sooner and more completely than in other countries, their impact was more visible. In all other respects the Philippine program was typical and serves well as a proxy for the Peace Corps as a whole.

In many ways this book is a cooperative effort. It could not have been completed without the assistance of many people, especially those former volunteers and staff members who shared with me their reflections, personal experiences, and memorabilia. A number will find themselves in the pages that follow; for those who do not, rest assured that your contributions were equally valuable and are deeply appreciated.

Three former volunteers deserve special mention: Rona Roberts of Lexington, Kentucky; Sister Sylvia McClain of Pittsburgh, Pennsylvania; and Patricia Auflick of Tucson, Arizona. They were all exceedingly generous in giving me access to a full set of their correspondence from the Philippines, saved all these years by their stay-at-home families and friends. These letters, written between 1970 and 1975, were essential in giving me a sense of what it really meant to be a volunteer in that time and place. Reading these letters provided a sense of immediacy that memory alone simply cannot do.

Former director Blatchford and his wife Winnifred scoured their attic to retrieve pertinent material from his days in office, material that he sent on regardless of whether it placed him in a good light. He also responded promptly and with good humor to numerous phone calls, letters, and faxes during a period of eighteen months. Terry Cappuccilli, formerly of the Peace Corps Library in Washington, personally guided me through its extensive collection of research materials. She and her predecessors systematically gathered and saved the raw material from which the Peace Corps's entire history will one day be written. We all owe them a debt of gratitude. May the library continue!

Special thanks are due to all the people in the Philippines who made my stay there so rewarding. The list includes friends and neighbors, coworkers, government officials, and the thousands of Filipinos who made me feel welcome wherever I went. In prominent places on that list are four whom I want to single out. Eugenia Jamias was an outstanding program officer who understood immediately the soundness of New Directions and put into place some of the best projects of the seventies. Her place in the personal Searles family history, however, is due to her wonderfully generous offer to care for Samantha (our cat) while we gallivanted through Asia. Modesto de Jesus was the first person I hired in the Philippines. He proved an excellent choice, serving ably for many years as the director of administration. After retiring he continued to serve the Peace Corps and his country by administering an educational scholarship program in the Philippines funded by former volunteers and staff. Elena Borneo—Mrs. B to one and all—became a legend in her own time. She gave solid guidance and friendship to two decades of volunteers and country directors. Helen Bolinas possessed that special knack that only a few have. She set a work standard that few could match, and displayed a natural grace that made each day a better one.

Jamias continues to work in the field of Third World development from her homebase in Manila. De Jesus died in 1994. His son now administers the scholarship fund. Borneo and Bolinas and their families emigrated to the United States to become part of the fast-growing, very welcome, 1.5 million-strong Filipino-American community.

Finally, to my family I reserve my greatest appreciation—for their willingness to pack up and follow me around the country and around the world as I searched for that special something that was always just beyond the horizon. To them I dedicate this book.

The End of the Beginning

1

If ever there was a time for the Peace Corps, it was at the beginning of the decade that a now forgotten optimist christened 'The Soaring Sixties.' The nation as a whole had emerged triumphant and nearly unscathed from World War II, at least compared with her allies and former enemies. The previous decade had been a period of unparalleled prosperity. The Korean conflict had caused a small but quickly forgotten ripple on the country's otherwise tranquil surface, as had Senator Joseph McCarthy's witch hunts. But the prevailing mood was upbeat. Many who would have been fortunate in an earlier generation to finish high school had become the proud possessors of university degrees. There was little or no inflation; home ownership, the ultimate expression of the American dream, had become ever more affordable; the dreadful specter of polio had disappeared; and the word *togetherness* had been coined to describe every family's goal. God was in his heaven and all was right with the world, or so it seemed to those fortunate enough to live in the United States.

As David Halberstam said in his memoir of the 1950s, "In that era of general good will and expanding affluence, few Americans doubted the essential goodness of their society. . . . They were optimistic about the future, . . . [and they] trusted their leaders to tell the truth [and] make sound decisions."[1] As the fifties gave way to the sixties, the level of confidence and sense of security that existed in the country were unique in American history, especially among the young, who knew nothing of the Great Depression and little of World War II. They were, as one of them wrote, ready, willing, and able "to express [their] faith that those . . . who [had] been fortunate . . . [would] want to apply [their] knowledge through direct participation in the underdeveloped communities of the world."[2]

With hindsight one can see obvious and great flaws in this picture of life in the United States. A significant minority of the nation's citizens were socially, economically—and in many states legally—

reduced to second-class status. Pockets of urban and rural poverty equaling that of the Depression dotted the landscape from New England down the Appalachians and across the Old South. The threat of nuclear disaster was ever present as the cold war's participants periodically rattled their sabers. And, as social critics bemoaned, the society was conformist, complacent, and consumption-driven to a degree that was certainly a cause for concern if not downright dangerous.[3] In assessing the 1950s, a recent scholar summarized the criticism aimed at it by declaring that "Americans enjoyed the wealthiest society in history, yet they were selling their collective soul, trading the nation's moral fiber for easy white-collar jobs that bought suburban homes and new cars."[4]

But these were the concerns of the few who lamented the nation's lack of purpose, not of the many who were delighted with the abundance at their fingertips. The latter group was ready to agree with the forecast made by *Life* magazine in its last issue of the 1950s that the country faced "a newfound good life coming out of our newfound leisure." The nation was moving inexorably toward a "life of plenty," its future was assured, its collective wisdom held the key to meaningful existence, and it was ready to soar as no other nation ever had.[5]

In such a climate it is little wonder that the charismatic new president, John F. Kennedy, was greeted enthusiastically when he called for the creation of a volunteer service organization that would allow young Americans to share their lives, their innate American ability to get things done, and their faith in the future with others less fortunate. The fact that the sharing would involve exciting travel to exotic places made the president's call even more appealing, and the favorable responses were counted in the tens of thousands.

The history of the early days of the Peace Corps has been told many times in books, journals, and magazine feature articles. Among the best of the books are Gerard T. Rice's *The Bold Experiment: JFK's Peace Corps*, Coates Redmon's *Come as You Are: The Peace Corps Story*, Brent Ashabranner's *A Moment in History: The First Ten Years of the Peace Corps*, chapters 8 and 9 of Harris Wofford's *Of Kennedys and Kings: Making Sense of the Sixties*, and Kevin Lowther and C. Payne Lucas's *Keeping Kennedy's Promise*. These accounts trace the Peace Corps's origins to the early morning hours of 14 October 1960, when candidate John Kennedy delivered an impromptu speech to ten thousand University of Michigan students and struck campaign gold. Several of Kennedy's aides—and the candidate himself—had from time to time discussed the political appeal of a pledge to create a youth organization that would do some sort of public service at home or abroad.[6] (Coincidentally, the Nixon campaign was considering making the same pledge, and each side was fearful that the other would take the plunge first.)[7] When Kennedy found himself at two o'clock on a frosty October morning in Michigan facing a totally unexpected crowd of cheering students, he challenged his audience to make the world a better place. Harris Wofford quotes Kennedy as having asked, "How many of you are willing to spend ten years in Africa or Latin America or Asia working for the U.S. and working for freedom? How many of you . . . are willing to spend your days in Ghana? . . . in the foreign service? . . . traveling around the world? On your willingness to do that . . . will depend the answer whether we as a free society can compete."[8] One of the students, Alan Guskin, remembered a quarter century later that "Kennedy's words . . . seemed to present to students on our campus a way to live our idealism, an opportunity to commit ourselves to the service of others."[9] The immediate response to Kennedy's off-the-cuff remarks was a rousing ovation from the students.

Wofford, then a Kennedy campaign aide, has called the groundswell of enthusiasm that swept the idea along "almost a case of spontaneous combustion." Sensing this, the Kennedy people made the program a centerpiece of a major foreign policy speech—which was widely acclaimed—and featured it in virtually every campaign stop from then until the election.[10] In the end, Kennedy won by less than 120,000 votes, a number that surely could have been the result of the immense appeal of a campaign pledge that no one had meant to make. When the new president in his inaugural speech demanded that Americans "ask not what your country can do for you, ask what you can do for your country," young American men and women by the thousands knew the answer: join the Peace Corps.

President Kennedy's choice of his brother-in-law and campaign lieutenant, Sargent Shriver, as the first director of the new agency was an inspired one. Reading the accounts of those who worked closely with him, one has the impression that Shriver was larger than life. Wofford wrote that "participating in the making of the Peace Corps [with Shriver] was an intoxicating and illuminating experience. [He] was not a tidy administrator, but he was a great executive. He did not delegate powers through an orderly chain of command, but he empowered people. He released their energies, backed their efforts, and drew on their insights. Wives of staff men tended to be jealous because Shriver harnessed their husbands' energies and loyalties—and weekends."[11]

Coates Redmon, one of the few women to participate in the organization's founding, recalled in *Come as You Are* that there were "two things that the senior staff of the Peace Corps dreaded most: One was not being asked to accompany Shriver on an important overseas trip; the other was being asked." Shriver was indefatigable and known for his all-work-and-no-play-or-even-sleep schedules. His day stretched from long before sunrise to well after dark; he would eat anything, go anywhere, meet anyone; he thrived on physical discomfort and would even seek out situations where an element of real danger might exist. All this while expressing his wonder that his much younger colleagues could not keep up.[12]

Lawrence Fuchs, the first Peace Corps country director in the Philippines, said, "Shriver was imbued with a missionary zeal to advance human understanding everywhere in the world."[13] Kevin Lowther and C. Payne Lucas, two veterans of the agency's first decade, wrote a critical appraisal of the Peace Corps in *Keeping Kennedy's Promise.* Although pointing out weaknesses and areas where improvement was needed, they described Shriver as one who "extended his personable style to the volunteers as well. In a very real sense he idolized them, and they in turn regarded him with awe and respect. . . . [Shriver] was the incorrigible optimist. He looked for the best in people. He expected volunteers and staff alike to meet the Peace Corps's unusually high standards. Shriver did not look for trouble; he looked for results."[14]

As Shriver learned, it was far easier to announce the conception of the Peace Corps than it was to deliver it. Various executive branch departments had areas of responsibility that they guarded jealously, even against their political allies. This was especially true at the State Department, which had a long established primacy in everything concerning foreign relations. The department was aghast at the thought of thousands of 'college kids' roaming about the world unsupervised, untrained in the niceties of diplomacy, and speaking out in ways sure to upset the delicate task of foreign relations. The department's solution was to recommend that the agency occupy an obscure corner of a new division devoted to coordinating all American foreign assistance programs. Called the United States Agency for International Development (USAID) and going through its own birth pangs, this new agency could be counted on to slow the Peace Corps's pace and potential for harm. Any Peace Corps proposal first would have to work its way through its own management structure, then step by step through that of USAID, the State Department, and—if the proposal were truly innovative or contentious—through the White House bureaucracy as well. Whatever merit the proposal had in the beginning would surely be snuffed out in the process.

The Peace Corps leadership, even with Shriver's drive and family contacts, was no match for the experience and authority of the State Department and its legions of management experts. A task force charged with organizing the nation's foreign assistance program sided with State, and—to the horror of the Peace Corps faithful—the president sided with the task force. Into this situation came an unlikely hero, Vice President Lyndon Baines Johnson. Johnson had fought Kennedy fiercely for the Democratic presidential nomination and lost somewhat ungraciously. In a political balancing act, candidate Kennedy had selected the senator from Texas to be his running mate, and now the two men were struggling to sort out their working relationship. Among the tasks Kennedy assigned to Johnson was the chairmanship of the Peace Corps National Advisory Council. Johnson had brought to the new administration one of his Senate aides, Bill Moyers, who, in turn, wrangled a transfer to the Peace Corps, where he played an important role in its formation.

With the Peace Corps's bureaucratic fate virtually sealed under the aegis of USAID, Moyers went to Johnson and begged his intercession with the president to permit the new agency a large measure of independence. This Johnson did with great success.[15] Although the details of what happened in Johnson's meeting with Kennedy are not public, the outcome certainly is. As the *New York Times* reported on 4 May 1961, "Peace Corps Wins Fight for Autonomy."[16] As embodied in the Peace Corps Act, sec. 4(c)(3), the final resolution gave the Peace Corps director the power to "promulgate such rules and regulations as he may deem necessary or appropriate," and it gave the secretary of state responsibility only for ensuring that Peace Corps programs "are effectively integrated both at home and abroad and [that] the foreign policy of the United States is best served thereby." In practice, these somewhat contradictory provisions were interpreted as giving the Peace Corps director ample latitude for independent movement.

Although the president had given the Peace Corps official standing by executive order early in his first year, it was still necessary for the new organization to win congressional approval.[17] The masterly way in which Shriver and Moyers courted and converted the nation's congressmen and senators is told both in Rice's scholarly study of the organization's early years and in Redmon's personal memoir covering the same period.[18] The outcome—passage by large majorities in both houses—masks an enormous effort to convince the Congress that large numbers of mainly young Americans could indeed do good in the Third World. The Peace Corps had to counter the opposition of people who were against foreign assistance in any form as well as those who, although generally in favor of sending American aid abroad, had genuine concerns about the usefulness of largely untrained, untried, and unknown volunteers. Both conservatives and liberals scoffed at Kennedy's Kiddy Korps: Senator J. William Fulbright, in many other respects a champion of a responsible American presence abroad, regularly questioned the wisdom of the Peace Corps and moved to limit its funding. Congressman Otto Passman, as powerful, egomaniacal, and destructive a congressman as ever held office, began a fifteen-year campaign to destroy the organization. (Passman remained the Peace Corps's nemesis regardless of the political affiliation of the Peace Corps director. In the fall of 1974, after a three-year stint as country director in the Philippines, I was a nonparticipating observer at a congressional hearing chaired by Passman at which his conduct nearly destroyed my faith in a political system that would permit such a man to exercise so much power.)[19]

Fortunately, lawmakers like these were a distinct minority. Far more shared the Shriver vision or at least sensed the high degree of enthusiasm that existed in their home districts for the idea. When President Kennedy weighed in with a press conference statement praising the Peace Corps and calling for congressional passage, victory was assured.[20] On 22 September 1961, he signed the Peace Corps Act in the Oval Office surrounded by a throng of well-wishers, including a beaming Sargent Shriver and a proud honorary founder, Hubert Humphrey.

The Peace Corps Act declares that the policy of the United States is "to promote world peace and friendship through a Peace Corps which shall make available to interested countries and areas men and women of the United States qualified for service abroad and willing to serve, under conditions of hardship if necessary, to help the peoples of such countries and areas in meeting their needs for trained manpower, and to help promote a better understanding of the American people on the part of the peoples served and a better understanding of other peoples on the part of the American people."

That Declaration of Purpose has remained unchanged for more than thirty-five years and has defied numerous attempts at simplification and restatement. It is one of those wonderfully broad statements of principle, not unlike the Constitution, that provide both fundamental direction and considerable flexibility. From the earliest days there has been general agreement that the mission of the Peace

Corps is "to promote world peace and friendship." That agreement, however, has not been extended to include the three goals through which the mission is to be achieved.

Goal One (to use Peace Corps terminology) is concerned with "meeting . . . needs for trained manpower," clearly an objective with economic and social development implications. Goal Two and Goal Three are concerned with "promot[ing] a better understanding" between Americans and the peoples of the host countries, clearly an objective with cross-cultural implications. Peace Corps volunteers and administrators alike have spent countless days, weeks, and months trying to determine the appropriate balance between Goal One and Goals Two and Three. In some respects the balance of this book is an attempt to show that such a debate is time wasted. Both are essential. Goal One cannot stand alone; the Peace Corps must always be a people-to-people program that operates and exists among the people of the host country. Goals Two and Three also cannot stand alone because both host country needs and the American character demand that the Peace Corps *do something* as well as *be somewhere*.[21] Brent Ashabranner, a former country director and Peace Corps deputy director, summarized the situation almost perfectly in 1971 when he wrote, "Volunteers [must have] a real job and the experience or training to do it. They give him a credibility overseas that he can not have without them. But the way he works with people, the way he makes them feel about themselves, the ideas and values he both imparts and receives through his associates—these are the important elements in Peace Corps service."[22]

Beyond the essential elements of the organizational mission, the act bestows upon the Peace Corps director, through the president, broad powers to recruit, train, deploy, maintain, and terminate "qualified citizens and nationals of the United States (referred to . . . as 'volunteers')." The act declares that volunteers are not to be "deemed officers or employees" of the United States, are not required to pass any "political test," and may be appointed "volunteer leaders" with supervisory or other special duties.[23] The act authorizes the hiring of American and host country nationals to perform management functions both abroad and in the United States. From the very beginning, Peace Corps administrators learned to interpret the act creatively, and it is a rare proposal that is turned down for failure to conform to the requirements of the Peace Corps Act.

The leaders of the Peace Corps made an early decision that they needed large numbers of volunteers in the field if the program was to make an impact. Large numbers were necessary both from the stand-point of doing something worthwhile in host countries—the Peace Corps wanted to be a player in foreign assistance circles—and also from the standpoint of building awareness of and support for the program in the United States.[24] Several of Shriver's advisors had rec-ommended a much more cautious approach involving a year or two of testing and evaluation to determine how the organization should function.[25] But this advice was rejected, much to the regret of those who later decried 'the numbers game,' and the far more exciting credo of learning by doing became the agency's operating philosophy. Larry Fuchs, in recalling his first day as a country director, described the difficulty he had in answering the question, What does the Peace Corps hope to accomplish in the Philippines? "What could I tell them?" he remembers thinking. "In five weeks 128 volunteers would report for action . . . [and be] assigned to remote villages to perform as 'educational aides,' a title and concept completely new to Filipinos, volunteers and myself."[26]

Following several whirlwind trips in 1961, Shriver and his team had signed up a number of Third World countries willing to re-quest volunteers. (In Peace Corps parlance the verb *request* is always used rather than the verb *accept* because the former reinforces the idea that host countries play an active role in seeking the volun-teers.) Ghana, Tanzania, Ethiopia, the Philippines, Thailand, India, Bolivia, Peru, and Brazil were among those on board by the end of the year.[27] Some of the countries were enthusiastic in their acceptance, some wary, and some calculating. The Philippines, for example, had a long and generally satisfactory experience with Americans serv-ing as teachers throughout the countryside. The country welcomed the prospect of more. In India Prime Minister Jawaharlal Nehru predicted that any American volunteers sent to India would "learn a good deal" from the experience, and he cautiously committed him-self and his country to receiving twenty or twenty-five of what he feared might be a new breed of imperialists. Other potential host countries concluded that the Peace Corps was important to the new American president and that requesting a few volunteers might just be the key to unlocking the American foreign aid treasure chest. Whatever the motivation, well before the Peace Corps's first an-niversary it had requests sufficient to require three thousand vol-unteers.[28]

In the meantime, applications had been pouring into the Peace Corps headquarters. From these thousands of applications the Peace Corps accepted perhaps one in five, using selection procedures that were lengthy, tedious, seemingly scientific, and probably badly flawed. Julius Amin, a member of the training staff for the first contingent of volunteers bound for his country, Cameroon, has provided an excellent summary of the selection process used in 1962. He describes it as one "designed to weed out as many applicants as possible."[29]

The fortunate few who survived the initial screening were sent to training camps administered by American universities, staffed by prominent academics, and run as if the trainees were destined to climb Mount Everest while simultaneously discussing deep philosophical issues in an obscure foreign language and displaying good manners, an outgoing personality, a seriousness of purpose, a commitment to American values—and, of course, the qualities that would make for a good volunteer. The fact that no one knew what these qualities were or how to determine whether they were present in any given individual did not prevent the selection boards from 'deselecting' a significant minority of the trainee population.[30] As Wofford remembered, it sometimes seemed as if selection officers expected that "the ideal candidate for the Peace Corps must have the patience of Job, the forbearance of a saint, and the digestive system of an ostrich" in order to pass their scrutiny.[31]

The Peace Corps leadership had an unbounded faith in the ability of America's best—the young men and women it had selected, trained, and sent abroad—to do good. This faith grew out of the wonderful optimism and confidence of the Camelot years, the belief that the American way was so right and so unique that simply sharing it with others would make those others better and that there was an innate capacity that permitted Americans to face even the most intractable problems and find creative ways to solve them. Volunteers were expected not only to carry out the requirements of their assigned jobs but also to initiate 'secondary projects' in the evenings and on weekends that would provide their hosts with a bonus.[32]

During much of the 1960s most Peace Corps volunteers worked in one of two broad programming areas, education or general community development, the latter being a catchall phrase covering all those activities that make communities function more effectively and more efficiently. Education volunteers taught English, math, and science in the high schools and colleges and all subjects at the primary level. They provided a classroom teacher where otherwise there would have been none, or they assisted the regular teacher if one was already in place. After school they coached sports teams, organized cooperatives, tended school gardens, taught adult literacy classes, and lived among their students and their families. In 1965 there were five hundred Peace Corps volunteers teaching throughout Ethiopia alone. Hundreds more were working in other African countries, in the Philippines, on several Caribbean islands, in Thailand, and, as the years passed, in dozens of other countries throughout the Third World.

If education was the perfect assignment for volunteers, community development was a close second. The needs of Third World communities, especially in the vast rural areas beyond the capital cities, were immense. Moreover, many of them were of a type that could be solved simply by the application of basic science and technology. The problems of contaminated water—or in some desert countries the very lack of water itself—could be overcome by digging the right kind of well. The multitude of problems caused by the haphazard disposal of human and animal waste could be reduced sharply by using properly constructed latrines and by building enclosures for domesticated farm animals. Groups of families could be brought together in cooperative gardening, marketing, and community action efforts. Community development could be aimed at alleviating the physical conditions caused by poverty as well as demonstrating that people working together could accomplish much that needed doing. The volunteer would provide the spark, the example, the encouragement, and the leadership needed to set the program in motion. Following the start-up period, program management would be turned over to the community.

While smaller groups of volunteers would work in programs that covered the spectrum of Third World needs, the education and community development volunteers would capture the attention of most observers, and they turned out to be a public relations dream come true. From its inception the Peace Corps was a favorite with the press, which documented its every move through the Shriver years and beyond. The *New York Times*, the *Washington Post*, *Time*, *Life*, the *Saturday Evening Post*, and even the *Wall Street Journal* paid homage to the Peace Corps vision and its fine volunteers. Peace Corps news appeared on the front page. On rare occasions the coverage had a negative slant, as in the overblown incident of a mildly critical postcard mailed from a volunteer in Nigeria. Volunteer Margery Michelmore, newly arrived, wrote home describing what for her was a novel scene—a man urinating in public. Unfortunately, the postcard, which had been dropped on the street and recovered by a Nigerian with anti-American feelings, became a *cause célèbre* that nearly forced the agency to leave the country.[33] Michelmore was brought home in disgrace. Similarly, the acceptance for training of a young man who had publicly and noisily challenged Jim Crow laws in Florida and campaigned for nuclear disarmament annoyed many southern politicians and Republican conservatives. They threatened to end support for the organization unless he was dismissed.[34]

Most press coverage, however, was salutary almost to a fault. Historian William Manchester concluded that in the early 1960s "the liberal hero of the hour, who in the 1930s had been the angry young workman, in the 1940s the GI, and in the 1950s the youth misunderstood by his mother, had become . . . the dedicated Peace Corpsman battling hunger, disease—and communism—with tools of peace."[35] Time Inc., a publisher with a special knack for reflecting the nation's mood, was right in step with that assessment. In 1964 its Time-Life Books division ended its twelve-volume, highly popular series *The Life History of the United States* with a chapter devoted to answering two questions: "What is the meaning of the remarkable tale [i.e., the history of the United States] which breaks off at this point? And what hint does our past offer about the chapters of America's story that will come next?" The author concludes that our past shows that the nation has met and overcome the most difficult of obstacles, whether natural or man-made, and that it has the capacity to continue doing so. He declares that "our tried institutions and the magic of our lofty ideals" will be able to overcome whatever obstacles the future holds. Illustrating this final point is a full-page picture of a Peace Corps trainee. Time Inc. sees in the steady, determined gaze of this handsome young man "the deep vein of generosity and idealism which links America's past with the world's future."[36] The fate of the nation and the world is in the reliable hands of the Peace Corps and its volunteers.

Time Inc. was accurately mirroring the opinion of the American public. Gerard Rice reports that successful Peace Corps applicants left their small towns across America "with brass bands playing and [their] picture on the front page of the local newspaper."[37] Letters home were avidly awaited by family and friends and taken to schools for 'show and tell' by younger siblings. Sargent Shriver became a household word not because he was a Kennedy in-law but because he was the personification of the Peace Corps. This popular enthusiasm eventually spilled over to politicians of all stripes. Congressmen and senators tripped over each other in their haste to visit volunteers on-site and be photographed with them. Later they returned to

Washington to give the Peace Corps's annual appropriations legislation overwhelming votes of approval.

The first five years were a time of frenetic activity at home and abroad for those involved in taking a formless idea and giving it shape and substance. The pace was exhilarating, demanding, and rewarding beyond what most people can imagine. At times the entire effort seemed to be driven by sheer enthusiasm alone. Yet out of it all came an institution that was a widely admired fixture of the American presence in dozens of Third World countries by the mid-1960s. Those of us who came to the Peace Corps in later years were never truly accepted by that original band of men—and a few women—who were there at the creation. They looked upon their experience as one that was unique, one that could not be duplicated by those who came later. It was theirs and theirs alone. One could sense that they begrudged our claims to membership of an equal standing. Such a reaction is certainly understandable. The act of creation is a once-in-a-lifetime event. But, as we who came later discovered, the basis for their claim to distinction was a bit premature. The act of creation was far from complete. Many a thorn remained among the roses, and these were demanding attention.

It would be uncharitable in the extreme to lay the blame for the problems that beset the Peace Corps during the second half of the 1960s solely at the doorstep of its founders. They had accomplished a great deal; in fact, without their vision, energy, and devotion to the cause, the Peace Corps would never have seen the light of day. Some of the problems to be faced were the natural consequences of the decision to learn by doing, to make the *number* of volunteers in the field a major indicator of success, and to reshape the program as experience dictated. Unfortunately, when the time came to make changes, the Peace Corps was not up to the task. In 1964 President Johnson had given Sargent Shriver the additional responsibility for Johnson's War on Poverty, appointing him head of the new Office of Economic Opportunity. Johnson asked Shriver to do for America's poor what he had done for the world's developing nations, but he did not relieve Shriver of his Peace Corps duties. As Lowther and Lucas point out, "At the very moment Shriver should have been making an intensive reassessment after four hectic years of unrestrained growth, the Peace Corps seemed rudderless."[38] Wofford remembered that "the Peace Corps . . . tried to [administer] the agency . . . by a kind of Quaker consensus among the several associate directors, and the general counsel [and] frequently . . . a much larger circle of staff colleagues."[39] Anyone who has ever attempted to manage in this fashion knows that the result is likely to lead to much talk and little action. Not until early 1966 would a new director be selected—nearly two years after Shriver had begun to devote most of his energies to the War on Poverty.[40]

Another set of problems facing the organization at this time was the result of circumstances well beyond the Peace Corps's control: Wrenching changes were reshaping the society from which the Peace Corps had emerged, and there was no escaping the consequences. The optimism and promise that marked the beginning of the decade disintegrated in a remarkably short time. The assassination of John Kennedy in 1963 is usually fixed as the event that marked the beginning of a mighty upheaval in American social and cultural values. Then came a growing awareness of the struggle for civil rights, which had been brewing since the late 1950s, accompanied by racial, generational, and sectional divisions. Poverty was discovered in the midst of the plenty that had characterized the popular version of life in postwar America. The Vietnam War and the draft added fuel to the fire. Out of nowhere, it seemed, the United States found itself sending hundreds of thousands of conscripts to fight a war for reasons that could not withstand close scrutiny. The nation had a selective service system that sent the poor, the uneducated, and the uninfluential to war whereas their more fortunate compatriots went to college.

Could it be, people asked, that America did not have the answers to the world's problems after all? And where were the justice and righteousness that Americans so proudly claimed for themselves? These questions were asked most frequently on college campuses as an emerging consensus begun in California spread across the country. Students demanded that teachers and administrators abandon their role of *in loco parentis*. Students no longer considered themselves empty vessels waiting to be filled with Truth by an all-knowing faculty. They wanted an equal voice in what they believed was a joint venture in higher education. With all of this ferment, the Peace Corps found itself drawing upon a pool of potential volunteers that was remarkably different from the one that existed in 1961.

These currents—the absence of leadership, the changes in the larger society, and the arrival of activist students—coming together as they did created tensions that threatened the very existence of the Peace Corps. Remembering that time from the vantage point of 1986, Senator James McClure said, "The [Peace] Corps, it appeared, was a noble experiment on the brink of failure—a victim of the political and social turmoil of the time."[41] And that turmoil was manifest both at home and abroad. Volunteers in Nigeria—unlike their docile cousins of five years earlier—threatened a sit-down strike when they perceived that the Peace Corps leadership was providing too little in the way of personal and professional support.[42] Others in the Dominican Republic openly criticized the American government's decision to send thousands of U.S. troops to interfere in a local uprising. This criticism infuriated President Johnson and was one of several events that led him eventually to reject an organization that he had done so much to create. In his memoirs, Johnson never mentioned the Peace Corps or his role in fighting for its independence. He even relegated Bill Moyers, the man who had given him such long and loyal service, to the role of nonperson.[43] On 6 March 1967 the *New York Times* reported, under the headline "800 Ex-Peace Corpsmen Protest War to President," that former volunteers were speaking out publicly against the Vietnam War. The kind of volunteers who conformed to the rules, did as they were told, and complained only to colleagues was fast disappearing. The volunteers of the late 1960s, like their counterparts in the society at large, demanded that their voices be heard. The paternalism with which the Peace Corps had treated its volunteers in the past was no longer acceptable, although several more years went by before the Peace Corps hierarchy could fully digest this fact.

Looking back on the late 1960s, it is amazing that the agency thought it could remain aloof on the issues of the Vietnam War and the draft. These were the defining issues on the home front from 1967 until 1970—and beyond. Yet each time a volunteer, or on rare occasion a staff member, raised a voice or wrote a letter or took a public stand against the war and the draft, it was treated as an aberration of the most grievous kind. Bruce Murray, a volunteer in Chile, was fired in 1968 because he had identified himself as a Peace Corps volunteer in a letter he had written to the *New York Times* expressing antiwar views. The *Times* did not publish the letter. Unfortunately, a Chilean newspaper did. The Peace Corps, torn between the need to maintain the support of the president and the Congress and the need to support an American citizen's right to free expression, settled for the former. The agency decided to make an example of the Chilean volunteer. He was abruptly terminated, immediately drafted by his local selective service board, and indicted when he refused induction. A year later, long after the damage was done, a Rhode Island court found both the Peace Corps and the local selective service board had acted improperly, and the indictment was quashed.[44]

A more difficult form of antiwar protest for the Peace Corps to control—but one that was even more damaging to its image and mission—was the action of a group of headstrong former volunteers (not all from the Peace Corps) calling themselves the Committee of Returned Volunteers (CRV). This radical fringe of the several-thousand-strong contingent of former volunteers then back in the United States was organized in 1966 under the leadership of several charismatic and outspoken men and women. Their antics captured the attention of the Peace Corps leadership, the media, and both the Johnson and Nixon administrations. Karen Schwarz, in a sympathetic account of the committee's activities, suggests that it lost the bulk of its initial membership during 1968 as its leadership "adopted increasingly radical points of view" but that its visibility and prominence increased as a result of the same action. The CRV publicly denounced the Peace Corps as an imperialist tool and participated in demonstrations against American foreign policy, some of which turned violent. It reached the height of its fame in May 1970 when, during a weekend demonstration in the nation's capital that was sparked by the American invasion of Cambodia and the killing of students at Kent State and Jackson State universities, the CRV staged a thirty-six-hour occupation of Peace Corps headquarters. Members unfurled a Viet Cong flag from an upper-floor window, clearly visible through binoculars from the White House, and distributed pamphlets to passersby on the streets below.[45] Ironically, although no one could have known it at the time, this weekend proved to be the high-water mark of the anti–Vietnam War movement, and the various protest organizations slowly began to fade away. The CRV was no exception. By 1971 it had disintegrated under the weight of revolutionary fervor that was too much even for its erstwhile radicals.[46] Nevertheless, the damage it caused between 1967 and 1971 was profound. Every part of the Peace Corps constituency was adversely affected: Congress, both the Johnson and the Nixon administrations, the volunteers and staff, the public, and—perhaps of greatest concern—the pool of potential volunteers.

At the same time the overall society was going through such a drastic change, it became clear that there were problems in the field as well. For several years the emphasis had been on establishing the Peace Corps as a going concern, sending thousands of volunteers into the field, and generating the kind of attention at home that would ensure adequate operating budgets from Congress and a sufficient supply of volunteer applicants to meet future personnel needs. Accepted as an article of faith was the unending need for American volunteers who, by their very presence, would bring about beneficial change to the people among whom they lived. As the years passed, however, it became obvious that the connection between mere volunteer presence and beneficial change was tenuous at best. Lack of requisite skills to accomplish a specific job that would meet an actual need in a particular location led to assignments with little real meaning. The matter of volunteer jobs, the thoroughness with which these jobs had been prepared before the arrival of volunteers, the relevancy of the training given volunteers, and the extent to which host countries needed these jobs filled were far more important than had been previously assumed.

Indications that this was true began to appear within a few years of the Peace Corps's founding. For example, when the first country director in the Philippines wrote a book about his experience, he talked at great length about the problems caused by the fact that volunteers in the Philippines were largely in what he labeled "nonjobs."[47] The Philippines had been one of the first countries to request volunteers. It was a country with a long and often happy association with the United States; it was home to many American military, business, and diplomatic personnel; and it had the social and economic development problems typical of Third World countries. The Peace Corps and the Philippines seemed to be a natural fit. The only problem was that the Peace Corps wanted to use volunteers in the education system, and the Philippines already had a surplus of teachers. The solution—a solution that would become a source of problems for volunteers and Filipino teachers alike until late in the decade when it was abandoned—was to assign volunteers as classroom aides without any defined teaching responsibilities. There was confidence at headquarters that once the volunteers were on-site they would find a way to be productive. Such, unfortunately, was often not the case.

Lowther and Lucas examined in great detail the many field evaluation reports from the 1960s and concluded, "Thousands of volunteers went abroad to 'develop' communities or 'change attitudes' only half comprehending what those attitudes were or why they required changing." They were referring to the popular community development programs that were widely used in Latin America and elsewhere. In these programs, after a few months of training in social welfare theory by an academically oriented staff, volunteers were expected to work miracles by organizing peasant communities so that they could define their own needs, develop programs for meeting those needs, and establish community-based institutions to perpetuate the practice. The occasional 'super vol' (a category many volunteers say never existed except in the imagination of public relations officers) might accomplish this, but for most volunteers it was impossible. As Lowther and Lucas point out, "Community development epitomized the Peace Corps at the height of its imagined power to remake the world."[48] Writing for a book of essays celebrating the twenty-fifth anniversary of the agency, one of the founders admitted that he was still haunted by "memories [of the] thousands of volunteers who never found *any* meaningful job in the course of their overseas tour."[49]

That these problems existed in the early and mid-1960s was no secret. The organization had a high-level evaluation group staffed by experienced journalists and run by Charles Peters, who remained a senior Peace Corps official until 1969. Peters and his staff evaluated programs throughout the Peace Corps world. On rare occasion, the evaluation reports praised someone or some program, but more often they concentrated on problems, of which they found many. Needless to say, there was great tension between field operations and the evaluators. As a former field operator, my sympathies lie naturally with the former. But the important point is that program deficiencies were uncovered and reported. In attempting to explain why the same deficiencies persisted year after year, Peters told Coates Redmon, "The reason a program could go bad, stay bad and not reach the attention of Shriver was that there was a conspiracy of silence."[50] No one wanted to be the bearer of bad news. Despite Peters's reports, the problems continued.

Inadequate and poorly planned volunteer jobs were clearly problems, but there were others as well. Much as the Peace Corps wanted to deny it at the time, and unfair as it is to those who served for higher motives, many men joined to avoid being drafted. The draft law provided numerous ways to obtain a deferment, and Peace Corps service was one of them. By following a college deferment with a graduate school deferment, then with two and perhaps even three years as a volunteer, an otherwise eligible American male could reach the magic age of twenty-six and be free. As one former volunteer remembered years later, "Many of us had come to Micronesia to avoid [being drafted], not in response to a heartfelt need to do good."[51]

In-country staffs in the 1960s and early 1970s had a member designated as the resident 'draft counselor' with the assignment of advising volunteers on ways to dissuade draft boards when they came calling. One of my first assignments in the Philippines was just that because the former draft counselor's tour had expired and he had gone home. Because I looked back on my tour of duty as a lieutenant in the Marine Corps with great pride, the assignment was awkward, to say the least. (Fortunately, the draft problem was ending and the assignment evaporated in a few months.) But all of this concern about the draft truly weakened the ethical base on which the Peace Corps was founded. Unavoidably it created suspicion among volunteers as to which had motives that were pure and which had motives that were suspect. One volunteer from that time remembered many years later, "Few of the volunteers [seemed] to be in the Peace Corps for the same rosy idealistic reasons of helping the world that had inspired me."[52] And this troubled her greatly. Despite all the denials that the organization made at the time with respect to the draft issue, it was as thorny an issue as it faced.

A second problem had to do with volunteer dress and personal habits. Drugs, sex, and rock 'n' roll reached the Peace Corps in the mid-1960s as it did in every segment of American society. Unkempt dress, beards and long hair, and the occasional use of drugs all caused trouble between volunteers on the one hand and host country nationals and Peace Corps staff on the other. Local citizens invariably viewed with suspicion volunteers who appeared to be flouting local ways, which were almost universally conservative in nature. Moreover, many staff members having been away from the United States during the 'revolution' failed to understand or to be able to deal with the volunteers' point of view. Men and women discovered that there was a generational gap between groups separated in age by no more than six or eight years. All of these currents—the lack of good jobs, the Peace Corps as a haven from the draft, and the arrival of different standards of conduct and dress—created a situation desperately in need of strong leadership and perhaps a miracle worker as well.

With the arrival of Jack Vaughn as the director in 1966 the leadership vacuum disappeared and the internal reassessment so badly needed could go forward. Vaughn began his task with great enthusiasm. He asked, according to Lowther and Lucas, "Did volunteers really have good jobs? Were staff living frugally? Were all those vehicles necessary? Were volunteer allowances too high? How good were their language skills? Did volunteer and staff really understand the host culture?"[53] Vaughn was asking the right questions, and as an article he wrote for the *Saturday Review* midway through his term in office shows, he was taking appropriate steps to correct matters.[54] But two problems prevented him from taking the forceful action needed. First, he was one of the founders. He had been a senior Peace Corps official from 1961 until 1964 during which time the decisions now causing problems had been made. He was simply too much of an 'old boy,' too much an author of the current program, to provide the vigorous, even hardhearted, action needed. Second, and very likely of more importance, he became director just as the full impact of the societal changes and anti–Vietnam War sentiments came to a head. His energies were sorely taxed dealing with the fallout from those problems. Sargent Shriver sympathized with his plight. Said Shriver, "[These nonprogrammatic issues] must have been his biggest problem. And God knows what I'd have done with [them] if I'd been there."[55] As a result, Vaughn's attention was deflected, by necessity, from the major organizational and philosophical reassessment that was required, and little was done on that front. Problems widely recognized to be plaguing the Peace Corps remained in place and unresolved as Nixon's replacement for Vaughn, Joseph H. Blatchford, roared into office in early 1969.

The use of the word *roared* to characterize Blatchford's arrival in Washington is both literally and figuratively correct. He was a thirty-four-year-old lawyer from southern California who brought his penchant for riding a black 180cc Yamaha motorcycle to the nation's capital. News photographs from his early days in office show him wheeling his motorcycle into the lobby of the Peace Corps headquarters—PC/W, in Peace Corps jargon—just a block or two from the White House, where it would remain until evening when he would crank it up again and ride on home. A few days after being sworn in as the third director, he gathered together more than fifty people, some of whom had no formal ties to the Peace Corps, and directed them to "look at the heart of the Peace Corps idea, at the volunteer concept, at service, at effectiveness and think about preparations for the 1970s." He quickly brought in his own management team; began rebuilding relations with Congress, many of whose members had become disillusioned with the Peace Corps; took a quick trip to visit volunteers in Kenya, Iran, and Libya; and began the process of becoming director. Within six months this bustle of activity produced the needed new organizational and philosophical foundations, an approach Blatchford dubbed New Directions.[56]

Blatchford came to the Peace Corps with solid credentials. In the late 1950s he and a group of like-minded friends had traveled to thirty cities in Latin America on goodwill missions. These trips combined his skill as a tennis player and the musical skills of some of his colleagues (several were jazz musicians) with a range of people-to-people activities designed to increase the level of understanding between the young people of Latin countries and the United States. That such an increase was needed at the time was readily apparent throughout South and Central America. Anti-American sentiment was widespread; on more than one occasion it had flared up in violence, the most prominent example of which was in 1958 during then vice president Nixon's ill-starred tour of Latin America. In Uruguay, Peru, and Venezuela mobs of demonstrators had shouted obscenities at Nixon, thrown rocks at the car in which he was riding, and spat on the vice president and his wife. Of the incident in Veneuela *Time* reported that "it required six truckloads of soldiers to escort Nixon's bulletproof limousine to the airport [safely]."[57]

Blatchford's work grew into an organization called ACCIÓN, which at its height had three hundred volunteers in community settings, primarily in Venezuela, and was supported with funds raised from private individuals and corporations in the United States.[58] Ironically, because of his Latin American experience, Blatchford had been asked to advise one of Shriver's working groups early in 1961 when the Peace Corps was in its formative stages. His advice (echoed by several other people with relevant experience) to keep the organization free from the partisan political process by making it a private nonprofit organization was rejected, understandably enough given the victorious Kennedy administration's interest in associating itself with the program's immense popularity.[59]

The *New York Times* described the new director as a "complex man, idealist and pragmatist, organization man and utopian, unquenchable optimist and realist." The newspaper's brief biography ended with the statement, "He puzzles his critics," because so much of what he stood for they did also.[60] He was a Republican in good standing. He had won his party's nomination for a seat in the House of Representatives but had lost in the November 1968 election by a narrow margin in a heavily Democratic district. He then managed to get his name on the short list of candidates being considered for the Peace Corps directorship and, given his superior qualifications, won the job. In his first meeting with Blatchford, Nixon was warmly supportive. He was interested in and knowledgeable about volunteers and what they were doing, and there was never as much as a hint that Blatchford was to do anything other than serve to the best of his ability. The only specific advice he was given concerned the president's worry that the agency was top-heavy, overstaffed, and organizationally adrift.[61]

Blatchford's memories of Nixon's intentions toward to the Peace Corps differ from those that were current among Peace Corps Democratic Party loyalists at the time. Karen Schwarz cites unnamed sources who claimed that Blatchford was "Nixon's way of saying 'F—— you' to the Peace Corps" and that Blatchford was "the worst thing that ever happened to the Peace Corps."[62] Moreover, in his diaries, H. R. Haldeman twice mentions that Nixon's intentions were not completely benign. On 12 July 1970, Haldeman records Nixon's desire "to cut Peace Corps and VISTA budget[s] down far enough to decimate them." Nearly a year later, in May 1971, Nixon is "worried about the Peace Corps and thinks we're making some mistakes there. . . . [Wants] to put a tough guy on it who hates the left-wing press and [who will] do something about it."[63]

Blatchford's recollections concerning his instructions and those contained in Schwarz and Haldeman are not necessarily contradictory. The group whose comments Schwarz reported was, according to one contemporary observer, "heavily populated by liberal Democrats who [had] a hard time accepting the fact that there is a two-party system, and that the other fellows won. . . . [And as a result] they have a prerogative to try to impose their own policies."[64] There is no doubt that there existed among old Peace Corps hands a long-felt antipathy, if one does not want to use a harsher word, toward Richard Nixon. Conspiracy theories abounded concerning the new president's plans for the jewel in the Kennedy legacy. Many feared that the coming tenth anniversary of the agency would be the occasion for a wake rather than a celebration. Accordingly, it is not surprising to learn that the sentiments Schwarz reported existed among this group.

Haldeman's notations were made well after Blatchford had been sworn in at an elegant Rose Garden ceremony in May 1969 when the president himself led the array of dignitaries in attendance. A picture taken at the occasion shows Blatchford, his wife, Winnifred, and Nixon all looking particularly happy and at ease with one another after the ceremony. (A smiling Henry Kissinger is visible in the background.)[65] One would hardly expect such a scene if the president's intentions had been to kill the Peace Corps and if Blatchford were the designated executioner. The meetings between the two both before and after the oath-taking, during which Nixon gave Blatchford his initial instructions, were cordial. As time passed, however, a series of events occurred that explain a change in Nixon's feelings. Four months after Blatchford was confirmed by the Senate, he called a conference in Fredericksburg, Virginia, to explain his program to the senior staff, including all the Peace Corps country directors.[66] After several days of speeches, work sessions, and one-on-one discussions, the entire group was invited to the White House for Sunday breakfast with the president. The affair was conducted with great style. The breakfast featured a band from Howard University, an inspirational talk by Congressman Guy Vander Jagt, a relaxed and talkative President Nixon, and a full array of treats from the White House kitchen. Later a smiling group of country directors posed with the president for a commemorative photograph. The assembled Peace Corps staff was suitably impressed with this display of administration hospitality. Unfortunately, the CRV, having learned of the honor being bestowed on the Peace Corps, took the opportunity to stage a protest demonstration in Lafayette Park directly across the street from the White House. The protest excoriated the president's Vietnam policy and the American armed forces and labeled the Peace Corps an imperialist tool. The media chose to publicize the demonstration rather than the president's friendly gesture toward an agency he was supposed to be undermining.

Shortly afterwards, in October and November 1969, Peace Corps volunteers in many countries participated in the Vietnam moratoriums that were becoming a regular part of the antiwar movement's activities. In May 1970 the CRV's occupation of Peace Corps headquarters, discussed earlier, made front-page news around the country, much to the president's annoyance. Even a quick scanning of *The Haldeman Diaries* shows how extremely sensitive Nixon was to adverse media coverage and how badly he overreacted to it. Little wonder, then, that it was a supportive Nixon that gave Blatchford his initial charge but that this support gradually eroded as the president saw evidence, or what he thought was evidence, of widespread hostility toward him and his presidency in the Peace Corps ranks.

Blatchford's own assessment of the situation twenty-five years later is that the president did lose some of his earlier enthusiasm for these reasons. But he recalls no time when Nixon actually indicated to him that this was so. In fact, Blatchford contends that Nixon originally gave more support to the Peace Corps and its director than any president other than Kennedy, as did many of the Republican members of the Congress. (Blatchford supports this latter assertion by pointing out that an effort led by Democratic senator Fulbright in 1969 to cut the agency's budget drastically was thwarted by Republican senators Goldwater and Percy.)[67] Blatchford did sense hostility from some of the president's advisers, especially John Ehrlichman and Patrick Buchanan, but in most instances he was able to deflect such hostility, and it did not greatly hamper his work.[68]

From his first days in office Blatchford's critics accused him of bringing partisan politics into the Peace Corps. The criticism is valid, although not very significant, if by partisan politics they mean he hired people who shared his own visions and loyalties. His two predecessors did exactly the same thing. Virtually all the men who played major roles in the founding of the Peace Corps—and many of those who played secondary roles—had been active in the Kennedy, Johnson, and Stevenson political campaigns, or in state and local Democratic politics, or were known to be sympathetic to the cause. As one of the founders remembered, "An awful lot of the first Volunteers and many of us on the Peace Corps staff had gotten our idealism stirred up by [working for Adlai] Stevenson."[69] When Jack Vaughn followed Sargent Shriver into office, one of his first moves was, quite naturally, to assemble his own team.[70] Thus it was to be expected that Blatchford would do likewise. Blatchford differed from his predecessors, however, in where he chose to look for his team. Shriver and Vaughn had recruited from academe, journalism, and a variety of civil rights, international, and, of course, political circles. Blatchford looked for a different kind of person—particularly for the critical overseas posts— whom he hoped to find among "the new breed of practical business-minded leaders" and who would be willing to devote their skills to Peace Corps service for a period of three to five years.[71]

The loudest and most outraged cries of political partisanship came in 1971 when Blatchford used an important Peace Corps policy, generally ignored by his predecessor, to terminate nearly one hundred staff members, including twenty-seven country directors.[72] The policy, originally called "In, Up, and Out" and later "the five-year rule," required that all American staff members, both those serving abroad and those serving in Washington, leave the Peace Corps no later than the fifth anniversary of the date on which they were hired.[73] The rule was instituted to ensure that the agency would never suffer the fate of other government bureaucracies: premature calcification resulting from an aged and spent permanent staff. In 1965 the five-year rule, which had previously been only an internal practice, was written into the Peace Corps Act. (Congressional acts are often worded to provide for periodic reassessment and fine-tuning, and the original Peace Corps Act underwent this process in 1965.) As a result, except in a few cases where a sixth year of service could be authorized, the five-year rule had the force of law. It was now obligatory. This new provision, however, was interpreted to apply only to service that occurred after 1965. Thus, even for those staff members who had already served several years, the clock was reset to 1965; they would not be affected until 1970.

To appreciate the appeal of this unintended loophole in the five-year rule for those then on board, one needs to understand that Peace Corps staff positions can be uniquely satisfying. Many former country directors look back on their service as the best job they ever had, regardless of how far they progressed in later life. My own reaction to being a country director was such that I often exclaimed to myself in grateful glee, "And they even pay me to do it!" (There has been no change in the situation since then. A recent staff member declared, somewhat indelicately, "You see, Peace Corps needs the five-year rule because we might be tempted to hang on to those bountiful tits forever.")[74] Little wonder, then, that the spirit of the law, that no one *should* serve more than five years, gave way to the letter of the law. By late 1971, some Peace Corps staff members had been in the organization for as long as nine years, and nearly a hundred were approaching or had exceeded five years. In November of that year Blatchford announced that the situation would be corrected during the first six months of 1972 by gradually replacing those who were serving beyond the five-year maximum.

Before the announcement not only was the law being ignored but the very reason for its existence was becoming evident: Many of the senior people, especially some in the field, felt that the old way was the only way. A number of country directors at the Fredericksburg conference "threatened to submit their resignations on the spot had Blatchford not promised to hold his more radical ideas in check."[75] But Blatchford, realizing that some in the 'old corps' could not change, took bold—and legally required—action to eliminate the problem.[76] A few people criticized Blatchford for not acting in 1970 when the law's first impact was to have been felt—a situation he blamed on the press of other business—but most of the critics concentrated on what they took to be a politically motivated purge of Democrats. These latter critics, however, claiming that "the whole thing reeks of politics," were wrong; they had forgotten why the rule existed in the first place.[77] It was not that Democrats were being replaced by Republicans. It was that those who objected to a new approach were being replaced by those who supported it. And, as everyone who had a hand in formulating the initial practice knew full well, that was the ultimate reason for the five-year rule's existence. Even Sargent Shriver, no friend of the Blatchford-led Peace Corps management, was reported to agree that "the rule should have been enforced across the board from the start," although he did lament that so many country directors needed to be replaced over a six-month period. The policy was meant to prevent managerial ossification, an unwarranted infatuation with the status quo, and a refusal to try a new approach. As the 1970s unfolded, this new approach would lead to the rejuvenation of the Peace Corps and allow it to escape the problems that threatened its very existence. Seen in this light, the renewed enforcement of the five-year rule was a necessary and proper management decision.

Blatchford came to PC/W convinced of the need to reevaluate the program, to define his objectives, and to find ways to implement them as quickly as possible. Although such an agenda led to charges that "from his first day in office, [he] projected the image of the somewhat brash, take-charge type," he knew that the longer he delayed, the more difficult it would be to make substantial changes.[78]

In hindsight, it is amazing that the five strategies that made up New Directions were so controversial. Today they seem what should have been seen as only a logical progression based on the lessons the Peace Corps had learned in the field and on the changes in the social climate that had occurred both at home and abroad. Yet one writer declared that "the change in its nature and role [was so] precipitous" that the organization's very existence was threatened.[79] Others saw in New Directions a conspiracy hatched by a Nixon administration still jealous of the Kennedy memory and determined to destroy its principal legacy by converting the Peace Corps into a "junior USAID." (The phrase was considered particularly disparaging because it implied that the Peace Corps would become a worse version of something that was suspect even in its senior manifestation.) It is supremely ironic to read accounts by members of the 'old corps' who were torn between claiming that they had already begun to make the programmatic changes that Blatchford instituted and charging that Blatchford's proposals would destroy the wonderful work that was the Peace Corps. Shriver groused, "I'd almost go as far as to say there were no new ideas . . . developed under Blatchford which were not already in operation . . . in the early days of the Peace Corps. But what he did do . . . was to negate the other purposes." Lowther and Lucas wrote that "Vaughn and his staff had already just about done for them" all that Blatchford and his team planned to accomplish with New Directions. Two current scholars, in a book examining the impact the Peace Corps has had on the field of anthropology, have asserted, "When Vaughn succeeded Shriver . . . he reordered priorities to concentrate on development activities per se. . . . Whether or not these new directions resulted in more effective development projects is an open question." The authors have even appropriated the phrase *new directions* and assigned it to Vaughn! Vernon Ritchey, a former Peace Corps public affairs officer, summed up the feelings of the opposition when he said, "I don't believe any of the precepts that accompanied the birth and early years of the Peace Corps can be found anywhere in the ideologies of the [Blatchford] administration."[80]

New Directions was an apt title for the program. It echoed a dramatic departure from the past in the same way that the New Deal and the New Frontier did; it was a happy pairing of words that could quickly focus discussion on a specific set of ideas; and it provided a rallying cry around which those who wanted to reenergize the Peace Corps could coalesce. Stripped of some of the rhetoric that accompanied it, New Directions can be reduced to five broad yet simple ideas.[81]

The first and most important was that volunteer jobs needed to be more immediately beneficial to host countries and in line with those countries' own development needs. The second, really a part of the first, was that volunteers needed to possess the required skills to do the job, acquired either through previous experience or through training provided by the Peace Corps. To ensure the availability of these skills, recruiting efforts would be broadened to include older men and women—with spouses and children if need be. New training programs would be established to provide the necessary skills to volunteers not possessing them, and training would be conducted in host countries to make it more realistic, practical, and in many instances less costly. (In the 1960s, training programs had been conducted in settings that approximated expected weather in the country of service but duplicated little else. For example, volunteers destined for Libya were trained in Arizona; those scheduled for the Philippines were trained in California and later in Hawaii.)

The third theme gave specific recognition to a concept that had always been a part of the Peace Corps but perhaps not fully implemented. The agency's relations with host countries were to reflect a true partnership, not one based on a donor-recipient mentality. Blatchford called it a spirit of binationalism. Although host country citizens had often been employed in logistical and administrative positions in the past, they were now to play an active, even paramount, role in making program decisions, and they were to fill policymaking positions on in-country staffs.[82] This concept so frightened some members of Congress that Democrat Wayne Hays declared, "It looks like it is going to be a full-time job keeping the wings of Mr. Blatchford clipped. . . . I am ready . . . to prohibit any funds being spent to hire foreign nationals to administer the Peace Corps."[83]

The fourth idea called for the Peace Corps to participate in multinational volunteer efforts whether under United Nations sponsorship or under one of the many nongovernmental international agencies. The original Peace Corps Act had recognized that such cooperative efforts might be useful, and this part of New Directions was simply a recognition that the authority to do so was there, even though little use thus far had been made of it.[84]

Finally, New Directions encouraged greater use of volunteers upon their return home to address the nation's internal needs. In contrast to the feeling at the beginning of the 1960s that the United States had much to give to the rest of the world, ten years later it was acknowledged that this country had its own needs to meet as well. Blatchford saw the returned volunteer as a resource to enlist in the efforts to address these needs. Returned volunteers had been tested by their service abroad, they knew that superficial solutions and quick fixes did not work, and they had demonstrated by the types of employment chosen upon returning home that their commitment level remained high.[85] Blatchford was confident that the mass of returned volunteers could be a constructive presence in the country and that it was they who should represent the Peace Corps, not the likes of the Committee of Returned Volunteers.[86]

Criticism of New Directions was directed primarily at the twin concepts of providing volunteer jobs more directly related to host country development needs and of recruiting people who already possessed the skills to meet those needs—or who could quickly be given the skills through training. The critics charged that too much emphasis on jobs would detract from the volunteers' interest and willingness to live and work among the ordinary people of the host country. They would be neither as skilled as the professional development workers nor as intimately connected with the local people as earlier volunteers had been. The host country—and the Peace Corps—would both lose, so the critics said. Moreover, the criticism continued, the attempt to recruit "blue-collar workers, experienced teachers, businessmen and farmers" would fail because such people would not want to serve; and even if they did volunteer, these people might be "precisely the ones with the least ability or inclination to develop their interpersonal skills."[87] The prospect of recruiting older people came in for special criticism. Some Peace Corps veterans feared that the presence of older volunteers would create "a different sort of Peace Corps. . . . Older volunteers [would be] less adept at learning the foreign language or adjusting to the living conditions. . . . The people-to-people component would disappear."[88] No one seems to have paid attention to the fact that *skilled* volunteers were meant to total only 30 percent of the volunteer contingent whereas the remaining 70 percent would continue to be recent college graduates with liberal arts degrees.[89] The critics conveniently forgot that older volunteers had already proved their worth by meritorious Peace Corps service. By 1969 Moritz Thomsen, for example, an American farmer in his fifties, had already served in Ecuador for four years and written a powerful account of his experience in a widely praised book, *Living Poor.*

New Directions did, indeed, bring new life. And nowhere is the validity of that statement more evident than in the Philippines, which adopted the new strategy wholeheartedly. Within five years the program shifted from providing volunteers to an educational system that already had a surplus of teachers to a program honored by the government of the Philippines in May 1974 "for redirecting the work of the Peace Corps toward livestock, fisheries, feed grains, nutrition, and other agricultural endeavors, thereby enlisting the best of America in the highest cause of all—the elimination of hunger and malnutrition."[90] The volunteers in the particular programs singled out for the honor—as well as their colleagues in teacher training, youth development, environmental services, and social development programs—all had the opportunity to be involved in meaningful work while coming to know Filipinos, both collectively and individually. This book will show that, while protecting and enriching the very best traditions of the Peace Corps, everyone benefited from the work that was done—the Philippines, the United States, and the volunteers themselves. The volunteers represented the United States in a way that was personal, human, and natural—a way that the official American community simply could not duplicate. And through it all they struggled with the immense challenges of living in another culture, a struggle that they look back on as a watershed event in their own lives.

The Philippine Peace Corps story is also one that is important to me personally. Like the volunteers' experience, mine was also a watershed event. The three years I spent living and working in that country proved to be superbly rewarding, although not every day was one that I would like to repeat. The introduction of New Directions programming was a major reason the satisfaction level was so high. The work was important, it was in accord with Philippine priorities, and we were *doing something* as well as *being somewhere.* Not everything we tried worked out well. In the Philippines, as everywhere, the organization had more than enough disappointments and setbacks as we struggled with the immense task of helping to improve the lives of millions of people. But we never doubted that the work we were seeking to do was worth the struggle.

The Call of Service 2

The story behind my joining the Peace Corps staff in the Philippines is a bit complicated, but it is helpful to hear because it says something important about the Peace Corps of the early seventies. Contrary to the criticism leveled against the Nixon and Ford administrations, the Peace Corps was not overrun in those years by unprincipled philistines intent on destroying a cherished symbol of the Camelot era. The volunteers and staff from that time were motivated by the same interests and concerns that had motivated Peace Corps people from the first day. They believed in the mission of the Peace Corps and wanted to make a personal contribution toward its attainment. My story is just one of many that validates that assertion. Perhaps its telling will encourage others from that time to tell theirs.

The story begins with a phone call one morning in the late winter of 1971 from the Peace Corps. The caller was recruiting candidates for the Peace Corps staff who would bring to the organization skills and experiences that would be different from those brought by the traditional candidates who had been recruited largely from universities, government agencies, and the world of nonprofit institutions. I certainly met that new standard. After completing three years of service as a Marine Corps lieutenant in 1958, I had spent eleven more climbing the corporate ladder in the United States and Europe. A quick look at my résumé would have yielded an image far more reminiscent of William Whyte's *Organization Man* than of Theodore Roszak's *The Making of the Counterculture*. I had read both books at critical times in my life. Whyte's was a popular book among the young, aspiring businessmen at Procter & Gamble, where I worked in the late 1950s. We read it for the insight it provided into the corporate world rather than as a criticism of that world. Roszak's book was assigned reading in 1970 when I was studying at Columbia Teachers' College, and it was hailed for its penetrating analysis of the origins of the new American society that had emerged in the 1960s. Try as I would, I could not embrace it. To make the picture of 'young man on the rise' complete, by the end of the 1960s I had a wife and three young children, a house in the Connecticut suburbs, and a growing bank account. This was hardly the kind of background that was common in the Peace Corps during the 1960s.

But in 1969 my career path took a sharp turn. In that year I had brought my family back to the United States from an overseas assignment in London, left the corporate world, become a full-time graduate student at Yale, and taken a position as a part-time high school history teacher in Westport, Connecticut. It was this combination of experiences, I learned later, that the Peace Corps found attractive. Here was a candidate with the desired corporate and management experience and a recently demonstrated commitment to 'doing good,' to use a phrase that has fallen out of favor but remains the best one available to describe what I hoped to accomplish.[1] The Peace Corps was interested in me, but also skeptical—as were members of my family and many friends—because the decision to leave the corporate world seemed at best reckless and at worst bizarre. Why, they all asked, leave a career destined to bring the fulfillment of the American dream for a pedestrian job as a high school history teacher?

Why, indeed? I asked myself that question more than a few times in the wee hours during the next two years as I completed a master of arts in teaching degree. I became a full-time teacher, the coach of a successful debate team, and a willing convert to a world where issues were more important than money. Even today, a quarter century later, my answer is still tentative, although certain elements of it are as clear now as they were then. The major reason was the cumulative impact that the turbulent 1960s had on me. This was a decade of turmoil and change that had affected the United States more profoundly perhaps than any other decade in the nation's history with the exception of the sixties of the previous century. Great as its impact was on the country as a whole, for me it had been even greater.

What many call the 'sixties' began in November 1963 with the assassination of President Kennedy.[2] Millions of Americans—the author among them—had been captivated by his youth, his promise of a new frontier, his marvelous rhetoric, and his conviction that the government could take the lead in bringing beneficial change to the country. But to my astonishment I was virtually the only person in my circle of budding captains of industry at Procter & Gamble who felt that way. During the 1960 presidential campaign, the forty-minute commute into Cincinnati with my car pool and lunchtime in the company cafeteria with my associates became periods of intense debate as I fought off the onslaught of those determined to prove that Kennedy would be bad for business and therefore bad for the country. Furious exchanges were replaced by long moments of sullen silence as friendships were tested and found wanting. In early 1961, my wife bore a son whom we named, aptly, John. In the fall of 1962 I was ready, even eager, to suit up in my old Marine Corps uniform to defend Kennedy's position in the Cuban missile crisis. He was the first and perhaps the only president who I have felt was truly *my* president. On hearing the news of the assassination, my instinctual reaction was to blame some undefined but menacing conservative political force for the destruction of a man who was vital to the country's well-being. (That I was quickly proved wrong did nothing to lessen my resentment.) The loss of Jack Kennedy was for me a personal loss. It was in the process of mourning his death that I began tentatively questioning the career path that stretched out before me.

Hard upon the heels of the Kennedy tragedy came an increasing awareness of the civil rights struggle. The combination of anger and resolve that had been building in the black community during the 1940s and 1950s had finally boiled over. An ever increasing coalition of black and white Americans was demanding the abolition of all forms of legally sanctioned second-class status for the country's largest minority group. Clergymen, academics, students, and people from all walks of life were joining to force the repeal of discriminatory laws and practices. These people, in their pursuit of principle, were performing acts that required genuine physical and moral courage. They were subjecting themselves to name-calling, beatings, and imprisonment to achieve something important. My friends and I read about the sit-ins, the marches, the prayer meetings, the jailings, the occasional triumphs, and the frequent setbacks, but with no personal involvement or risk. And despite feeling that something important was passing me by, I continued my climb up the greasy flagpole of success. The nearest I came to the civil rights movement was to ask a roving trio of musicians at a fancy cocktail party to play "We Shall Overcome," by then the unofficial anthem of the struggle. They had no idea what I was talking about and returned to playing the songs that Harry Belafonte had made so popular.

Then in 1964 President Lyndon Johnson announced with much fanfare his quest for a Great Society and its accompanying War on

Poverty. He was determined to eliminate poverty and all of its dreadful consequences and, moreover, he was convinced that the United States had the resources and the willingness to complete the task. The newspapers were filled with descriptions of desperate situations in the Appalachian Mountains, in the backwaters of the South, and in the ghettos of the large cities. Once again the nation had set its sights on a goal worthy of attainment, a goal I shared, yet one that had virtually no support in my community. Living in a lovely semirural town in Connecticut, we were surrounded by neighbors who, except for a few 'natives,' commuted to New York City or held management positions at corporations headquartered in other nearby suburbs of New York. Our community's response to the Great Society is best illustrated by a skit that was included in the town's annual musical production in 1966. The highlight of the skit was the discovery by the town fathers (in real life all well-paid executives) that the town qualified for money from the War on Poverty program. Having no sewers, water mains, full-time fire department, police department, or high school, the community actually 'suffered' from the conditions that the Great Society was committed to overcoming. The humor lay in the fact that the town had eschewed these amenities by choice, not necessity, in order to maintain its bucolic ambiance. But in the play the town fathers, recognizing easy money when they saw it, successfully applied for a grant. By the end of the skit the government had discovered the ruse and reclaimed its money, in the process giving the audience several good laughs at the federal government's folly. That, and a feeble attempt by some families to experience the plight of the poor by surviving for a week on a poverty-level food budget, was about as close as our community ever got to the War on Poverty, but the feeling grew that the important things in life were passing me by.

The escalation of events in Vietnam also had its effect. At first the Vietnam War and the demonstrations against it made little difference in my life or that of my colleagues. By the end of the decade, however, especially after we moved to England in 1967 on a business assignment, I began to see things differently. My British and European friends simply could not accept the American contention that one of its vital national interests was at stake in Vietnam. Given the painful experiences that the British, French, and Dutch had with colonies in that part of the world after World War II, they could easily detect in official U.S. pronouncements the same sort of rationalizations their own governments had employed to justify maintaining colonial empires and a wholesale interference in other people's lives.

Increasingly, I came to share the concerns that had led so many Americans to question the war, and I began to look upon the war protesters with more sympathy. The discrepancy between what I professed to believe and what I was actually doing became too great to hide even from myself. Not only did I feel guilty about not doing my share of the work on behalf of causes I supported but I felt I was missing out on the action. When 1968—arguably the most traumatic year in that traumatic decade—brought with it the murder of Robert Kennedy and Martin Luther King Jr., President Johnson's abandonment of his office and his Great Society, the violence at the Democratic Party convention in Chicago, the continued escalation of a mistaken war, and a sense of disorder and disarray throughout American society, I could no longer ignore what writer Robert Coles rather grandly labels the "call of service." That phrase certainly was not on my lips then, and I find it pretentious now, but it does convey the sense of what I was feeling. A great national debate was taking place in the United States that would determine the country's course for years to come, and I was not part of it. And, what was equally disturbing, if my life continued on its present course, I never would be.

The activities of the business world left me largely unmoved. From the beginning I had been troubled by the vast amount of energy, talent, and money that was devoted to purposes of seemingly little consequence. Returning to the United States in 1958 as a recently discharged Marine Corps lieutenant, I had stopped in Cincinnati for a daylong series of employment interviews with executives in the advertising department of Procter & Gamble. My lasting memory of the day is of grown men, intensely devoted to what they were doing, rushing around clutching bars of soap and packages of detergents as they worked to convince people to buy Procter & Gamble products. It was my first visit to a major corporation, my first job interview, and my first attempt to deal with my postmilitary life. In fact, until a few months previously when I had decided against a Marine Corps career, I had given little thought to how I would go about earning a living. And, with a pregnant wife and a young daughter awaiting my return, I did need to earn a living right away. When the company offered a job, I happily put my doubts aside and went to work. However, I never lost the feeling during the next eleven years that I was working very hard but with no sense of personal satisfaction. And my unease intensified in direct proportion to the amount of money I earned. The company decided what I would do, where I would go, and with whom. We lived in certain neighborhoods, we went to certain restaurants, we dressed in a certain way, and we attended the same parties. Rather than sitting back and enjoying it, I chafed at the conformity and regimentation of it all. Those few with whom I shared my concern usually found it odd that my response to the good life was so negative.

The sense of being a bystander continued to trouble me throughout the sixties. Historically important events washed over us without leaving a mark, or so it seemed. The feeling of being left out intensified when we were transferred to London in 1967. We had eagerly accepted the offer to make the move partly to get away from the sterile environment in which we were living and partly for the excitement and adventure that living abroad would bring. What I had not realized was that living in another country only increases the feeling of noninvolvement. One is suspended between a permanent home and a temporary home, observing both but being part of neither.

Finally, there was the matter of wanting to break free from the pressure to conform. For most of my adult life I had been responding to someone else's initiatives rather than my own, doing what was expected and following the path of least resistance.

For years two obstacles stood in the way of change: the need for a paycheck and the lack of courage to alter course. By the end of the 1960s the first concern had been reduced to a question of how much is enough. For a decade the combination of an ever-increasing income and a reluctance to spend at full capacity had permitted us to establish a comfortable financial cushion. Although I would still need to work, I could consider alternatives to business. That left only one obstacle to overcome: the missing element of boldness. What would it take to convert inclination to resolve? The answer came from two unlikely sources: the rock 'n' roll musical *Hair* and the movie *To Sir, with Love*.

Opening on Broadway in the fall of 1967, *Hair* defined one of the sea changes of the 1960s. Never before had musical theater so accurately caught the mood of the country's young and portrayed it in such an exhilarating and challenging way. *Hair* has a minimal plot—it tells the story of a recently drafted young man's last fling with his friends before reporting for induction into the army. But its primary impact was achieved through a distinctive and revolutionary use of sound, lighting, and staging. These elements created, in the words of a contemporary critic, an "extreme climax of disorientation when movement and color explode and time ceases to be."[3] The musical, with its tremendous commercial success, provided recognition—even approval—for the distinctive elements of that emerging alternative lifestyle: rock 'n' roll, the new sexual freedom that the Pill brought, the widespread use of marijuana, an enlightened view on racial matters, a rejection of previously accepted standards of dress and deportment, protests against the Vietnam War, and a hedonism that were all but incomprehensible to the staid puritanical middle class of which I was very much a part.

Hair soon moved across the Atlantic to London, where we saw it in mid-1968. My initial reaction was fiercely negative. I found the music cacophonous, the actions of the characters scandalous, and the immorality depicted on the stage unacceptable. If anyone had cared to look, my facial expression must have been the same one worn by the stern and disapproving farmer in the Grant Wood painting *American Gothic*. But after the intermission a different message began seeping through. I saw that the musical was also about liberation and the breaking down of arbitrary ways of judging people and events and that being different was not the same as being wrong. The knot in my stomach loosened, my grey flannel suit and rep tie no longer seemed essential to my self-worth, and one foot even began to keep time with the strange beat coming from the stage. I did not embrace the specific values that the characters in the musical shared—I was too much a New Englander and a product of the previous generation for that. I did accept the proposition, however, that like the characters in *Hair* I was far freer to choose among life's alternatives than I had thought.

To Sir, with Love is a British movie in which the American actor Sidney Poitier portrays an engineer recently arrived in London from a former British colony and in search of greater opportunity to practice his profession. He finds an interim job as a secondary school teacher to tide him over until he finds a professional position. The principal of the school takes advantage of Poitier's newness and need for employment to assign him to a disruptive, undisciplined class of rowdies, students none of the experienced teachers will accept. The plot is predictable but nevertheless moving. Poitier, as a movie reviewer commented, "must not only subdue these near-hoodlums, he must somehow win their respect and teach them something."[4] He does this so successfully that in the end the students award him their ultimate accolade. They call him sir, an honor they deny to all of their other teachers. Poitier's character has brought out the best in his students and erased the worst. As he sees them graduate—an outcome no one would have predicted at the beginning of the school year—he tears up an employment contract as an engineer and commits himself to teaching. The final scene shows Poitier's first meeting with another bunch of rowdies as a new school year begins. The audience knows, however, that this group, perhaps even worse than its predecessor, will turn out just fine. "In the end," *Time* magazine's movie critic concludes, "Poitier makes his point: the world can use more sirs."[5] The movie is unabashedly sentimental as one tear-jerking scene follows another. But that was irrelevant. For me the burning question as I left the London movie theater was how I could become one of those sirs. The answer proved to be quite simple.

In June 1969 I left the corporate world and returned home from England to enter Yale Graduate School's Master of Arts in Teaching program, simultaneously becoming a part-time history teacher and library monitor in a nearby Connecticut high school. The 1969-70 school year was a tumultuous one at Yale. In addition to the anti-war demonstrations that were then common at most colleges, Yale and New Haven were the scenes of several major rallies for the darlings of the radical chic fringe of high society: the Black Panthers, a militant and, some suspected, violent segment of the civil rights movement. University president Kingman Brewster caused a great commotion when, as a trial of several prominent Black Panthers got under way, he declared that no black man could get a fair trial in the United States.[6] Many of Yale's alumni of the Old Blue set called for his scalp, but his faculty and students were equally vocal in their support. In May 1970 the city erupted as the civil rights and anti-war movements joined one fine Saturday morning to bring downtown New Haven to a halt. My most vivid academic memory of the year was of a scolding given to a whole class of aspiring public school teachers by two philosophy professors who accused us of wasting time attending class when we should have been out in the streets. The atmosphere at Yale was a far cry from what it had been fifteen years earlier when I had been an undergraduate. In those days an exciting weekend was defined as one in which the beer supply lasted through Sunday.

But why is all of this personal history relevant to the larger picture of the Peace Corps and its New Directions in the 1970s? Because it demonstrates that the people drawn to the Peace Corps staff at the time of New Directions were, like me, motivated by the same idealism as that which motivated their predecessors. There was no influx of highly charged conservative ideologues, as the critics of the Peace Corps of that time would have it. The same sort of committed individuals were attracted as had always been. Among the staff members recruited in the spring of 1971 were a former Jesuit priest with ten years of administrative experience in Korea, the principal of a large high school in Maryland, several people who had earlier served as Peace Corps volunteers, and two experts in agricultural development. Each of us had our special reasons for joining the Peace Corps program, but we were united in having a common interest in doing good. If there was anything that distinguished those of us destined for country directorships from those of a decade earlier, it was that more of us had management experience in business, education, or government. The earlier group had more people who, although they might have worked within an organizational framework, did not participate in the management of it (for example, university professors or journalists). The important point is that charges such as Karen Schwarz makes in *What You Can Do for Your Country* are patently untrue. Schwarz claims that following Nixon's election the Peace Corps "filled up its senior positions with incompetent patronage appointments" and sent people who were unfit to overseas staff positions.[7] It is time to challenge that statement. Another writer on Peace Corps matters, T. Zane Reeves, makes a similar charge in *The Politics of the Peace Corps and VISTA*. Reeves states that the coming of a Republican administration in 1969 caused the appointment of people who "held conservative ideological values" and who "redirect[ed] volunteer recruitment toward recruits whose values [were] compatible with the conservative redirection."[8] It is impossible to find a conservative ideologue in me. Yet I was recruited as a country director, three years later I was promoted to regional director, and a year after that I rose to deputy director of the Peace Corps. As with Schwarz, one must ask of Reeves, Where is his evidence? My own story contradicts the charge, as do the recollections I have of the men and women with whom I worked in the Peace Corps during five years of the Nixon and Ford administrations.

The few who have written about the Peace Corps of that period have been misled by the dark cloud of Watergate and by their assumption that the agency can be understood by looking at what was said or done in Washington. The Nixon scandal has blinded them; they do not see that what happened was in reality a necessary reorientation of the program at a time when its continued existence was threatened. In this respect it is important to remember that the budget for the year before Blatchford's arrival passed the House by only ten votes and that Republican senators Barry Goldwater and Charles Percy had to rescue Blatchford's own first budget from Democratic senator William Fulbright's determined assault. The Peace

Corps was not dealing from a position of strength at the end of the 1960s; it was doomed if strong corrective measures were not taken. Moreover, the measures that were taken not only provided the necessary new directions but also were implemented without any loss to the organization's cherished cross-cultural ideals. In fact, without New Directions the opportunity to practice these ideals would have disappeared, leaving the world and the United States a poorer place.

The hothouse atmosphere that characterizes PC/W and the danger of reading too much into what goes on there is discussed in detail in chapter 8. At this point it is sufficient to point out that only three things of importance happen in Washington: setting overall direction, recruiting volunteers, and raising funds from Congress. The rest, to borrow from William Shakespeare, "is a tale told by an idiot, full of sound and fury, signifying nothing."[9] The real work of the Peace Corps is centered in the field. Most of what goes on in Washington matters little to the volunteer's daily existence. Only by understanding this fact can one make sensible judgments about the significance of what happens at headquarters. Many people who have written about the Peace Corps have yet to come to grips with this reality and as a result have overinterpreted Washington-centered activities and underinterpreted what happens abroad.

The degree to which one is attracted to the Peace Corps is rarely related to which party controls the White House. The attraction depends on a congruence of Peace Corps purposes and personal motivations. Where the congruence is close, the attraction is high; where distant, the attraction is negligible. There have been people on the Peace Corps roster who were hired solely as a result of political connections—and I worked with some during my Washington years—but they were always a tiny number compared with the vast majority who were in the agency for far more appropriate reasons. And this larger group controlled the important issues.

My two years as a high school teacher turned out to be sufficiently rewarding for me to consider making education a lifelong career. Although my real-life students were hardly in a class with Sidney Poitier's movieland students (mine were largely college-bound offspring of relatively affluent parents), the satisfactions were just as he portrayed them. So also were the days when things went wrong. One day I lost control of a class so completely that my department head had to rescue me. On another occasion I became so angry with a student who barred the doorway to my classroom that I tossed him out into the hall. But these difficult moments aside, I did get great pleasure out of a daily routine that included some learning, some good relationships, and a sense that my being there was important.

Then in March 1971 came a phone call from Blatchford's staff recruiter, G. Douglas Burck, a former Procter & Gamble marketing executive and travel industry pioneer, that would alter the course of my life. The thought of an overseas position with the Peace Corps had instant appeal. Both my wife and I had enjoyed living abroad, and an exciting vacation trip to East Africa in 1969 made the idea of living in the Third World less daunting than it might otherwise have been. What little we knew of the Peace Corps we liked. It would certainly satisfy my need to do good; it would keep me involved with young people; it would be for only three years, after which I could continue my career in education; and it certainly would be challenging.

We immediately called friends in Washington who had worked in the Kennedy and Johnson administrations, one of whom had even spent some time at the Peace Corps as a junior staff member during the early days. I found their negative reactions puzzling at the time. They reported that the Peace Corps was passé. Nobody paid attention to it, and besides, wasn't I a little old for all that kid stuff? They pointed out that the big names—Shriver, Moyers, Vaughn, and the other founders—had moved on, leaving people of little consequence in charge. They even described how the Nixon administration, for which they naturally had little regard, had announced a major reorganization of the government bureaucracy in 1971 that included merging the Peace Corps into a larger bureaucratic structure called ACTION, thus effectively emasculating it. (ACTION and its impact on the Peace Corps is discussed in chapter 8.) My puzzlement concerning their comments was genuine. The Peace Corps mission was one of enduring importance, not a matter of fashion that could be in favor one day and out the next. Thirty-eight was certainly not too old. It never entered my mind that the program could be affected by partisan politics or that it mattered much which party was in the White House. In hindsight, I realize that in 1971 I was naïveté personified. But that did not matter; once again we ignored the advice of our friends.

Burck immediately arranged for a series of interviews in Washington to coincide with my coming spring vacation. I arrived bright and early one April morning and within a short time was ready to accept any offer they might make. Part of the reason for my enthusiasm was simply the thrill of being in Washington (as embarrassing as such a sentiment may be in these skeptical times). In 1971 the offices were located near Lafayette Square, a small, well-kept public park facing the White House, that enduring symbol of the nation.[10] The presidential mansion was easily visible from the Peace Corps building, and many of the executive offices had magnificent views of the White House and the Capitol beyond. One of the most important interviews of the day, as it turned out, took place in one such office. Philip Waddington, one of three regional directors at the time, had responsibility for Peace Corps programs over a vast piece of geography that stretched from the remote islands of Micronesia through the southern part of the Asian continent and from there across North Africa to Morocco. I sat facing Phil at his desk. Behind him, a bank of windows presented a picture postcard view of the White House and its grounds. Spring was in full bloom and the setting was glorious. Only the most jaded of cynics could have looked upon that scene and felt no stirrings in his soul. (Three and a half years later I was to occupy that same office. From time to time I would need that view to restore my spirits as the frustrations of the bureaucratic wars in Washington threatened to turn me into one of those jaded cynics.)

Another reason for the enthusiasm I felt, one that was considerably more pertinent to the issue at hand than the potency of national monuments, was the high quality of the discussions I had with the six or eight senior officials with whom I met. I was impressed with their stories of the good that could be accomplished by relatively modest changes in the way Third World countries managed their health care, sanitation, nutrition, and agricultural programs. They talked to me about New Directions, the bold set of guidelines they had given themselves, and they stressed the newly increased importance of placing volunteers in worthwhile jobs that would contribute something of value to the host country. I was as yet unaware of the deadly seriousness of the dispute between those who supported the primacy of Goal One (doing a needed job well) and those who preferred to emphasize Goals Two and Three (building strong personal relations between Third World citizens and Americans). In addition, being of firm New England stock, I thought that the emphasis on work was not only appropriate for the Peace Corps but a foundation stone of the natural order as well. I was struck by the fact that these men (no women were as yet in important positions) were displaying the same sort of intensity that I had found thirteen years earlier at my Procter & Gamble interview, but with one crucial difference: These men were intensely devoted to something *important*. By the end of the day the Peace Corps people were spending their time convincing me of the validity of the organization and the new life they were instilling in it, and I was concentrating on convincing them that I belonged on the team. We both succeeded.

There was only one awkward moment during the day, and that came when I was asked about my political affiliation. The position for which I was being considered, country director, required White House approval. The basic intent of the process of political clearance is to ensure that these positions, usually called schedule C or excepted appointments, are staffed by people who reflect the views of the sitting administration. In answer to the question about my political leanings, I was able to say—truthfully—that I had always registered as an independent and never had taken an active role in any political campaign. In answer to another specific question, I reassured my interviewer that I had not worked against President Nixon's election in 1968. The man asking the questions carefully avoided asking whether I had voted for Nixon, and I carefully avoided giving any indication. I believed then, and still do, that the Peace Corps suspected that I was not in the Republican camp but that they really did not care as long as there was no evidence of active opposition that could cause embarrassment when they sought political approval for my appointment. It was far more important from their standpoint that I meet their tests of motivation and skills than that I meet any test of political creed or party affiliation. My interview experience strongly supports the view that Blatchford and company were not driven by partisan considerations and did not feel held in check by the political approval process, despite what their critics were saying then and continue to say now.

With the interviews over, I was ready to become part of the Peace Corps, but the bureaucratic wheels in Washington turned slowly. Although reassuring noises were made from time to time, nearly two months passed before the official letter of appointment came through. It informed me that I had been appointed deputy director in the Philippines, subject to completion of a security check by the FBI, physical examinations for all five members of the family, and a completed application form for official passports, the type of passport issued to government employees.

The appointment as *deputy* country director was expected, because it was meant to provide a few months of on-the-job training before I took up the position of country director. What came as a shock was the assignment to the Philippines. I had known from the start that my ELO status (English language only) precluded an appointment to a Spanish-speaking country in Latin America or a French-speaking country in North or West Africa. There remained, however, a long list of countries in East Africa, the Pacific, and parts of Asia where English was acceptable for official purposes and where I could learn the rudiments of the local language for social purposes. Dreams of Kenya, Malaysia, India, Nepal, and Afghanistan danced through our heads as we awaited the fateful letter of appointment. There was only one country on our list of undesirable posts: the Philippines. We had heard dreadful stories of violence and corruption there, and my only personal experience in the country was as a Marine on liberty outside the American naval base at Subic Bay. That experience did not suggest the Philippines as a good place for raising a family.

After reading the letter of appointment, we began to pay closer attention to the news coming out of the Philippines and to search out recent articles that had been written about it. Virtually all of what we found emphasized civil unrest, terrorism, corruption, and near chaos. *U.S. News and World Report* described conditions on 29 March 1971, under the headline "Engulfed in Strife": "For more than a year, violence and disorder have been escalating. Students have been rioting in the streets; Manila has been paralyzed by a transportation strike; terrorists have hurled Molotov cocktails at passing vehicles and planted bombs at U.S. installations; crime and corruption have soared; and the Government itself is torn by political warfare." Accompanying photographs showed a crowd of angry men burning the American flag and an obviously worried President Ferdinand Marcos pleading for calm in a nationwide radio address.

Several weeks later, *National Geographic* carried an article describing the organized violence that was being directed against a number of indigenous tribal groups living on the southern island of Mindanao. According to the story, settlers from the more populous sections of the country had moved into Mindanao under federal government sponsorship. When they found that small groups of unassimilated ethnic peoples stood in the way of their plans, the settlers hired mercenaries to drive the aboriginals from their ancestral lands. The magazine showed a picture of one badly wounded woman, describing her as a "victim of the violence that stalks Mindanao's uplands."[11] From our vantage point in suburban Connecticut, the Philippines appeared to be facing problems far more severe than those which could be addressed by Peace Corps volunteers.

Then acquaintances who had recently returned from a two-year assignment with an American oil company in Manila assured us that, although what we had heard was true, there were many features of the Philippines, especially the warm and friendly people and the natural beauty, that offset the disadvantages. They showed us pictures of a beautiful country with exotic names like Zamboanga, Cebu, and Cagayan de Oro. They described to us Banauwe, a self-declared eighth wonder of the world, with its ancient rice terraces carved into mountainsides centuries earlier. They told us of the friendship with which they were greeted wherever they went, and they said that even Manila was manageable—or nearly so. They summed up their feelings by saying, "If you don't want to go, ask the Peace Corps to send us." Having heard just what we wanted to, we filled in the security clearance forms, took our physical examinations, and obtained our official passports.

Tucked away in a drawer of my desk is a battered and worn "Official Passport United States of America" issued on 7 July 1971. Official passports are a deep maroon, in contrast to the blue of the ordinary passports and the black of the diplomatic passports. An official passport does not provide the diplomatic immunity or license to ignore the laws of other countries that diplomatic passports do, but it does open many doors that otherwise might remain closed. There is an unspoken recognition among government workers around the world that they have things in common with one another. The maroon passport identifies its carrier as a member of that group. I took inordinate pride in that passport during the next five years as it gradually became for me an important status symbol. Not uncommonly, well-traveled passport holders will fill all of the pages of a passport with various visas, permits, and tax stamps before the passport's expiration date. At that point, the American passport authorities attach a foldout strip of twelve additional pages to the original booklet to provide extra space. An especially heavy travel schedule could require a traveler to need a second strip of additional pages. My passport had not one accordion file insert, not two, but three—a total of thirty-six extra pages needed to record my travels throughout the developing world. When the third insert was added, I knew that my high standing in the hierarchy of world travelers was assured.

By the time the passport arrived, I had nearly completed a six-week familiarization program for new staff members at PC/W. The Peace Corps has struggled for years to learn how to prepare people, both staff members and volunteers, for living and working abroad. By 1971 the organization had learned how truly difficult a task this can be, but it had not yet learned how to handle it well. The training program in which I participated was successful primarily in helping us to master the bureaucratic necessities of life in the field: how to propose a program of work for volunteers, how to request volunteers with particular skills, how to handle medical emergencies, how to relate to the rest of the official American community, and, of course, how to understand and implement New Directions. We were introduced to the absolute prohibitions that the Peace Corps insisted upon: no recreational drug use, no involvement in local political affairs, no living in expatriate communities, no ostentatious lifestyles, and no participation in any American intelligence activities. (The Peace Corps and the CIA have always kept their distance, although a rumor to the contrary occasionally surfaces. One of my own children once wondered if I might be one of 'them,' as did a college classmate who should have known better. There has, however, never been any credible evidence to support these rumors.)[12]

The training program provided little in the way of advice for staff who would be bringing spouses and children. In this respect, little had changed since 1961. The mission and the concerns of volunteers have always taken precedence over those of staff families, and this was a cause of discord in some staff homes. As mentioned earlier, there was more than a little resentment toward Sargent Shriver from the wives of staff members who were often away for long periods or working late and on weekends when home.[13] The same situation continued throughout the 1970s, and it probably still exists. The culture of the Peace Corps reflected the fact that nearly all volunteers and many staff members were single or, if married, childless. Family concerns were simply not high on anyone's agenda. The strong reaction by many in the field against Blatchford's decision to admit volunteer families was a reflection of this bias, as well as of the extra work required to support a volunteer family compared with supporting a single volunteer or a married couple. (In many respects, the institutional attitude was similar to the one we young Marine Corps lieutenants had often heard in the past: If the Marine Corps wanted you to have a wife, it would have issued you one.) The single day my wife spent at the training program did little to prepare either of us for the realities of family life in a city like Manila and, as did most of the people in our situation, we learned how to cope by coping.

But the thing those of us destined for the field wanted most from the training program was for it to be over. We knew that the real work we had signed on to do could only begin after we reached our destinations, and anything that interfered or delayed that event was accepted grudgingly. Finally, the last day of staff training arrived. I do not recall any ceremonial or formal send-off. We were just handed travel orders and plane tickets and sent home to pack.

Packing was one thing. Dealing with the children's uncertainties was another. And because my wife and I had never moved as children, we simply did not understand how little the children—aged thirteen, twelve, and nine—looked forward to the prospect of once again saying good-bye to friends and once again moving to a foreign country. Tears and long faces became a regular part of the home front immediately preceding the move as they came face to face with the inevitability of transferring schools, making new friends, and facing the unknown in Manila.

Years later, in 1993, as part of the research for this book, I wrote to a woman who had been in Peace Corps/Philippines with us. She and her husband were among the farmers who responded to Blatchford's New Directions by becoming volunteers, bringing along their four children—as the new policy permitted—two of whom were teenagers. She described the experience as wonderful for the family, except for the older children. Her conclusion twenty-five years later was that only volunteers with young children should be accepted for Peace Corps service. Teenagers, she explained, had enough to do working through the confusions, conflicting emotions, and challenges that mark that passage. The additional burdens imposed by a different culture and losing all one's familiar support structures made the already difficult task of achieving maturity doubly so.[14] My own children agree with that assessment, although looking back none of them admits to having regrets about undergoing the experience. In 1971, however, we gave little thought to the children's point of view and went on with our packing.

The last of the chores to be completed before the big move required a quick trip from our home in Connecticut to Ontario, Canada, to put our summer cottage in order for the planned three-year absence. This did not take long, and we were headed back to Connecticut within a few days. It was a Saturday afternoon, and we were driving along the New York Thruway north of Albany—I remember it as if it had happened yesterday—when a news bulletin datelined Manila came over the car radio. Unknown terrorists, the broadcaster announced, had thrown hand grenades into the crowd at a political rally in Manila, killing and injuring many. The Philippine government blamed the attack on armed insurrectionists intent on creating chaos as a first step toward full-scale revolution. (The next day the New York Times reported that ten people had been killed and sixty-six wounded, including all eight of the senatorial candidates appearing at the rally.)[15] We rode along in stunned silence while all of the fears that we had pushed aside a few weeks earlier came flooding back. We had to face the uncomfortable fact that being posted to Peace Corps/Philippines would be much different from our experiences as London expatriates. There our older two children had been able to roam that exciting city freely with the help of safe and friendly taxis and the London underground system. They and their friends had chased the Beetles and the Rolling Stones—just then enjoying their early years of success—and other pop stars all over town with hardly a second thought for anything more serious than perhaps getting a bit lost. The ominous paragraph from *U.S. News and World Report* about violence and chaos flashed through my mind. The headline "Engulfed in Strife" now took on a much more personal meaning than it had earlier. Was I really going to take my family into what could easily be described as a war zone? Suddenly the call of service that had sounded so clearly when the Peace Corps first contacted me began to ring hollow, and my response to it seemed an act of utmost selfishness.

Fortunately, momentum and the fear of looking foolish carried the day. Our packing was completed, the house was rented, the movers were almost at our door, the good-byes had been said, and the plane tickets were in hand. It would take an immense act of will to turn everything around, and we would have looked pretty silly in the process. There was nothing to be done; we were committed—revolution or no revolution. We were on our way to the Philippines.

The flight to Manila was uneventful except for a number of suspenseful minutes as the plane was boarding at JFK Airport in New York when we found ourselves short one child. I had been counting luggage since we left home. Our worldly belongings at this point, in addition to one cat, added up to eleven suitcases, and I was determined to land in Manila with every one of them. But it was in making a similar count of our party of five that I discovered our youngest child was nowhere to be found. Just when I was wondering how forceful my powers of persuasion would be in getting a jumbo jet to postpone its flight schedule for the sake of a missing child, he popped into view from the direction of a passenger TV lounge.

To say that I was nervous and uncertain at JFK is probably an understatement, but my condition was nothing compared with what it was when we stepped off the plane onto the broiling tarmac in Manila after the ten-thousand-mile trip across the United States and the Pacific. Manila Airport in the early 1970s was a combination of lunatic asylum, den of thieves, and ongoing mass demonstration—or so it appeared to us that first night. When we entered the international arrivals building, we found ourselves in the midst of a sea of commotion as people called and waved to one another, surging to and fro in frantic search of those they had come to welcome, while many shabbily dressed men ran about grabbing pieces of luggage and racing off with them to destinations unknown. What we did not understand at the time was the social occasion Filipinos make of departures and arrivals of family and friends. The idea of a relative or friend arriving unmet is unthinkable. One traveler might be met, or bid farewell, by a dozen or more family members, friends, babes in their amah's arms, and other children of assorted ages. Those saying good-bye would be thrusting last-minute gifts into the already overburdened traveler's hands, while welcoming parties would be gleefully receiving the expected gifts from abroad. Multiply this by the two hundred or more passengers arriving or departing at any given time and one can visualize a meaning for the word *bedlam.*

Fortunately for us, in the crowd were the dozen or more members of our own welcoming party, all clamoring to be helpful, friendly, and supportive—and instead they were overwhelming us. As we passed through the customs and immigration desks into the public areas, the chaos multiplied by a factor of ten. The carefully guarded belongings I had squired halfway around the world disappeared into what we were assured were friendly and trustworthy hands, but I wondered if we would ever see them again. As the hordes of people and noise grew louder, my new Peace Corps colleagues acted as if nothing were amiss. My welcoming party was hardly distinguishable from any of the others. They were perfectly at ease in this mass of people; they were dressed Filipino-style in colorful *polo barongs;* their English was sprinkled with words I did not understand; and they had everything under control. At that moment, I doubted that I would ever be as cool, self-possessed, and acculturated as they so obviously were.

The sights, sounds, and smells of a Third World tropical city are among the most powerful stimuli in the world. The senses are fiercely assaulted by the unfamiliar. The hot humid air, even at night, wraps itself around one like an unwelcome woolen blanket. The smell of raw sewage mingles with that of frying garlic, and both permeate everything. The streets teem with people, especially children. As our caravan of Jeep CJ4s and Wagoneers left the airport and passed through the outskirts of Manila into the heart of the city, we saw a bustle of activity and a lifestyle that were incomprehensible to us weary and jet-lagged newcomers. We had looked upon ourselves as seasoned travelers. Obviously, we were wrong.

The signs of poverty were everywhere. We passed families preparing to bed down in squatters' huts that were nothing more than large shipping crates. And as we looked closer we saw that these were the better homes. Others lived in shacks made from cast-off cardboard, sheets of galvanized metal, and building materials 'borrowed' from nearby construction sites. Many youngsters wore only T-shirts, which was a bit of a shock for us puritanical New Englanders. Although we did not know it at the time, our reaction to the many bare bottoms we saw was precisely the same as another New Englander's reaction had been seventy years earlier. Pattie Paxton was one of the thousands of American school teachers who had heeded her government's call to bring the benefits of American education to her country's new colony in the Pacific. She wrote that her first reaction was acute embarrassment as she asked herself, "Weren't missionaries teaching the people to cover their nakedness?" Later she concluded, as did we, that "it now seems a sensible way to dress children in hot weather."[16]

The forty-minute drive was an unforgettable introduction to our new home. A short time later my wife wrote to friends, "Manila is the worst. . . . The streets are full of garbage and smells. The traffic is unbelievable, traffic laws nonexistent or ignored. The air is terribly polluted, too many vehicles send clouds of black fumes into the already gray air. Manila Bay is polluted. Drainage is a problem that causes flooding during rains. The roads are full of potholes. . . . There are large areas of shacks and beggars with palms up at every traffic light."[17] What had I done to my family in this insane effort to heed the call of service? The next morning—Day One of what now threatened to be an interminable thirty-month stay—I began to think of excuses that would provide a face-saving way to cut the tour short and go home. The phrase *culture shock*, which we had discussed in theoretical terms in staff training, had become a living reality. The cumulative effect of jet lag, anxiety, foreignness, and doubt had done its work. I could see no light at the end of the tunnel.

This accounting of our arrival in Manila is accurate, but it would be misleading to leave it at this point. Within a remarkably short time—no longer than a few weeks—we began to discover the real Philippines, one that we happily called home. Once we adjusted to the frantic rhythms of Manila and began to work with Filipinos, to travel in the provinces, and to become involved in the work of the Peace Corps, the initial impressions faded away. In the end, rather than seeking acceptable excuses for going home early, we extended our stay for an additional six months. We learned, as most Peace Corps people do, that wherever one is sent there is more than enough to share and admire. All we needed to do was adapt. We accepted what we could and put aside for later consideration what we could not. We may have arrived untutored, but by the time we left we had become a part, expatriates though we were, of a country and a people whose hospitality we had enjoyed immensely and whose respect we hope we had earned.

To Hurl a Brick or Kiss His Hand

3

Volunteers are sent to countries that are alike in many ways, but each is also unique. These countries, especially in the years before former Soviet Bloc nations began to request volunteers, are variously described as underdeveloped, developing, or Third World. (A few of the most desperately needy qualify for the term Fourth World.) They are nations where large percentages of the people are poor, the availability of the basic necessities of life can rarely be taken for granted, the apparent modernity of the capital never extends beyond the city limits, and the indigenous culture is different in both substance and form from that of the United States. But to acknowledge these similarities is not to say that there are no major differences among them. Each country is a product of its own history and culture, and each presents the Peace Corps with its own set of challenges and satisfactions. Although all country directors in the early seventies were following the same guidelines, we were each doing so in circumstances that differed from those our colleagues faced. It was the need to understand these circumstances and to do our work within the structure they imposed that made the task so stimulating and at times so frustrating. The Philippines was representative of the whole in being both similar to the other countries yet also very much the product of its own distinctive historical process.

Like most of the people sent abroad by the Peace Corps, those of us who went to the Philippines had at best a hazy and misinformed image of the country. As one of my colleagues from the 1970s remembered later, when he decided "to commit a minimum of two years in the prime of [his] life to venture off to some faraway Asian land, [he] was not certain whether the Philippines was spelled with two l's, two p's, or both, let alone where it was or what it would be like living there."[1] Most of us were able to locate it on the map; we knew that the United States had 'liberated' it twice, once from the Spanish and once from the Japanese; and we had heard disconcerting

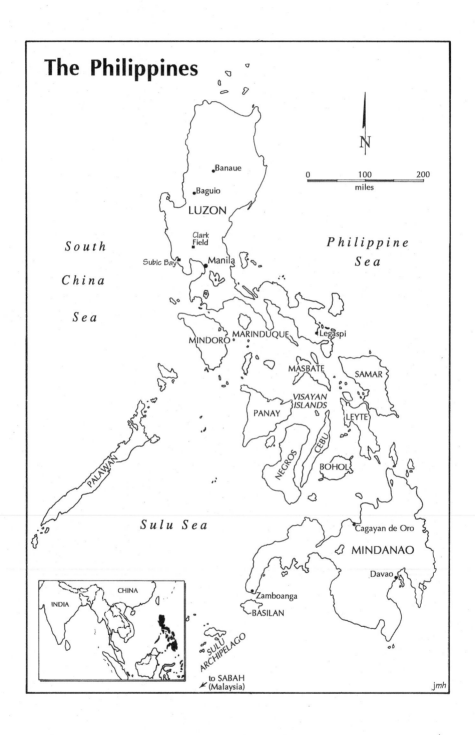

The Philippines

Banaue

Baguio

LUZON

Clark
Field

Subic Bay

Manila

South

China

Sea

Philippine

Sea

N

0   100   200
miles

MINDORO

MARINDUQUE

Legaspi

MASBATE

SAMAR

VISAYAN
ISLANDS

PANAY

LEYTE

CEBU

NEGROS

BOHOL

PALAWAN

Sulu Sea

Cagayan de Oro

MINDANAO

Davao

Zamboanga

BASILAN

SULU
ARCHIPELAGO

to SABAH
(Malaysia)

CHINA

INDIA

jmh

stories about the country's poverty, endemic violence, corruption, and disorder. Beyond that we were hard-pressed to say more.

Our lack of knowledge did more than simply cause us embarrassment when we found ourselves working with Filipinos who knew a great deal about U.S. history. It also made the transition from an American environment to a Filipino environment even more difficult than it already was. What meets the eye in the Philippines is often not at all indicative of reality. Manila, the nation's capital city and its largest metropolitan area, has a western facade that fools nearly every visitor. And as long as newcomers remain only visitors, they will continue to be fooled. Beneath the surface is a culture that one distinguished Filipino commentator has described as "only and entirely itself."[2] Although there are discernible reminders everywhere that many influences have combined to create the Philippine culture, it can only be understood on its own terms, not by reference to one or another of the contributing cultures. For the volunteer living in the Philippines, one of the most crucial aspects of the culture to understand is the ambivalent, almost schizophrenic, way Filipinos regard Americans. At times anything American is held in the highest esteem. At other times Filipinos display a degree of resentment and suspicion of things American that borders on hatred. One does not find the former sentiment in a pro-American segment of the population and the latter in an anti-American segment. Both exist, sometimes simultaneously, in nearly all segments. Early in my stay I needed to enter the American embassy in Manila one day while a vigorous, even nasty, anti-American demonstration was taking place outside its main entrance. Gathering my courage I began to ease my way through the mob. Seeing me, one of the young demonstrators smiled, said, "Hi, Joe" (every American is called Joe), escorted me to the guard at the gate, and gave me the Filipino equivalent of "Have a nice day."

Theodore Friend, a longtime observer of the Philippines, has puzzled over "the fond dependence and acute resentment that mark the Philippine side of the relationship [with the United States]."[3] This is understandable only in the context of the relationship between the two countries that has now existed for nearly a century. That relationship brought the two countries into a warm and close association, and a sense of trust in and gratitude for American involvement in Philippine affairs developed. At the same time it also provided ample reasons for Filipinos to feel the reverse—reasons that led to disappointment and anger, as well as uncertainty about the wisdom of continuing the special relationship with the United

States. Both the constructive, mutually supportive experiences and the ones that severely tested Filipino goodwill are part of the historical record, and neither can be ignored. Their complexities have been examined by historians in great detail on both sides of the Pacific, and a number of excellent works are readily available for those wishing to embark upon a full-scale reading program.[4] For the purposes of this study, however, a brief examination of three of the most important periods in Philippine-American relations will serve.

By the end of the nineteenth century, Spanish rule had been the dominant force in the Philippines for more than three hundred years. Happily for the Philippines, as the Spanish Empire began to break apart, its iron grip on the archipelago gradually weakened. The new ideas about nationhood and independence that had affected so many other parts of the empire finally reached Philippine shores. A middle class emerged made up of *mestizos* and *criollos,* many of whom saw themselves not as Spaniards but as Filipinos whose fortunes were linked to the future of the islands, not to Spain. (In the Philippine context, a *mestizo* is of mixed race, usually of indigenous and Chinese blood, but also of indigenous and Spanish or European blood; a *criollo* is a Caucasian born in the Philippines whose roots in Spain or elsewhere have withered.) During the same time, a smaller but more radical group of Filipinos emerged from the countryside determined to drive Spain from their shores and declare independence. Spanish intransigence drove the dissimilar groups into each other's arms, and a full-fledged revolution began in the mid-1890s.

Meanwhile, Spain became embroiled in a dispute with an angry United States that was eager to show off its newly self-declared status as a world power. The two countries had increasingly quarreled over Spain's treatment of the last vestiges of its empire in the New World—Cuba and Puerto Rico. The fact that the Philippines was also on Spain's diminishing list of colonies, however, was of little importance to most of the Americans who were urging that the United States intervene directly in Spain's Caribbean affairs. President William McKinley even claimed to have had absolutely no idea where the Philippine Islands were when he first heard of them. Such ignorance was not the case with the brash, young would-be imperialist, Assistant Secretary of the Navy Theodore Roosevelt. One day in early 1898, while his boss was away, Roosevelt ordered Commodore George Dewey to take his squadron of cruisers, frigates, and unarmed merchantmen to the Philippines and prepare to destroy the Spanish fleet that made Manila Bay its home.[5] (Roosevelt used the recent unexplained sinking of the battleship *Maine* in Havana Harbor as a convenient excuse for doing so.) As a result, shortly after open hostilities began in the Caribbean, Dewey was in a position to instruct his gunnery officer in Manila Bay, "You may fire when ready, Mr. Gridley." His order quickly sent the decrepit Spanish fleet to the bottom of the bay, and Commodore Dewey unwittingly began the process that rather quickly would make the United States an imperial power.

Not knowing what plans, if any, the United States might develop for the islands, Dewey, anchored aboard ship in Manila Bay, invited Emilio Aguinaldo—a key rebel leader exiled by the Spanish—to return to the Philippines under American auspices. This Aguinaldo did with alacrity. Within a few months he had raised a substantial army, taken control of large portions of the countryside, and surrounded the city of Manila. On the political side he had declared the Philippines independent, written a constitution, and declared himself dictator.[6] Meanwhile, Dewey waited for his superiors to decide on America's course of action. Unfortunately for Aguinaldo and his independence movement, the McKinley administration decided to annex the Philippines and treat it as a colony. Aguinaldo and his followers, incensed at what they considered evidence of American deceit, broke off contact with what they now saw to be a conquering military force.[7]

The war that followed made the three-month affair in the Caribbean with the Spanish look like a schoolboy fist fight, although the United States has always called the Philippine conflict an 'insurrection' in order to use semantics to deny the legitimacy of the Aguinaldo government. (An insurrection is considered an uprising against an established government—in this case the occupying Americans—whereas a war is between two sovereign powers.) Eventually a peak force of seventy thousand American troops was engaged in a pacification program that seemed never ending to the troops fighting the battles. One popular ditty that reflected a common sentiment among American soldiers found its way back to the United States courtesy of an American school teacher, Philinda Rand, in a letter she wrote to her family:

> It's home, boys, home,
> It's home we ought to be
> It's home, boys, home
> In God's country,
> Where the ash and the oak and the bonny maple grow,
> It's home, boys, home,—it's home we ought to go.[8]

Given the strangeness of the Philippines to the common American soldier and the oppressively hot, humid climate that is so much a part of these tropical islands, it is little wonder that the anonymous poet chose "the ash and the oak and the bonny maple" to represent home and God's country.

The early expectations of a quick victory over the insurrectionists gave way to a more pessimistic assessment once the Filipinos abandoned traditional military tactics and took up guerrilla warfare. In response, the United States forces adopted a policy of using "acts of violence and brutality designed to speed up the [war's end]."[9] The tales that emerged from the war are indeed gruesome. Americans burned barrios, killed civilians, tortured and murdered prisoners, and destroyed food supplies. Despicable acts by one side were followed by equally despicable acts by the other. Filipino forces tortured and killed prisoners, mutilated their bodies, stole food from the villagers (even those upon whom they depended for security), and hacked to pieces people suspected of collaborating with the Americans.[10] As a later generation of American soldiers would learn in another Southeast Asian country, guerrilla warfare was a bloody, untidy business.

The American military in the Philippines consisted of a core staff of regular army men, many seasoned by the Indian Wars in the United States, and a larger number of volunteers recruited mainly from the farms and small towns of the western states. This pride of the western frontier did not represent its country well. One historian, David Bain, imagined how Americans back home must have responded to the widely published accounts of atrocities committed by their boys. "Burning houses? Shooting prisoners? Torturing civilians? What, people might have asked, had happened to American youth?"[11] The evidence suggests that racial antagonisms had something to do with it. Soldiers recited ditties, sang songs, and wrote letters that left little to the imagination. One of the less offensive marching songs of the American troops was included in another letter home from Philinda Rand. The chorus, sung to the tune of "Tramp, tramp, tramp the boys are marching," went as follows:

> Damn, damn, damn the insurrectos
> Pock marked, khakiac ladrones,
> And beneath the starry flag
> We'll corral them with a Krag.
> Then we want to see our own beloved home.

(*Insurrectos* are the rebels, *ladrones* are thieves; a Krag was the newest type of army rifle; the meaning of *khakiac* remains a mystery.) Rand added as a postscript: "This is a typical soldier-song written by a man in Iloilo, an American, of course. He is not over refined, and the writer has evidently had a hard time here, but it's rather good I think, and, it is, as I said typical."[12]

In 1901 the main Filipino force under the command of now *Generalissimo* and *Presidente* Aguinaldo retreated to a mountainous region one hundred miles north of Manila to lick its wounds and prepare for the next phase of the struggle for independence. In what must be considered one of the great feats of bravery and skulduggery in the annals of military history, an American general from Kansas, Frederick Funston, along with four other American soldiers and a few Filipino scouts from the small provincial town of Macabebe, brazenly entered Aguinaldo's camp under cover of a ruse, captured *el presidente,* and brought him out of the mountains to American headquarters. Funston and the other Americans had pretended to be prisoners of the Macabebe scouts, who themselves pretended to be rebel reinforcements for Aguinaldo. (The Filipino scouts were recruited by the Americans from among a small ethnic group whose members had a long and well-established hatred for Tagalogs, the larger ethnic group from which Aguinaldo drew most of his forces.) The ruse worked perfectly with only minor casualties on either side.[13]

By this time a growing number of the middle class had concluded that armed resistance was futile. Resistance turned to acceptance and that in turn became active collaboration, especially in the larger towns where the American troops could provide protection from rebel reprisals. After his capture, Aguinaldo followed suit. He rather quickly agreed to surrender terms from an erstwhile enemy, as he had once before. He swore allegiance to the United States on 1 April 1901, appealed to his former subjects to lay down their arms on April 19, and retired to the countryside. Aguinaldo spent his remaining years in obscurity. In the 1930s he campaigned for the Commonwealth presidency but with very little success. He attended the independence celebration in 1946 but was overshadowed by many other notables. His only victory was that he lived a very long life and in the process outlived all of those against whom he had struggled so long before.

Some historians have not been kind to Aguinaldo's memory. Renato Constantino has declared that Aguinaldo, although "at heart a Filipino who wanted to see his country free," was even more a member of the middle class "eager to protect and enhance [his] privileged economic position."[14] According to Constantino, Aguinaldo was happy to accept something less than complete independence in return for an implicit acknowledgment that the educated and monied group would have a dominant position in the new order.[15] The former *generalissimo*'s decision to acquiesce, although not particularly courageous or patriotic, was probably quite pragmatic. As he said in his April 19 declaration, "Let the stream of blood cease to flow [and let us welcome] the freedom . . . promised . . . through the magnanimity of the great American nation."[16]

The American government had crushed a legitimate and broad-based movement for Philippine independence, explaining to the world and to its own people that the Filipinos were not ready for self-government, that they would need a generation or two of American training before they could be trusted to manage their own affairs. Largely ignored was the fact that this action was in sharp contrast to the United States' own historical tradition or to the way it had welcomed Spain's former colonies in the New World as independent states. The old Spanish masters had been banished only to be replaced by a new set. The Americans might turn out to be benevolent masters compared with the other imperial powers, but masters they were nevertheless.

Rarely did the Peace Corps hear Filipinos discuss the war their ancestors had fought with the American army. Our hosts were much too concerned that they might be considered rude or insensitive if they did so. It was only when we read the young demonstrators' banners with the bright red slogans painted on them that we understood the depth of their resentment. And even then we tended to see the resentment as limited to a small group of angry university students, rather than as a manifestation of a far more widely shared sentiment.

President McKinley's reasons for taking the Philippines have been vigorously debated, but his intentions toward Filipinos have generally been accepted at face value. Margaret Leech, McKinley's biographer, maintains that once having made the decision, "for the rest of his life he placed the welfare of the Philippine inhabitants second only to that of the American people."[17] He instructed William Howard Taft, the first American governor of the colony, to "bear in mind that the government [you and your colleagues] are establishing is designed not for [the United States'] satisfaction, or for the expression of our theoretical views, but for the happiness, peace and prosperity of the people of the Philippine islands, and the measures adopted should be made to conform to their customs, their habits and even their prejudices." Taft personalized his own understanding and acceptance of this fundamental policy of government by using his famous phrase "little brown brothers." Modern historians are fond of pointing to the condescension inherent in the appellation and questioning Taft's real feelings.[18] They forget, however, that Taft used this term when many Americans in the Philippines were using *nigger, scrubby leper, half-devil, half-child,* and similar epithets as descriptives of their unhappy hosts. In the context of the time and the place, Taft's use of "little brown brothers" seems forgivable.

Taft embarked on one of the most unusual campaigns in the history of imperialism, one he christened a "campaign of attraction." He would make the benefits of accepting American rule so attractive that no one would think of fighting against it. In return for stability, peace, and economic development, the United States asked Filipinos to forswear the rebellion, accept employment in a new civil service, and quietly await the time when their tutors would decide that they were ready for independence. This was a bargain that most Filipinos were ready to accept. In a short time the anger over the thwarted revolution was submerged below the level of daily consciousness, and the working relationship between the two peoples steadily improved. American civil engineers built roads and bridges, sanitation experts installed sewers and other disposal systems, doctors and nurses brought hospitals and clinics up to current standards, teachers moved out into the provinces carrying the benefits of American education to the masses, and government specialists established the bureaucratic necessities of a national government. It is the last two of these efforts—the dispatch of American teachers to the provinces and the creation of a national government—that in the long run had the greatest impact on Filipino memories of the American colonial presence.

Philinda Rand, a young woman from New England, was one of the teachers who joined in the experiment to export American education to the Philippines. Rand, a Radcliffe College graduate of the class of 1899, along with some of her friends and hundreds of other American men and women, had heeded the government's call to go to the Philippines and, in McKinley's words, "to educate the Filipino[s] and uplift them."[19] They were to do this by introducing American educational techniques and by teaching English. The Philippines has no common language. There are eight major languages and more than a hundred dialects in use throughout the seven thousand islands. This multiplicity of languages represented a major obstacle to nation building. The introduction of English as the language of instruction was meant to remedy the situation by providing the common language that was lacking.

A call had gone out across America for teachers to go to the Philippines to participate in "a tremendous experiment in training for democracy." Teachers were offered a salary of $125 per month (as much or more than they could earn as teachers in the United States) and transportation in return for a three-year commitment to serve in the islands. One should not overestimate the appeal represented by the salary. Counterbalancing it were the newspaper reports and the tales of returning soldiers that the Philippines was a land of desperate "insurrectos, whole tribes of headhunters, and horrible tropical diseases."[20] (Remarkably, seventy years later my reaction to an invitation to be part of the Peace Corps in the Philippines was tempered by similar concerns. Armed uprisings continued to burst out in remote parts of the country, tropical diseases were still to be feared, and unconfirmed reports existed that some small ethnic groups living in the far reaches of the provinces continued to practice headhunting.) Nevertheless, motivated by a combination of altruism, desire for adventure, need for a job, and the opportunity to join a boyfriend or fiancé stationed in the Philippines, thousands accepted the call during the next forty years. The influx of American teachers quickly peaked at 1,074 in 1902. Gradually, as Filipino teachers were trained and placed in the school system, the number of American teachers dropped until only a few remained in 1950.[21]

One of the first large groups of teachers arrived on the U.S. transport ship *Thomas* at the end of August 1901. Reports of the number of teachers aboard vary, but the consensus seems to be 550 to 600.[22] As a result of the commotion created by the arrival of such a large group at one time, the American teachers in the Philippines became widely known as Thomasites, and the label was applied to all who came, regardless of how or when.[23] Judging from the letters home, diaries, recollections, and contemporary newspaper reports, the Thomasites were a remarkable lot. Philinda Rand was typical in many respects. She was single, well educated, adventurous, and clearly one of the new women who were emerging in America as the nineteenth century ended.[24] She readily admitted that she signed on as a teacher for the adventure, but she was also one who took her role seriously. She struggled with the daily task of teaching young Filipinos, without adequate books or supplies, in schools open to all sorts of weather and home to roaming farm animals.

Rand's letters are sprinkled with uncharitable descriptions of her students. She complained about the absence of New England virtues such as diligence, punctuality, seriousness of purpose, and respect for education. Yet—and of more importance—the letters also contain many references to Filipinos she came to cherish as friends, to the country and its great natural beauty, and to the never-ending challenge and satisfaction of learning to live in another's culture. She persevered for more than five years before saying farewell to a land she had grown to love. Many years later she expressed her great pride in having been one of those who worked to "weld heterogeneous groups of Filipinos from many provinces into a single nation by giving them a common tongue, English."[25] The love and respect for the Philippines and its people were reciprocated. While Philinda Rand and her housemate, Margaret Purcell, another Thomasite, were living in the province of Panay before the end of anti-American hostilities, rumors of an imminent attack by revolutionaries circulated. The two women became frightened. "What about us?" they asked their Filipino neighbor when they heard her making plans to ensure her own family's safety. "Oh," she said, "in that case, you would come right in with us." The two Americans were "very glad to know that [our neighbors] were sufficiently our friends to have considered us."[26]

When we were in the Philippines in the 1970s, we met older Filipinos who told us that the Thomasites were really the first American Peace Corps volunteers. These people had known both groups and recognized immediately the many similarities. They said we shared the same personal characteristics and motivations and worked for local acceptance with the same intensity. And they were right. The letters and recollections of these early teachers are indistinguishable from those of Peace Corps volunteers two generations hence—except that the latter had a more professional vocabulary for discussing cross-cultural matters. Although some of us were annoyed by the comparison because we had never heard of the Thomasites and were reluctant to share our special distinction with them, we could not avoid seeing how deep the affection was for our forerunners.

The long-term contribution these thousands of American teachers made in the Philippines between 1900 and 1950 is a matter for debate. Some critics charge that the presence of American teachers did more to stunt the growth of national consciousness than it did to stimulate it. They condemn especially the introduction of English as a new national language because of its nonindigenous roots. Contrary to Philinda Rand's recollection of using English to weld together disparate people into a nation, the critics charge it did just the reverse. As long as English was the language of education, the move to adopt a single national language called Pilipino based on Tagalog (a language spoken in central Luzon) was doomed, and the unifying impact of a common language was lost. Still another critic has charged that the imposition of English was "the most effective program of cultural [intervention] ever devised."[27]

Others claim that the emphasis on education as the cure-all for Philippine ills masked more urgent needs such as land reform and the redistribution of wealth. These critics tend to shrug off as mawkish sentiment the great fondness Filipinos have for the memory of their American teachers. Seen from their nationalist point of view, the American actions, even if well intentioned, once again led not to an end desired by Filipinos but its opposite. Nationhood was delayed, not hastened.

The second area in which Taft's policy of attraction made a permanent difference in Philippine life was the manner in which he brought Filipinos into the colonial government. From the earliest days they worked in the civil service, rose to positions of political control in the provinces, and within a few years served in the legislative bodies that governed domestic Philippine affairs. As an ever larger number of the educated, influential, and well-to-do Filipinos accepted the attractions Taft offered, the number of their cohort not in the American camp diminished to a relative handful.

Even former leaders in the rebellion became important government officials once they pledged allegiance to the American cause. Among them was Manuel Quezon, who had been a major in Aguinaldo's army until the general's capture, at which time he surrendered to the American forces as well. From 1907 until 1916 Quezon was one of two Filipinos accredited to the U.S. Congress as nonvoting members. He worked diligently and successfully in Washington to build a base of support for the islands. In 1916 his efforts culminated in passage of legislation granting the Philippines a large degree of autonomy in internal matters and a promise of eventual independence.[28] In 1934, as the leader of the ruling party in the Philippines, he masterminded the passage of further legislation in Washington that established a Philippine commonwealth and set a 1944 date for full independence. In 1936 he became the first president of the Commonwealth of the Philippines, and in 1941 he was elected to a second five-year term in office.

Quezon was the most important of the Filipinos who participated in the American-sponsored government, but he was certainly not alone. Thousands of his colleagues did the same as opportunities for self-government grew under the colonial regime. As Karnow concluded, "From start to finish of America's rule, the Filipinos essentially governed themselves under increasingly light U.S. supervision." Political parties were formed, debate was vigorous, and after 1916 agitation for independence was not only permitted but expected. Quezon in exasperation once complained, "Damn the Americans! Why don't they tyrannize us more?" as he found it more and more difficult to arouse his fellow Filipinos in the continuing debate over the timing of Philippine independence.[29]

But troubling questions remain concerning the long-term effect of the policy of attraction. Were Quezon and the other elite co-opted by the Americans? Did this small group of Filipinos, not at all representative of the majority, settle for far less than they could have won if they had continued fighting? Did they recognize, as David Joel Steinberg has suggested, "the mutuality of advantages found in collaboration" and, in effect, sell out the mass of the Philippine population to protect their own positions of prominence?[30] And finally, by giving political power to the elite in the early days of the rebellion and continuing to give it in ever-increasing amounts, did the United States establish an oligarchy that has sat heavily upon the people ever since? Filipino historian Renato Constantino is among those who answer these questions in the affirmative. The United States, in the interest of "creating a market for American goods," he insists, put into positions of authority Filipinos who shared a common interest in markets, land, and profits—interests that were virtually identical to those of the Americans.[31] The elite had no interest in making the economic and social reforms that would have eased the plight of the majority of the Filipino people. In fact, their personal and class interests were precisely the opposite.

The debate over these questions will not be settled here. For the purposes of this project it is enough to show that forty-five years of colonial government can be interpreted by Filipinos in two ways. The first interpretation highlights the rapidity with which local people were given responsibility for their own affairs and the degree to which they controlled their own destiny. The second concentrates on the undemocratic nature of the national government it produced, the absence of any major reform efforts during the period of American control, and the establishment of a nation that was so dependent upon the United States as to never have the capacity to be truly free.

The bitter result of the Japanese attack on the Philippines in December 1941 is well known. The uneven match between the Philippine-American forces and the invading enemy led to the evacuation of

President Quezon, Vice President Sergio Osmeña, and General Douglas MacArthur along with their staffs and families in early 1942. A large portion of the army left behind fell into the hands of the Japanese, from whom they suffered cruelly for the next thirty months. Others vanished into the remote countryside to battle the Japanese as guerrillas. One American who did so served with a Filipino guerrilla unit for two years before MacArthur's return. Afterward, he recalled that his life was often in Philippine hands. On one occasion, when it was necessary to seek refuge in a rural village, a local teacher explained that he and his neighbors would hide the American. When asked by the dubious American why they would do this, given the Japanese warning that such action was punishable by death, the teacher said, "The Americans are our brothers."[32] His experience illustrates one of the most memorable things about the war in the Philippines: the way Americans and Filipinos joined in defending the nation. In contrast, when the Japanese forces overthrew the British in Hong Kong and Malaya, the Dutch in the Dutch East Indies, and the French in Indochina, the local populace stepped aside to let the imperialists fend for themselves.

MacArthur's parting words, actually spoken on his arrival in Australia, have become the stuff of legend. "I shall return" reverberated throughout the Philippines giving hope to the millions of Filipinos beginning to sense the hardships and humiliations awaiting them under Japanese occupation. MacArthur's use of the first person singular in wording his promise was a source of controversy at the time. Some of the general's critics took it as yet another sign of an egomaniacal personality. MacArthur's biographer, William Manchester, reports, however, that the wording was carefully crafted by the Quezon government to assure Filipinos that it was MacArthur's personal promise, a promise they could rely on, not one from the United States, whose credibility was suspect as a result of the failure to send reinforcements as promised.[33]

In October 1944 MacArthur returned to the Philippines with a powerful American army. He had kept his promise, and liberation was at hand. In February 1945 he announced the restoration of the Commonwealth, now led by Sergio Osmeña, following Quezon's death. But like so many other experiences shared by the United States and the Philippines, World War II left the latter with a residue of anger, suspicion, and resentment toward its reputed benefactor and liberator. The Filipinos felt they had been abandoned in early 1942. The United States had promised to send a relief column to the islands, but it failed to arrive; instead, the Americans pulled their defensive perimeter back to the Hawaiian islands and turned their attention to the war in Europe. At that time Quezon complained, "America writhes in anguish at the fate of a distant cousin, Europe, while a daughter, the Philippines, is being raped in the back room."[34] Even making allowances for Quezon's frequent use of hyperbole, the metaphor he chose to describe American action is particularly ugly.

Later, the U.S. Army liberated the country but in the process reduced Manila to utter ruin. The American strategy forced the enemy to stand and fight in Manila, thereby ensuring the city's destruction. Trapped and without hope of survival, the Japanese turned savage, extracting from the civilian population a horrible price. Approximately 100,000 civilians in Manila were murdered by marauding Japanese soldiers in less than a month while American forces struggled to destroy the enemy.[35]

The stories of the atrocities committed against women, children, the sick, and the aged rival the worst of those from the notorious Japanese rape of Nanking in 1938. One woman who was a young, pregnant wife in the spring of 1945 remembered a quarter century later that "the Americans had decided to risk the whole city for the sake of the few American lives in Santo Thomas [a prison camp] while the Japanese went on a rampage." She continued, her anger just barely controlled even after so many years, "I spat on the very first American soldier I saw that unspeakable day. . . . I had not eaten or slept for more than a week. . . . My husband had been tortured by Japanese soldiers in my presence and then led out to be shot. Our home had been ransacked. . . . I had seen the head of [an] aunt . . . roll under the kitchen stove. . . . I had heard the screams of the girls I had grown up with as they were dragged [away to be raped]. . . . So this was Liberation. I was no longer sure what was worse, the inhumanity of the Japanese or the helpfulness of the Americans."[36] In the end Manila was reduced to rubble, more completely destroyed than any allied city other than Warsaw. For many Filipinos it has never been clear that such destruction was necessary or that liberation had to be so crushingly painful for those being liberated.

More than two decades later, a Peace Corps volunteer living in the province of Leyte—site of MacArthur's return to the Philippines in 1944—found himself squarely in the middle of a debate on the significance of the country's liberation. He and a young Filipina teacher, who later became his wife, were asked to judge essays written by local college students commemorating the American landing at Leyte Gulf. As he recalled, "Most of the essays were vapid attempts at regurgitating [the official line], but one had as its thesis the notion that the Philippines was not *freed* by MacArthur's landing, and celebrating the landing was a monument to subservience to American military might." When the volunteer and his fellow judge selected it as the winner, the local sponsors were devastated. They quickly canceled the reading of the winning essay at the annual celebration of the landings—which, of course, would include a host of visiting American dignitaries. Regardless of whether there was an underlying grain of truth in the winning essay, there was no way the traditional Philippine high regard for smooth interpersonal relations would permit such a direct insult to their American guests.[37]

Several months after the Leyte landings, many Filipinos watched in astonishment as the victorious Americans organized the return to power of the same Filipino elite that had governed before the war. Many of these elite had collaborated with the pro-Japanese regime, and some had also escaped the bloody liberation by fleeing to the mountains north of Manila with the Japanese commanding officer. Yet, despite these embarrassing facts and a pledge to bring to justice all such traitors, the United States directed that Osmeña call into session the legislature that had been elected in 1941. It was impossible to field a quorum without including those members who had held positions in the collaborationist government. The inclusion of the collaborationists made those who had resisted the Japanese or suffered at their hands even more infuriated than they would already have been at the sight of the old oligarchy's return to important positions in the postliberation government.

Filipinos are capable of keeping alive two seemingly contradictory memories of the American-Philippine relationship. One is of a country and the valiant general who represented it, whose love for the Philippines was steadfast, whose deeds and encouragement did much to secure the nation's freedom and independence, and whose special relationship with it was a source of satisfaction and pride. The other is of a fair-weather friend who failed to support them in an hour of great need, who saved their capital city by destroying it, and who made a mockery of loyalty by ignoring the extent to which the Filipino elite had aided the common enemy.

Remembering with bitterness that the United States had poured many billions of dollars into the recovery of its former enemies, while providing a relative pittance to rebuild the Philippines, the woman who survived the battle for Manila wrote disparagingly in 1967 about the American ambassador "who throws in our face with every speech he makes" the fact that Washington provided financial aid to the Philippines after the war. From her vantage point the money had been *earned*, it was a repayment for services *rendered*, it was what being *family* required, and it was too little by far to be considered adequate compensation.[38]

Despite the trauma of liberation and the disappointment about the return of the "ossified" (as Karnow described them) but familiar elite into government positions, the coming of independence for the Philippines on 4 July 1946 was welcomed with great joy. General MacArthur was a prominent guest of honor, and the entire world marveled that a former colony had been released peacefully. The next twenty years saw the Philippines struggle with the challenges of true self-government and the constant reminders that there was indeed a special relationship with the United States. Uncle Sam continued to be a source of reassurance and of resentment. Philippine elections often had a hidden American component, as the former colonial master tried to ensure the selection of a candidate who would favor its interests. The involvement of the CIA in Philippine affairs was one of the worst kept secrets of all time. Yet the resentment level was not high because American support had been a key factor in eliminating the threat to national stability represented by the Huk rebellion, a communist-led insurgency that had gained wide popular support in several rural provinces.[39] As the cold war developed, America's major interest in the country shifted to its two strategic military bases there: the huge naval base at Subic Bay and the even larger Clark Air Force Base in central Luzon. These bases formed the heart of America's plan to defend its interests in Southeast Asia, and their continued availability to American forces was of utmost importance. In return for assurances that the bases would remain available, the United States sent large amounts of financial aid and development assistance to the islands. But many Filipinos considered the presence of the bases an affront to Philippine sovereignty and a demonstration to the entire world that the country was nothing but a vassal of its great and powerful neighbor across the Pacific. Independence had been gained, but the ambivalence remained.

Below the surface there continued to be "fond dependence [alongside] acute resentment." There was a tendency to "mirror American styles even while resisting American presences."[40] A generation of Filipinos argued mightily to get American military bases out of their country, although a large portion of the same generation wanted the country to become the fifty-first state of the Union. (In 1971 a public opinion poll that had been conducted in southern Luzon under the auspices of the American embassy indicated that in excess of 80 percent of the people there favored statehood.) The issue of the American bases colored nearly everything that the United States did in the country. The bases issue remained a problem for many years until, as discussed in chapter 9, a combination of natural disasters and the end of the cold war made the whole question moot.

The Philippines proudly entered the world's roll of independent countries on 4 July 1946. Then, in a moment of combined annoyance and assertiveness, the government changed its 'birthday' to June 12, the date of Aguinaldo's original declaration of nationhood in 1898. The Philippine embassy in Washington in June 1995 displayed a large banner declaring "97th Anniversary of Philippine Independence." The significance of July 4 has been written out of Philippine history, and what once was referred to as the American protectorate is now often called the American occupation. The tension that always accompanies any attempt to understand Filipino attitudes toward the United States was perfectly expressed by a Filipina author who wrote in 1969 with reference to Uncle Sam, "One must either hurl a brick [at him] or kiss his hand."[41]

The simultaneous existence of these contradictory and incompatible elements in the Filipino psyche can only be understood in the context of the country's historical roots. From the initial confusion over American intentions when Dewey first met Aguinaldo to the question of U.S. military bases on Philippine soil, American actions have often given rise to feelings of both appreciation and animosity. Good intentions have been seen as paternalism, material assistance as self-serving, the grant of home rule as the creation of an oligarchy, free trade as exploitation, and a protective military umbrella as a threat to sovereignty.

The Peace Corps was no exception. There were times when the helpful American became the insufferable American, when the agricultural expert became the know-it-all, when the change agent became the meddler. Precisely where the invisible line lay between the former and the latter was difficult to decipher, and volunteers often found themselves at a loss to understand what it was that they had done to cross that line. One volunteer, struggling to decide if he was the change agent or the meddler, described his dilemma in 1975: "I couldn't draw the line between development and cultural imperialism. I would go to the barrios and survey families, catalog their particular health problems and dream of ways to eradicate them. But then I'd catch myself and wonder whether my solutions . . . weren't really just [those of] an American trying to sell the American Way. . . . Other times . . . I'd vaccinate children or teach a mother about nutrition or [demonstrate] how to construct a cost-less water filter and then I knew what it was all about: helping people help themselves! My motivation . . . would be restored tenfold."[42] Quite possibly the reason it was so difficult to decide which role one was playing was that much of the answer depended on the Filipino response. Sometimes we triggered the reservoir of goodwill toward Americans; sometimes we triggered its opposite. Their response determined our own. We failed to understand that theirs was a historically conditioned one, not necessarily a comment on us personally. In time, as we developed strong working relationships with our hosts, and as we together turned some initial programming disasters into successes, we did get better at not sending the offensive signals, and they became more willing to forgive our lapses.

New Directions in the Philippines

4

The concept of volunteer management (the conscious, systematic, and continuing effort to organize and direct volunteer activities in order to accomplish desirable objectives) is anathema to most volunteers. Volunteers cherish their autonomy and see themselves as independent agents of change needing little or nothing in the way of supervision and direction to be effective. A former volunteer with whom I corresponded a few years ago stated that his "contact with Manila was minimal," the proudest boast a volunteer can make.[1] Another remembered that his "guiding light in the 70s . . . was to interact as little with Peace Corps program managers as possible."[2] At times this built-in bias against an institutional affiliation expressed itself as outright hostility toward anything and everything connected to the Peace Corps. One angry volunteer who served in the Philippines in the late 1970s was expressing this sentiment when, in reference to a meeting he had attended, he wrote, "The usual standoff between staff and volunteers was repeated. . . . Occupying the high ground, optimistic, and armed with the mike, the staff stood staunchly together in opposition to volunteers who vainly strove to voice two years of accumulated experiences, grievances and frustrations."[3] For this volunteer all that had gone right during his period of service—and his was an especially productive two years—was due to his own efforts; everything that had gone wrong or had been difficult was the fault of the staff. His words reflect feelings that, though not universal, were common enough to be of concern to every country director. As sociologist David Riesman discovered after interviewing volunteers in the Philippines during the mid-1960s, volunteers have "an almost paranoid, prickly and unforgiving attitude towards headquarters, whether in Manila or in Washington . . . [and they have a] resistance to even mild regulation."[4] Riesman's discovery certainly remained valid during the 1970s.

Yet despite the reluctance on the part of volunteers to acknowledge it, the Peace Corps staff's major function is volunteer management. A high proportion of staff time is devoted to it and its many component parts: creating programs that fit host country needs, developing job assignments, working with local officials and supervisors, preparing training programs, and providing moral and program support once a volunteer is in place. The in-country Peace Corps staff—both the Americans and the host country nationals—are the great unsung heroes of the organization. Usually people who write about the Peace Corps ignore their existence. When the staff presence is acknowledged, it is to assign them blame for things that went badly; rarely are they singled out for praise when things go well. Whether we were country directors or officials in Washington, those of us who depended on the staff knew full well how essential they were. The manner in which they carried out their responsibilities and the institutional framework within which they worked often proved to be the deciding elements in a program's success or failure—and in the success or failure of individual volunteers.

Too little has been written about the subject of volunteer management partly because of the 'generalist' bias of the founders, partly because the five-year rule has led to the departure of staff members just as they were finally learning to do their jobs, and partly because of the instinctive resistance to the idea among volunteers. The literature of the Peace Corps is either volunteer-centered, concentrating on the experience of an individual or at most a few volunteers, or Washington-centered and concerned with the larger issues of history, politics, and public perception. There is a need to explore a third aspect of the Peace Corps experience: the operational policies and procedures meant to transform a basic resource (the volunteers) into a force capable of achieving the organization's three goals. With respect to the Philippines, this discussion can be divided into four broad topics: how the Peace Corps evolved in the country, how it dealt with the issues of programming priorities and training policies, how it worked within the institutional framework of the Philippine government, and how the Peace Corps related to the official American community in the Philippines.

The Philippines in 1961 was an obvious and willing candidate to host a large contingent of Peace Corps volunteers, having enjoyed a close, although occasionally contentious, relationship with the United States for over sixty years. The islands were economically undeveloped, with a large portion of its forty million people living in poverty.

The government was in the habit of receiving American aid, and there were fond memories of the thousands of Thomasites who had earlier served in the Philippine education system. So it naturally followed that in 1961 an agreement was quickly reached between the two governments for a Peace Corps presence. On September 1, the first Peace Corps country director arrived in Manila to prepare the way for the 128 volunteers—the first of many contingents to come—due to follow him five weeks later. Remembering his initial reaction several years later, Larry Fuchs wrote, "No one really had any idea of what the job of Peace Corps representative would be." (For a time the position of country director was called "representative" to minimize the idea of a hierarchical bureaucracy.) As he quickly learned, the job was a daunting one. He and a few staff assistants had to "find houses for three hundred volunteers; [establish] a Peace Corps office in Manila and four field offices; contact principals and teachers at several hundred schools; explain the Peace Corps to Filipino officials and the press; study and discuss requests from more than thirty Filipino agencies desiring new programs; organize medical care for volunteers; establish in-country training programs; prepare dialect training materials and twelve [training] institutes; greet, entertain and guide approximately forty visitors from Washington; attempt to strengthen a vaguely and weakly conceived program; and most enervating of all, deal with the daily crises in the health and morale of volunteers."[5] One can almost make the case that Shriver's preference for learning by doing was essential to the program's existence simply because, had people known in advance just how difficult the task would be, no one would have been willing to undertake it.

Within a year one-third of all the Peace Corps volunteers in the world were working in the Philippines. By mid-1963 there were 630 volunteers there—the largest group in any one country—of whom more than 500 were working as educational aides. These were the jobs that Fuchs later characterized as nonjobs. The volunteers were assigned to elementary schools throughout the islands and told to "help" the Filipino teachers. They were not to teach classes because the country already had a surplus of teachers, and volunteer teachers would simply have reduced the number of positions available for Filipinos. Neither the Peace Corps nor the Philippine government wanted to increase unemployment rates among teachers, but the pressure for numbers was intense. Hence the creation of the educational aide job. Volunteers already face many difficulties in adjusting to living and working in a new culture, but the adjustment becomes even more difficult if there is no meaningful work for them to do.

Fuchs admitted to being slow to recognize the problem, but toward the end of his first year he explained he "was comfortable and objective enough [about the program's weaknesses] to give appropriate empathy to the pain, frustration and hostility of volunteers."[6]

Wherever there are volunteers displaying pain, frustration, and hostility, one is likely to find a substantial level of job dissatisfaction. For most of the 1960s PC/P continued to place most volunteers in the educational system. As late as 1969, 95 percent continued to work in the primary and secondary schools. However, substantial improvements were being made in finding more meaningful work for volunteers in the educational setting, many becoming co-teachers. The problem with job dissatisfaction remained, however. It was not until New Directions began to take hold in the country and volunteer jobs were found in other government agencies that the prospects for meaningful work improved. But, as the discussion that follows will show, the problem never did completely disappear; job dissatisfaction remained a serious concern for both volunteers and staff. And the need to provide every volunteer the opportunity to do something as well as be somewhere continues to be a primary concern.

The Peace Corps experience in the Philippines during the early years had also revealed other serious flaws in the original concept. Fuchs recalled that the Washington staff had firmly believed that only a minimum level of administrative, logistical, and programmatic support would be required in the field. Volunteers would be selected and trained in the United States, they would receive what job support they needed from their respective Philippine agencies, and they would be able to take care of themselves in all other respects. At the end of his twenty-one-month tour of duty, Fuchs concluded that PC/W had been wrong on all counts.[7] Volunteers were not supermen and superwomen; most of them were young Americans who only months earlier had been universally called college kids; the selection and training programs conducted in the United States were inadequate; and host country agencies were unprepared to provide the personal support many volunteers required. The initial small staff was stretched to the breaking point as it struggled to provide the personal and programmatic support needed. Three out of the original five staff members left the Philippines at the end of the first year, and Fuchs himself left before the end of his second year.

It gradually became clear that the management of Peace Corps programs in Third World countries demanded a far more complex administrative structure than originally contemplated. By 1970 Peace Corps/Philippines had twelve regional offices spread around the islands, a large headquarters in Manila, and a staff of seventy or more. The administrative apparatus required the services of specialists in personnel, finance, and logistics. Each of the regional offices was staffed by an American regional representative, a Filipino assistant representative, and an American or Filipino secretary. The headquarters in Manila contained a medical clinic, a library, a motor pool and repair shop, as well as the offices of the country director, his deputy, and a number of support services. In the far south the organization maintained an in-country training center on the outskirts of Zamboanga.[8] The Ayala training center, as it was called, was located about six hundred miles south of Manila in a tropical setting that was magnificent to behold. Tall palm trees swayed in the ocean breezes; the water, whose waves lapped gently on the coconut-strewn shores, was clear and warm; and the main house and its outbuildings were models of tropical architecture with their use of native woods, bamboo, and woven palm fronds. The center and its surroundings typified the natural beauty that graces so much of the island nation. On occasion the more adventurous of the American embassy personnel would spend vacation time at the site, enjoying its tranquility and proximity to the exotic Moslem city.

In every respect PC/P—and programs in many other countries as well—had developed into a full-fledged bureaucracy that was far removed from its origins. Shriver's habit of labeling every policy statement "interim" to indicate his belief that nothing should be fixed and unyielding gave way to a formal set of procedures and policies. Country directors found that they had to be far more than the personal representatives of their boss in Washington; they had to be managers of complex organizations as well.

During the 1960s the organization in the Philippines went through a process that mirrored what was happening to the agency in Washington and throughout the world. The lofty levels of idealism and optimism that had characterized the early years gave way to a more realistic appraisal of what could be accomplished and how to go about doing it. The need for better jobs became undeniable, as did the need for aligning the work of the Peace Corps with the host country's own development priorities. It also became clear that a head count of volunteers was not the most appropriate standard by which to measure success. As the decade ended, the number of volunteers in-country began to fall. Dissatisfied with the education program, volunteers resigned, and their posts were phased out. The Philippine Department of Education realized that its real needs would not be met by large numbers of volunteer co-teachers. The need for change was apparent, but a catalyst was needed to make it happen. That catalyst proved to be New Directions.

Phil Waddington, the man who later hired me for the Philippines job, was sent to Manila as country director by Blatchford in December 1969, shortly after New Directions was announced. It was Waddington who began the long, slow process of changing the program's basic thrust in that country, but in October 1970 he was promoted and called back to Washington. His successor lasted only seven months, and five months after that, in December 1971, I replaced the man who had been interim country director. As a result of the rapid turnover in country directors, the changes that Waddington had started were slow in taking shape. By mid-1971, however, the first of the New Directions volunteers began to arrive and the planned program redirection was under way.

The most important change was a realignment of Peace Corps programming priorities so that they would correspond with those of the Philippine government. The decision to emphasize education ten years earlier had been a matter of expediency, the creation of the educational aide job permitting the quickest deployment of the largest number of available volunteers with the least amount of specialized training. Given the nearly universal respect for education in both the United States and the Philippines, it was a decision that had been easily rationalized. When the time came to reassess the wisdom of that decision, however, its flaws had become obvious. New Directions shifted Peace Corps emphasis to involvement in areas of agriculture production and social development in line with contemporary economic development theory.

The first objective for any developing country, according to that theory, must be self-sufficiency in food production. Without it there is an almost insurmountable obstacle blocking meaningful economic development. If a poor nation must use most of its hard currency to purchase food, it cannot make the essential investments in infrastructure development that must precede any measurable improvement in economic activity. Money that would otherwise be spent on transportation systems, factories, natural resource development, and modern technology must instead be used to buy rice, corn, and canned goods. In the years immediately following World War II, that was the situation prevailing in the Philippines. The country imported large quantities of rice, dairy products, canned goods, and even fruits and vegetables. In addition, the country had one of the world's highest rates of population growth, making a gloomy outlook even bleaker. With always more mouths to feed, more hard currency was needed to buy food from abroad and even less was available for genuine development projects.[9] The economic take-off point theorized by economist W. W. Rostow kept receding ever further into the distance.

Rostow's point was that a fully developed and modern agricultural sector freed other resources, both human and financial, which could then be used to move an economy forward. In one of his seminal works on economic development theory Rostow said, "In fact, agricultural revolutions have been required to permit rapidly growing and urbanizing populations to be fed without exhausting foreign exchange resources in food imports or creating excessive hunger in the rural sector. . . . [They have] played an essential and positive role, not merely by both releasing workers to the cities and feeding them, but also by earning foreign exchange for capital formation purposes."[10] Rostow had first presented his ideas about economic development in a series of lectures delivered to an academic audience at Cambridge University in 1959. In the words of an early reviewer of a collection of these lectures, Rostow's ideas "swept the popular imagination and influenced national leaders, especially in poorer countries aspiring to prosperity under democracy."[11] By the beginning of the 1970s, Rostow's terminology and conceptualizations were in use by development workers around the world. We in the Philippines used the phrase *take-off point* as if it were a nearly visible place just around the corner. The Philippine technocrats with whom we worked did not worry about *what* to do—Rostow had told them all they needed to know—the worry was about *how* to do it. (The discovery that Rostow's theories vastly oversimplified the situation was not to be made for some years to come; in many countries the problem of an underdeveloped economy remains as intractable as ever.)[12]

In addition to delaying or even precluding economic development, the need to import food invariably led to higher food prices with drastic consequences for the poor. Without money to buy an adequate amount of imported food and without knowing how to make the most nutritious use of local foodstuffs, a large segment of the population suffered daily from the effects of malnutrition. When the lack of a wholesome diet was coupled with haphazard sanitation and the absence of basic preventive health measures—both common in the developing world—the result was a constant state of debilitation that sapped the will to work and provided a fertile ground for diseases of every type to flourish. What untrained observers saw as indolence among the poor in the Third World was far more likely to be an energy deficiency resulting from bad diet and poor health. The dreadful scenes of mass starvation that accompany famines are more the exception than the rule in the Third World. The greater problem is the consequence of long-term—if not lifelong—dietary deficiencies and endemic diseases that make a mockery of the idea that people in the Third World hold the key to their own development.

The government of the Philippines was well aware of the problems caused by its outdated agricultural sector and of the need to increase the people's understanding of the importance of basic sanitation and the practice of good nutrition. It had well-trained technocrats in key positions of leadership, it had established bureaucratic structures to carry out appropriate programs, and it had assurances from the United States and other countries that financial assistance would be made available. Moreover, by the late 1960s the prospects for achieving food self-sufficiency had improved dramatically with the development of a variety of productivity-enhancing technologies, including the availability of a special strain of high-yielding rice, the staple food for most Filipinos. This miracle rice was developed during the 1960s at the International Rice Research Institute located at Los Baños, an American-funded agricultural research facility not far from Manila. Its impact on the world's food production capacity—and the impact of similar miracle varieties for corn and wheat—is difficult to exaggerate. Properly planted and tended, the new strains of rice could double, even triple, annual production levels.[13] (In brief, the breakthrough came as a result of breeding plants with stronger stalks so that they could hold the heavier yield of grain produced by using modern fertilizers, herbicides, and irrigation.) As the director of the Overseas Development Council concluded in 1970, "It is realistic for the first time in history to consider the eradication of hunger for the overwhelming majority of mankind."[14]

In the Philippines the ultimate goal was in sight—if Filipino farmers could be taught to make use of the new developments and if the needed resources, especially fertilizers and high-quality animal feeds, could be provided. The government knew how to increase crop yields by a factor of two or three. It also knew how to shorten from two years to seven months the time needed to raise a hog to market size, how to use farm ponds to grow high-protein fish to feed farm families, and how to use cash crops to supplement rural family incomes. It had the money to provide small loans (a key ingredient in the plan) so that farmers could purchase the necessary fertilizers and farm implements, and it certainly knew the essentials of good health and nutrition. What it lacked was sufficient manpower and a sense of urgency at the extension agent level to carry the new ideas to the majority of the population who were subsistence farmers. And, as every development worker sooner or later comes to realize, it is at the barrio level that the success or the failure of the government's programs is determined.

Once the Peace Corps began to adjust its role to fit more closely the goals set by the Filipinos charged with planning the country's economic and social development, it immediately became clear where the volunteers could be most useful: in the delivery of services designed to increase agricultural production and to address basic diet and health concerns at the local level. The agricultural sector of the Peace Corps program eventually came to include projects in livestock and poultry husbandry, the production of rice and other foodstuffs, the delivery of credit to small farmers, and the development of a small-scale fish farming industry. The social development sector soon included projects in rural health services, nutrition education, social welfare activities, and a variety of small business, youth, and town planning initiatives. Without abandoning the field of education, we did continue with the shift in emphasis that had begun earlier: Volunteers were placed in colleges and universities as teachers and administrators; other volunteers provided in-service training for Filipino teachers of English, math, and science; still others worked to bring modern methods of physical education to the country's school system. Peace Corps staff and Filipino education officials agreed that volunteers would be placed in jobs only where there were no qualified local people and that the jobs must be important to the education system. There were to be no more nonjobs.

By August 1973, with the arrival of the first of three groups of volunteers due within a ten-month period to work in the rural credit project, the transition to New Directions was well past the midpoint. Of the 350 volunteers in the country at that time, more than half were involved in agricultural programs.[15] Most of the remaining were in other priority programs or in highly specialized jobs where the organization could provide volunteers with rare skills. (As an example of what was done in this latter category, four volunteers over a period of five years helped to save an endangered species of eagle in a remote part of the island of Mindanao.)[16] On the morning of the first rural credit group's arrival, a Manila daily newspaper declared, "With the coming of these technicians, the Peace Corps in this country has changed. We can recall when the first groups of PCV's came over . . . most of them landed in the schools. [Now they are being] assigned to the most pressing problems of the country-side."[17]

With the major change in program direction, one would expect that the characteristics of the typical volunteer would change as well. And they did, but far less than the critics of New Directions had predicted (and also far less than the Peace Corps publicity apparatus was implying). For the most part, volunteers remained recent college graduates. It was not by chance that a huge influx of new volunteers arrived each summer; the fact was that their availability coincided with college graduation. One difference between the volunteers of the 1960s and those of the 1970s was that more of the new arrivals had bachelor's degrees in animal science, home economics, biology, agricultural economics, or business. In addition, many had grown up on farms or participated in 4-H Club activities or worked in community settings that would have provided them with some relevant, but often limited, real-life experience related to the jobs they were to perform. But there were also many whose academic training had been in the traditional liberal arts fields. They were destined for programs where the needed skills could be taught in training sessions. The rudiments of nutrition, sanitation, and many aspects of personal health are not difficult to acquire. They may, in fact, be more easily acquired than the teaching and community organizing skills that the volunteers of the 1960s needed. There were no real differences in motivation and idealism between those who came as part of New Directions and those who came before, except for the draft avoidance issue among the earlier groups. (Once the draft lottery system was put in place, the Peace Corps refused to accept applicants likely to be called up, so that problem eventually disappeared.)

Another major change in the volunteer population that was readily apparent came as a result of the decision to recruit volunteers with substantial amounts of experience, even if they had spouses and children. We usually had twelve to fifteen families on the roster at any given time, with a combined total of as many as twenty children. And what a fine collection of volunteers they were! Rollin and Betty Heller had farmed in Illinois for thirty years before their arrival in the rural credit program.[18] Lloyd and Catherine Johnson had raised hogs in Minnesota for many years before they and their four children joined a livestock production program.[19] David and Martha Deppner had managed a flock of twelve thousand laying hens in Ohio before they and their children joined the same program.[20] George and

Monita Timmons were Kansas farmers and George had been mayor of their hometown when they came to the country to teach agricultural marketing skills to a provincial governor's planning board. When their youngest son, Gary, who had accompanied them, turned eighteen, he also was sworn in as a volunteer.[21] Lowell and Helen Lambert had thirty years of farming and ranching experience when they decided to do as their son had done ten years earlier: join the Peace Corps.[22] There were others in the social development programs, in education, and in highly specialized jobs where only one or two volunteers were needed. As a group, and as individuals, they added immensely to the program.

Not only did they have more highly developed skills than their younger colleagues but they also provided the latter with moral support and perspective that was often badly needed and gratefully accepted. One woman remembered that the Timmonses "were surrogate parents for a whole group of volunteers serving on Panay, offering everything from simple recipes for the novice cook to advice on how to decide whether to marry that Filipino boyfriend or girlfriend. Culture shock would have been a lot tougher without them."[23] Far from being inflexible or unable to acculturate, as the critics had predicted, the older volunteers became part of their communities as completely as did the others. There is no question that families were more costly than individuals would have been or that more staff time and effort were needed to support families with children. Offsetting these considerations was the fact that families as a rule accomplished all three of the Peace Corps goals more successfully than did single volunteers. The Philippines is a family-oriented country, and the reception that families received was heartfelt, open, and welcoming.

To be fair, some others did not share my enthusiasm for volunteer families. An early country director in Korea recalled in 1995, "Unsuccessfully, I argued against [the acceptance of families]. Perhaps for my speaking out I was awarded an early family that had three or four young children. [They] were a major distraction, burden, and cost. . . . The value of a family . . . eluded me."[24] It could be that we in the Philippines were just fortunate in the quality of the families sent to us. Or, and this is the more likely reason, the difficult living conditions that prevailed in Korea, especially with respect to schooling for American children, the totally nonwestern nature of the Korean culture, and the hurdle of learning an especially difficult language, all came together to make it a poor location for families. In any event, the Philippine experience proved that families could be successful in at least some Peace Corps countries and that the added expense and staff time needed to support them was worthwhile.

The education and age profiles of the volunteer population were not the only characteristics that had changed. The innocence of the earliest volunteers was gone. Volunteers were now assertive, confident in the legitimacy of their own voices, and no longer willing to accept those in authority without question. This change clashed violently with the Peace Corps's traditional tendency to look at volunteers as the source of problems, not as problem solvers. Although the authors probably did not intend to convey this impression, Lowther and Lucas devoted page after page to criticizing volunteers on their job performance, their insensitivity to cultural differences, and their general lack of maturity.[25] In doing this they were simply reflecting the prevailing view of the 1960s in Washington that what was right about the Peace Corps was a result of action by the leadership, and what was wrong was the result of the inadequacies of a small number of volunteers who had inexplicably slipped through the rigorous selection and evaluation process. PC/W devoted enormous time and energy to developing procedures that culled those whom it considered unworthy, they badly overreacted to what were often fairly minor volunteer indiscretions, and, rather than correct the flaws in the program, they insisted that volunteers alter themselves to fit the program. It was a shock to learn upon arrival in-country that volunteers were expected to make even bad assignments work, rather than for the staff and the host country agency to admit fault and to solve the problem or transfer the volunteer. An early Peace Corps evaluator told Shriver that the weakness of certain projects in Guatemala, Sri Lanka, and Pakistan resulted from involving too many volunteers graded 'average' by training site psychologists.[26] To his credit, Shriver rejected this assessment, but the tendency to blame the volunteer persisted. Fuchs, despite his heroic efforts and considerable success in getting the Philippines program up and running, never got over the habit of calling volunteers 'boys' and 'girls.'

Under New Directions the Peace Corps volunteers were a bit older (they were on average twenty-seven instead of twenty-four years of age) and had some real-life experience. These volunteers were also far more accustomed to having their voices heard than were their predecessors. It was clearly time to jettison the paternalistic attitude toward them. Administrative changes in mid-1969 removed "restrictions on the volunteers' freedom to manage their own affairs." These changes were announced in the *Peace Corps Volun-*

teer (an agency publication sent to all volunteers) under the headline "New Policies: Untie Some Apron Strings."[27]

In the Philippines we took these changes one step further by asking volunteers to help manage the agency's affairs as well as their own. Volunteers made the training more relevant to actual field conditions, and they redesigned programs so that they would be more effective. As they worked, it soon became apparent that these men and women had a great deal to offer. After all, who should know better what worked and what did not than the people who had actually filled the assignments. Like the staff in many other countries, PC/P included volunteers in staff meetings, established a practice of meeting with them every six months in small groups throughout the country, insisted that staff members always be willing to hear volunteer concerns, and accepted the premise that job and adjustment problems could be the organization's fault as well the volunteers'. This transition was not always easy. Some staff members resented the equal voice given volunteers; some volunteers abused the policy by using it to excuse poor performance. But on the whole everyone benefited when volunteers were brought into the decision-making process and were treated as responsible adults rather than as college kids with an inherent tendency to mess up.

Peace Corps/Philippines had a large full-time staff in 1971. The professional segment included the country director, his deputy, and the heads of the management and financial sections; the people responsible for developing new projects with local agencies and organizing the training programs for new volunteers; the medical staff; and seven regional representatives located around the country. (The number of regional offices had already been reduced from an earlier twelve.) Seven professional positions were held by Filipinos. The administrative and support positions were all filled by Filipinos, some of whom had been with the Peace Corps since its first year in the Philippines. It was they who provided the institutional memory that the rapid turnover in American staff precluded. Ironically, given Fuchs's unsuccessful plea in 1961 for at least a modicum of staff support, by 1971 the administrative structure could almost have been called bloated. Concurrently, Congress, under the prodding of Congressman Passman, was about to cut Peace Corps funding midway through the fiscal year, threatening Peace Corps's very existence.[28] Although this potential crisis was eventually resolved in Washington, all spending not directly related to essential volunteer support activities was ordered cut. The staff in the Philippines was able to reduce its employment rolls by 20 percent, close several more regional offices and the central training facility in Zamboanga, replace some departing American professional staff with equally qualified Filipinos at a lower cost, reduce office space in Manila by 30 percent, close an unneeded vehicle repair shop, and tighten controls over administrative spending. Needless to say, there were some who predicted dire consequences, but as the months passed, the grumbling stopped and the agency continued to function normally. President Nixon's warning to Blatchford that the Peace Corps seemed overstaffed and top-heavy had proved correct, at least for the Philippines.

PC/P also reintroduced the concept of volunteer leaders. The Peace Corps Act had from its inception provided that volunteers "whose services [were] required for supervisory or other special duties or responsibilities" could be enrolled as volunteer leaders.[29] Larry Fuchs used them extensively during his tenure and cited many by name in his book, *Those Peculiar Americans*.[30] But the practice had been abandoned because the volunteer leaders had gradually become merely messengers for the ever-growing staff, and other volunteers resented the existence of a special class of volunteer. When the volunteer leader positions were brought back, seasoned third-year volunteers were assigned to positions that carried the same type of programming responsibilities carried by some of the regular staff. These volunteer leaders had previously done well in the programs they managed, and they brought a special kind of authenticity to their jobs. Not everyone, however, applauded the move. Some of the existing staff members resented the fact that volunteers were being given staff responsibilities and threatening the higher status that staff membership was meant to imply. Others believed that it was unethical to ask volunteers living on modest allowances to do the same job being performed by staff members earning much higher Foreign Service Officer salaries. These criticisms had some validity, although experience soon proved that the benefits far exceeded the disadvantages. The important consideration was to provide knowledgeable program direction; it really did not matter whether that direction came from a volunteer or a staff member. The budget cuts that every country director had to deal with prevented the hiring of enough staff to do the required job. The solution to use experienced volunteers in this capacity worked well.

At the same time the basis for volunteer support structure changed from geography to program. For example, rather than assign a staff member responsibility for all volunteers in the Bicol region (basically the southernmost part of the island of Luzon), he was assigned responsibility for all volunteers working in a specific project area (e.g., the fisheries program) regardless of where they were located. This change placed a significant travel burden on the staff, but it also concentrated responsibility along programmatic lines. It recognized the greater importance of doing something rather than just being somewhere. The work to be done became the organizing principle, and this allowed for much better technical support for volunteers, as well as much closer coordination with Filipino officials.

Experienced volunteers also played a key role in that other essential staff function: training. PC/P was fortunate to have a dedicated and experienced cadre of trainers, both American and Filipino, who never ceased their search for ways to improve. The first and most important step forward—taken in 1970—was the move to bring training into the host country. Initially, volunteers for the Philippines were trained on a university campus in California. Later, training was moved to Hawaii in an effort to provide a more realistic setting for those destined for tropical countries. Finally—what in hindsight was the logical choice all along—volunteer training was brought into the Philippines where training activities could be tailored to meet the requirements of both the job and the culture. (Many other countries made the same decision, and the massive training sites in Puerto Rico and Hawaii were closed, although with much harsh criticism of Blatchford for doing so.)[31]

Peace Corps has traditionally divided a volunteer's tour of duty into two phases: training and service. In the Philippines we concluded that this was an artificial distinction. Volunteers never actually *complete* their training, if by training one means the process of learning to do a job in a different culture. They continue to learn throughout their tour. In addition, given the varying requirements of different jobs even within the same program—for example, the farmer clientele of two volunteer agricultural extension workers might be completely different—some volunteers became aware of their particular training needs only after they were on the job. As a result, the director of training for the Philippines, Mel Beetle, and his deputy, Arturo Aportadera, devised a continuous training program. An eight-week training period was followed by eight or twelve weeks on the job, and that would be followed by two or three more weeks of training tailored specifically to an individual volunteer's needs. Additional training programs would be scheduled over the next year as required to meet changing job responsibilities. This approach worked well both for skills training and for cross-cultural training. Critics of the early 1970s condemn the shortening of training programs from an initial twelve weeks to eight as a penny-wise and pound-foolish attempt to save money.[32] At least for the Philippines, this criticism misses the point. The initial training period was reduced to eight weeks, not to lower training costs but to do the job better. And this example is perhaps the best response to those who condemned the Peace Corps management for enforcing the five-year rule in late 1971: The agency had become set in its ways and tended to see change as a threat rather than as a solution. Many could not see what was obvious: The sharp division between training and service was needlessly limiting the organization's ability to reach its full potential.

Peace Corps/Philippines also eliminated the survival-of-the-fittest environment that had permeated so much of the earlier training efforts. As I wrote to Waddington in December 1972, "Essentially our approach is rooted in the belief that people who join the Peace Corps are mature, committed, and capable people who have a unique and valuable opportunity to be of service to others. . . . Our job as staff is to ensure that each volunteer achieves his full potential for service. . . . Peace Corps [has been] too quick to conclude that an individual cannot fill the new role, and we gently 'counsel him out' (a euphemism for getting him to accept our own negative view of his potential)."[33] The conclusion that a new approach was necessary became inescapable when an analysis of previous training programs showed that often 25 percent of volunteers 'failed' during training and a further 25 percent 'failed' during the first twelve months of service. This meant that half of those so energetically wooed and recruited had gone home before they really had an opportunity to make any contribution at all. (Lowther and Lucas reported that volunteer attrition rates were "scandalously high," and Fuchs had earlier lamented that "as many as 40 percent of the volunteers scheduled for service in the Philippines had been 'selected out' of some training groups.")[34] The truly disturbing element in all this was that many interpreted the high failure rates as evidence that the Peace Corps and its training staff were doing an *excellent* job rather than as evidence to the contrary. One of the founders recently complimented Shriver for being willing to drop "as many as a third of a volunteer group . . . from a training program" to ensure high quality.[35] It never seems to have entered anyone's mind that no other elite group suffered such a high casualty rate and that the Peace Corps should not either.

Everything that I believed told me that failure rates of this magnitude pointed to inadequacies in the institutional Peace Corps more than to the inadequacies of the people who wanted to serve in it. I still recall with disbelief hearing a staff member from Malaysia describe with glee how he fed new arrivals highly spiced local food at their first meal—and in Malaysia highly spiced is very highly spiced indeed—to let them know what they were in for. This approach was more reminiscent of fraternity hazing than it was of a soundly based training program. In summary, our intent was to shift the emphasis away from making volunteers prove to us that they were worthy toward making the staff prove to the volunteers that we could provide the support and resources they needed to survive the inevitable periods of loneliness, self-doubt, fear, depression, physical discomfort, and frustration that are part of the Peace Corps life.

Finally, and perhaps most dramatically, PC/P eliminated the traditional qualifying process for trainees with its formal assessments, psychologists, and review boards. Previously those selected for Peace Corps service had been forced to undergo a three-month trial before being sworn in as actual volunteers. In the meantime they were called trainees. This was a nerve-racking period for everyone. Volunteers knew that they were constantly being observed and evaluated, but they had no real idea of the standards against which they were being measured. As Julius Amin reported in his study of the Peace Corps in Cameroon, a volunteer from the first batch of trainees destined for that country recalled that "selection was clandestine . . . [and] plot-ridden." Another from the same group found the Peace Corps guilty of violating its own policy of flexibility. Still others compared Peace Corps training unfavorably with military training. "In the army, they break you down at the beginning of training, then they ease up. . . . In the Peace Corps they never stopped breaking you down." The result for the Cameroon program was predictable: More than 20 percent failed in training. Perhaps even worse, many of those who survived recalled their training with acute resentment rather than with a sense of pride in their accomplishment.[36]

The reason that volunteers did not know the standards on which selection decisions were based was that there were none. Despite ten years of experience in preparing people to serve as volunteers, no one had been able to develop a set of standards that was helpful in predicting which trainees would be successful and which would not. After several years of the boot camp training model, the Peace Corps eventually realized that there was no connection between the ability of trainees to climb a rope or do push-ups and their ability to perform well as volunteers. It was more difficult, however, for the Peace Corps to abandon its reliance on some sort of elaborate, seemingly scientific, method of psychological assessment. During the 1960s it was common practice for a board of trainee assessment psychologists to rank all volunteers on a scale of one to five. Those ranked one were considered hopelessly unfit for volunteer duty, whereas those ranked five were considered to be surefire candidates for attaining the status of 'super vol.' A major controversy arose around the question of whether 'threes' should be sent abroad. The debate raged for several years until sufficient field experience allowed some sort of objective assessment to be made. The result was that "no necessary connection existed between those volunteers who seemed the best in training and those volunteers who turned out to be the best in the field."[37] Even the possessors of the mighty 'five' ranking had their share of disappointments, and more than a few of the 'threes' enjoyed great success. There is no way of telling how the lowly 'ones' and 'twos' would have done in-country because none of them were allowed to make it that far.

Even as the 1960s ended, the Peace Corps was still attempting to use psychology to identify those trainees who would succeed and those who would fail. As a good friend and fellow country director remembered in 1995, "We made [a] revolutionary change [in Korea] in our training program for volunteers. . . . The value added by using psychologists on the staff of training programs was difficult to identify. I could quantify only negative returns [and] a waste of scarce funding support."[38] So he eliminated them. In the Philippines the training staff was more intent on easing the guilt of trainees who had made the decision to resign than it was in helping them stay and do well. We desperately needed an approach that would signal our faith in them, not our doubts. Here were grown men and women ten thousand miles from home having made their commitment to the Peace Corps, but the Peace Corps was making it plain that it had not yet made a commitment to them.

The solution chosen was remarkably simple. Rather than making trainees spend the three-month period under the constant worry that they would be found wanting and sent home, PC/P swore them in within two or three days of their arrival in-country. It was important that they know right from the start that they were part of the organization; everything would be done to ensure their success, not to weed them out. It is important to point out that standards remained high even when volunteers were sworn in immediately upon arrival. Those who were obviously not qualified went home. But the vast majority who had the potential to expand into their sometimes larger-than-life new roles did not have to endure the anxieties and distractions of a subjective and flawed evaluation procedure.

The result of the efforts to humanize the training environment was a marked increase in the retention of volunteers. During the thirteen months preceding the change in philosophy (from March 1971 to March 1972), 131 trainees arrived in the Philippines. By the end of three months, 26 percent of them had been 'deselected,' 'counseled out,' or allowed to quit even before they had set foot on their job sites. In the first five months under the new program, 141 men and women arrived in-country. After three months of training and two months on the job, only 9 percent had left the program.[39] Critics will charge that the quality of the volunteers in the field must have dropped, although there is no evidence that such was the case, nor is there any evidence that the widespread screening procedures used in other programs worked. But there is ample evidence from many other arenas that people perform better in supportive environments than they do in those marked by constant screening, skepticism, and suspicion.[40]

One of the best aspects of New Directions was its willingness to delegate more responsibility and authority to the field. As Blatchford said in 1969, "We must [have] the flexibility to respond to specific local problems; thus we have provided for local option wherever these seem necessary."[41] Country directors were freed from the burden of centralized decision making that had characterized so much of the Peace Corps of the 1960s. Nowhere is that better illustrated than in the fact that the staff in the Philippines was able to take control of so crucial an activity as training and impose its own collective philosophy on it. The fact that the changes were good strengthens the case for field-based decision making and in hindsight shows that the early ways relied too heavily on a strong centralized decision-making process that delayed progress rather than enhanced it.

One of the major tenets of New Directions was a belief, affirmed in 1970 by Blatchford in an article in *Foreign Affairs,* that Peace Corps activities "must be rooted in local desires and in projects administered by local people."[42] This meant that the agency and the host country, usually in the person of a representative of the national government, needed to cooperate much more effectively than previously. Projects needed to be planned so that they would complement the country's own efforts to stimulate economic and social development. Volunteers needed to work within the government's institutional structures; Peace Corps staff had to be in close contact with the officials responsible for the programs both at the national and the local levels; and Peace Corps programs needed to be subject to the same evaluation procedures as the government's own programs were.

In order for the volunteers to do work of this kind in the Philippines, PC/P needed to establish close relations with the senior government officials who managed the key development programs. Without support from the top, little could be accomplished at the working level where most volunteers would be placed. Fortunately, the support was found in three important cabinet-level departments: the Department of Agriculture and Natural Resources (DANR), the Department of Health, and the Department of Social Welfare. The Department of Education retained its close association with the agency as did such public and private organizations as the Presidential Arm for National Minorities, the Philippine Amateur Athletic Foundation, the YMCA, and several independent colleges and universities.

Staff members worked with these organizations to develop ways to use volunteers, to establish guidelines for volunteer qualifications and training, and to develop volunteer jobs at appropriate points in the system. Later, after volunteers had arrived and were at work, Peace Corps and Philippine officials met to evaluate progress and to make whatever changes were appropriate and necessary. Although the above is an accurate description of how the programming process was supposed to work, no Peace Corps veteran will be surprised to learn that it did so only imperfectly, especially during the early years of a project. There were simply too many variables, any one of which could go wrong and cause serious problems. Just as the first volunteers in the Philippines in 1961 had to endure "pain, frustration and hostility" while the Peace Corps learned how to do its job, the first of the New Directions volunteers had to endure similar feelings while the staff learned theirs.

The Peace Corps staff's most senior contacts within the Philippine government were with the secretaries of the various departments. Generally, however, it worked with bureau heads in Manila and in the field with regional directors and local supervisors. In three years I met the Philippine president only once, and that meeting occurred somewhat by chance.[43] President Ferdinand Marcos ruled as an elected president from 1965 until September 1972 and as a dictator from then until 1986. He welcomed the Peace Corps but paid it little attention. He left that task to the various technocrats who managed the nonpolitical aspects of his government. He did, however, make an impact on the Peace Corps when he proclaimed martial law, an act that profoundly changed the environment in which the Peace Corps operated and its relationship to the government.

By 1972 virtually all contemporary observers had concluded that the Philippines was in a state of near anarchy. A revolutionary force under the name of the New People's Army was active in several parts of the country. Student unrest, occasionally violent, marred the nation's campuses and often disrupted normal activities at the president's palace, government office buildings, and the American embassy. The elections of November 1971 (for provincial governorships and eight seats in the Senate) were excessively violent, even by permissive Philippine standards, as politicians used 'guns, gold, and goons' to win heavily contested elections. The Philippine police constabulary reported that 131 people had been killed and 107 wounded in political incidents, a new record of dubious distinction.[44] One volunteer newly in the country had more than her share of opportunities to experience the dangerous side of living in the Philippines. As she wrote to a group of prospective volunteers, "Some of my experiences haven't been pleasant ones. . . . I was present when the 6th and 14th floors [of the city hall] were bombed. . . . I was also present [a few weeks later] at the attempted assassination of Mrs. Marcos." Yet, she concluded, "I can truthfully say . . . I do not regret . . . [joining] the Peace Corps."[45]

Criminal violence in the streets was commonplace. A few weeks after our arrival, my wife was accosted in broad daylight at a busy intersection by three young Filipinos brandishing knives. They grabbed her purse, but she held on with all her might. After a brief struggle, the would-be thieves decided that this woman wanted to keep her purse more than they wanted to steal it, and they fled. It was only after she stormed into my office in a fury over the incident that she realized the danger she had been in and collapsed in a heap on a nearby sofa.

Restaurants regularly required their patrons to check all of their weapons before being seated, and men riding in that unique Philippine vehicle, the jeepney, often carried weapons. Volunteers used jeepneys regularly as a means of transportation, and we cautioned them to avoid making eye contact with anyone carrying a weapon, especially if the men had been drinking. (Making prolonged eye contact in the Philippines is considered overly assertive under any circumstances.)

Philippine legislators spent most of their time squabbling about irrelevant issues and posturing to achieve political advantage. And to put the finishing touches on a badly deteriorating political situation, in the summer of 1972 floods of biblical proportions struck Luzon's rice fields, and a severe drought ravaged the corn crop in the south. An American resident of Manila, Beth Day, declared that an "unholy alliance [of man-made and natural disasters] had turned the beautiful city into a frightened hotbed of demonstrations and random violence, earning it the doubtful distinction of being one of the most dangerous and lawless cities in the world."[46]

It was in these circumstances that Marcos took action one evening to declare martial law.[47] Early the following morning I received a worried call at home from PC/W giving me the news. (There were no newspapers that morning because Marcos had suspended all publications, so I was unaware of his declaration.) What, Washington wanted to know, was the situation? And were the volunteers safe? My reply was that martial law was less cause for alarm than one might think, that perhaps it could restore some order to a chaotic situation, and that volunteer safety was enhanced by martial law, not diminished. My response was fully consistent with the feelings of a large majority of ordinary Filipinos in 1972. Six or seven years later, it would be a different story as Marcos's true nature became widely known, but in the beginning his declaration of martial law had a broad base of popular support.

One looks in vain for sympathetic accounts of the declaration of martial law written within the past ten years. Everyone now knows too much about Marcos's fatal shortcomings as a human being and as a national leader to see in the declaration anything other than a first step toward the attainment of absolute power. At the time, however, we lacked the hindsight of later observers. Raymond Bonner, the author of a fascinating study of Marcos's relations with the United States, flatly states that it "is not Monday morning quarterbacking" to see in the declaration "a grab for personal power and riches." He implies that anyone failing to see this in 1972 was either a dupe or someone with a hidden agenda. He dismisses the fact that writers for the *Washington Star*, the *New York Times*, and the *Christian Science Monitor* and a bipartisan element in Congress supported Marcos as simply evidence of the pervasiveness of the dupes and the hidden-agenda folks.[48]

In 1972 it was rumored that the United States had played a major role in the declaration of martial law. Some said that the CIA had actually initiated the move; others reported that the United States had given explicit approval for Marcos's action; and yet others said that the approval was only implicit in order to give Washington credible 'deniability' should Congress make a fuss over the change in our Asian 'showcase for democracy.' The startling thing about the reports was that the Filipinos seemed not to be concerned about the possibility that the CIA was involved. There was such broad support for martial law, or at least recognition that it was necessary, that any possible U.S. involvement was welcomed, not censored. In later years, when public attitudes in the Philippines toward Marcos turned negative, the reports of American complicity were seen in a different light. Then, in keeping with long tradition in such matters, the CIA's involvement became one more item on the long list that had caused such contradictory feelings toward the United States. It was one thing for the Americans to be involved in an action that had popular approval; it was quite another when that approval disappeared and martial law came to be seen as a device to give Marcos free rein to plunder his own land.

Some volunteers were upset because the declaration of martial law violated deeply held principles, and a few refused to serve under it. Two who made this decision were a couple in their sixties who traced their commitment to democratic principles to the Spanish Civil War in which they had been ardent supporters of the Republican cause. Although they had settled into their jobs with the Department of Social Welfare and were well liked and respected by their colleagues, they absolutely refused to serve the interests of a totalitarian regime. They found it shocking that their country director did not share these sentiments. Most of the staff and volunteers, however, accepted martial law as a necessary move given the rampant corruption, violence, and inability of the elected government to govern—conditions readily verifiable simply by personal observation. A veteran Philippines volunteer endorsed the New Society, as Marcos called his new government, in a letter to new volunteers by saying that the Philippines "has a stable and potentially highly efficient system of government right now" and just might be able to make more progress implementing its "ambitious development plans."[49] A middle-aged volunteer spoke for most of us in 1973 when he wrote, "Martial law has made a difference—people are not as frightened as they were. . . . [We no longer have to] walk past 35-45 men fondling armalites, rifles, shotguns and pistols on the way to pick up the mail."[50] Another volunteer compared "the rough time of pre-martial law" with the "much more peaceful and safe" time afterwards. He went on to declare, "I for one have faith in President Marcos and the New Society," a statement he probably would want to disown today, but it was a common sentiment then.[51]

Nevertheless, there was something truly troubling about living in a country where all democratic processes had been abolished. One volunteer was greatly upset to learn that his Filipina wife was on the police constabulary's list of people to be brought in for questioning. (She never was, and the couple remained in the country for a full term.)[52] PC/P received a shock when a telegram arrived saying, "Shooting of PCV not intended. Director Tan investigating incident." It turned out that no one had been shot. A volunteer had been working near an army encampment—a common feature of martial law in some provinces—when a stray round was fired. He took it personally when it landed nearby, and he had complained to his Filipino boss.[53]

The midnight curfew caused some inconvenience for those who lived in urban areas, especially when they found themselves in violation of it. Early one Sunday morning a sergeant from Camp Cramé called my house—Camp Cramé being the place where political prisoners and other 'backsliders' were detained. He informed me that my daughter was in custody after being picked up in a sweep of a local nightclub of doubtful reputation, doubtful at least from the parental standpoint. Needless to say, there was anger and acute embarrassment, and not all of it was directed at martial law. On Monday, the PC/P grapevine quickly reported that several volunteers had been swept up during the same raid. Through the long night of detention the director's daughter and the volunteers studiously avoided looking at each other, not knowing who might tell on whom. Little wonder that some thought families a bad idea!

In time martial law became a condition of service that was accepted like all of the others. It provided a constant source of conversation and some unintended humor by its frequent use of some outrageously clumsy propaganda. But it would be several more years before the true nature of the Marcos regime would become apparent and be subject to universal condemnation.

Just as volunteers want to think of themselves as independent people unfettered by any restraints or conditions imposed on them by the larger Peace Corps, the Peace Corps itself wants to imagine that it operates independently of the rest of the official American presence. But in each instance such is not the case. Peace Corps/Philippines, like every country program, is an integral part of the American ambassador's country team, which includes the senior diplomats from the embassy plus the heads of the other American government agencies working in the country. In the Philippines of the 1970s these included the United States Information Service, the United States Agency for International Development (USAID), the Joint United States Military Assistance Group, and, of course, the CIA. On occasion the team would be joined by a representative of the commanding officer at one or both of the huge American military bases: Clark Air Force Base and Subic Bay Naval Base. Visitors from Washington—senators,congressmen, key staff members from congressional committees, and senior State Department officials— were also invited to sit in on team meetings, and I recall that their presence tended to make these already formal and tightly structured meetings even more so.

The country team met weekly in a secure area within the embassy building that was like nothing I have ever seen. Those members of the team not already on the premises would receive an initial scrutiny by the Marine Corps guard stationed at the main entrance. Then we would proceed to a large interior room without windows where another Marine guard stood watch. After passing his inspection, the team members would be ushered into a boxcar-sized, bulletproof, soundproof, tamper-proof, everything-proof high-tech structure that stood in the middle of the room. Each member had an assigned seat at a long conference table, with the highest ranking members sitting at the ambassador's end of the table and the rest of us trailing off toward the other end. (Needless to say, the Peace Corps's assigned seat was much closer to the table's foot than to its head.) The ambassador would enter last and take his seat. Then the rest, who had been standing stiffly at their designated places, would take theirs. The format of the meeting rarely varied. The ambassador would make some opening remarks, ask questions, make some assignments, and then ask for reports. Each of those present would review what had happened in the previous week and present plans for the coming week. I was awestruck by the whole procedure and by this collection of imposing men, many of whom I came to admire.

The United States was represented by two experienced, able, and distinguished ambassadors in those years: Henry Byroade and William Sullivan. Ambassador Byroade—it was rumored that his nickname was Hank, but it was never used in his presence—had been the youngest general officer during World War II, and he had represented his country either covertly or openly in China, Egypt, South Africa, Iran, and now the Philippines. He was not terribly interested in the Peace Corps, but he was supportive and on occasion went out of his way to indicate his endorsement of its work. In August 1972 when a planeload of 120 new volunteers arrived bringing the first of the Peace Corps volunteer families, Ambassador Byroade showed a keen interest in them. Our relationship had only one difficult moment. When I was promoted from deputy country director to country director, PC/W failed to ask his blessing, an expected courtesy that ambassadors hold dear. He first heard about it from me at a country team meeting. His pique was genuine and obvious to all. After a long silence—it was probably only a few seconds, but it seemed endless—he moved on to another subject. I had some sympathy for his annoyance because I myself learned of the promotion only when my mail from Washington began to be addressed to Country Director. After a week or so of this I called Washington and discreetly asked what was going on. The reply, "Oh, didn't Phil call you?" was both a happy confirmation of my new position and a sobering reminder that my concerns and Washington's were not necessarily the same.

Ambassador Sullivan was a personable and outgoing man who seemed to enjoy his work immensely. He had been deeply involved with Henry Kissinger in the peace negotiations with Vietnam, had helped select bombing targets while ambassador in Laos, and had expected to open diplomatic relations with North Vietnam from his post in Manila. When the latter event failed to materialize as the peace negotiations dragged on, he devoted his considerable energies exclusively to the Philippines.[54] He took an active interest in the Peace Corps. On one occasion he and his deputy chief of mission, Lewis Purnell, and their wives visited a training site some distance north of Manila. The ambassador arrived casually dressed—a rarity for many in the diplomatic service—in a huge American army helicopter, giving both the volunteers and the local populace a great thrill.

In late 1973 Sullivan and Purnell were helpful in resolving what could have been an embarrassing situation for the Peace Corps not only in Manila but also in Washington. Unbeknownst to any of us in the Philippines, a ceiling on the number of volunteers who could serve at any given time had been imposed following a trip to the country by President Nixon in 1969. Nixon's visit was short—less than twenty-four hours—but long enough for him to become concerned about the large number of Americans in the country and by the strong anti-American feeling among a small but vocal body of Filipino dissenters.[55] As a result, he ordered that personnel ceilings be set for all American agencies in the country. Because the volunteer rolls were dropping sharply at the time and had remained at relatively low levels for a few years, the ceiling never had any noticeable impact on the Peace Corps. Its very existence had faded from memory by early 1974. However, the new programming thrust was in full swing at that time, and the ceiling had been exceeded by about one hundred volunteers. Although clearly in the wrong, albeit innocently, the Peace Corps was at the mercy of the deputy chief of mission who had discovered the problem. After a bit of negotiation, Purnell acquiesced to the suggestion that some creative counting be employed to solve the problem. The ceiling established a maximum number for 'volunteers'; it said nothing about 'trainees' (not a surprising fact because when Nixon had issued his directive in 1969 all training was still being done in Hawaii). Purnell agreed to deduct from the totals all those in training, which brought PC/P close to the ceiling. No one mentioned the obvious fact that the spirit of the ceiling had been violated, nor that there was no longer a distinction between trainees and volunteers. The whole episode was an indication that the new approach to working in the Philippines had the embassy's full backing. If the program had not grown beyond the confines of the educational system, the outcome would have surely been a strict enforcement of the ceiling and a quick reduction of the number of volunteers in the country.

At a time when Manila was the focal point of much of America's activity in Southeast Asia, the Peace Corps was not important to the mission in the Philippines—the word *mission* denoting the collective official American presence in a foreign country. The Peace Corps was hardly much of a bargaining chip when it came to achieving American strategic interests, which primarily related to ensuring continued access to the military bases and to protecting economic interests. Our relative unimportance meant that we sometimes had to assert ourselves to get our story in front of visiting members of Congress who would vote on the Peace Corps budget. The early 1970s were tough times. Every year the fight for an adequate appropriation from Congress was long and hard. The Peace Corps needed every friendly vote it could muster, and previous experience had shown that the case for the Peace Corps was most persuasive when it was made in the field. Accordingly, whenever a congressman or senator visited the Philippines, the Peace Corps wrangled an opportunity to present its case. The only problem was that the more important the legislator, the less time the official schedule allotted to the Peace Corps.

When Senator Daniel Inouye of Hawaii—a key member of the Senate Foreign Relations Committee—visited in 1973, the Peace Corps did not fit into the schedule at all. Because our pleas for time went unheeded, we had to take matters into our own hands. One of the staff, Charlie Shiraishi, was from Hawaii and had met the senator. He managed to get us invited to meet the visiting dignitary in his hotel room just as Inouye was preparing to return to Washington.

While he shaved, we made our pitch through the open bathroom door. Peace Corps volunteer Andrew Hammond, from the pioneering New Directions program called Group 43, took the lead in doing so because he could speak with the authenticity and conviction that only an experienced and successful volunteer could. The three of us crammed into the session every pertinent fact that we could think of to impress the senator. As the hurried meeting ended, Inouye reached into his carry-on bag and handed Hammond a bottle of scotch whisky (a gift he had received from his Filipino hosts). We never found out if the senator's generosity reflected a gesture of support for the Peace Corps and our presentation, or if it simply meant that he had no use for what in the Philippines was a precious commodity. When the folks at the embassy learned about the meeting, they could not decide whether to admire the Peace Corps for its unmitigated gall or to be exceedingly angry at us for diverting the senator's attention from 'important' state matters.

The part of the mission with whom the Peace Corps was most often involved was USAID. Volunteers worked in many programs that were also being supported by USAID personnel and resources. Because USAID was generally working at a macro level and volunteers were working at a micro level, however, daily contact was not the rule. A built-in bias against USAID existed among many volunteers and staff members, perhaps reaching back for its origins to 1961 when the Peace Corps successfully fought off a plan to be merged with the USAID bureaucracy. There was certainly lingering animosity in the Peace Corps in Manila from the Fuchs years when, as he described in *Those Peculiar Americans,* USAID provided him with "administrative and logistical support, which to describe it most charitably was erratic."[56]

Another part of the problem emanated from an unfortunate holier-than-thou attitude that the Peace Corps sometimes projected. Peace Corps personnel lived in Filipino settings, not in the exclusive enclaves that housed most Americans and other expatriate residents. Most Americans in the official community wore coats and ties, whereas volunteers and staff alike dressed in the far more comfortable and colorful *barong tagalog* or the *polo barong*. The *barong tagalog* is an elaborately embroidered long-sleeve shirt traditionally made from cloth woven from *piña* or *husi*, which are natural fibers. It was worn for important meetings and on formal occasions. (With the collar buttoned, it is equivalent to 'black tie.') The *polo barong* is also heavily embroidered, but it has short sleeves and is usually made from a cotton-synthetic blend. It is for informal wear.

USAID personnel, many of whom were doing important work, resented the implication that they were somehow less worthy because they chose not to live like the Peace Corps. One USAID man groused to a volunteer, "Peace Corps is afraid that someone else might get a little credit for trying to help people, too."[57] Possibly the problem was simply that a basic difference existed in the way the two organizations carried out their respective missions: Peace Corps worked at the point where a service was delivered and USAID worked on the delivery system itself. People not connected with either USAID or the Peace Corps had difficulty understanding why a slight hostility between the two always seemed to be simmering just below the surface. In 1972, the U.S. General Accounting Office reviewed all aspects of the aid program in the Philippines. Although generally supportive of the overall effort, it did single out for criticism the lack of coordination between the Peace Corps and USAID programs.

The Peace Corps and USAID did cooperate on occasion, often with good results. One outstanding example of close cooperation among a variety of American agencies in the Philippines, including the Peace Corps, took place during the summer of 1972. For forty days Luzon was assaulted by heavy rains as a result of a stalled weather system. When the rain finally ended, much of the island was under water. In Manila it was virtually impossible to tell where the flooded land ended and Manila Bay began. For days, an American task force headed by USAID delivered food to isolated barrios in the disaster area. A newly arrived batch of volunteers joined in the effort along with members of the U.S. military and several nongovernmental assistance agencies. The volunteers involved remember this exhausting, dirty, and seemingly endless task as a high point of their service.

More typically, individual volunteers would link up with individual USAID workers to help one another. One volunteer couple worked with a USAID-funded regional development commission. Both volunteers benefited from the USAID support and in turn gave USAID insights into the way the local community functioned that the agency otherwise would not have had.[58] Another volunteer, working in one of the livestock programs, Lloyd J. Johnson, provided sound advice that we should have paid more attention to. Writing in 1973, he said that "greater cooperation between other agencies . . . [was] desirable; some of my best work [was] because I was able to work with a man from USAID, but [my doing so] was actually opposed by at least two PCV's, one [a volunteer leader] working on the

Peace Corps staff."[59] The resolution to the Peace Corps/USAID problem was not found during my time. Neither organization could put aside its own unique institutional culture long enough to accept the other as an equal. For its part the government of the Philippines valued both American agencies and saw no contradiction in using USAID to help accomplish one part of its program and the Peace Corps to accomplish another. In May 1974 the DANR honored both agencies for their respective contributions to Philippine agriculture by giving each the same award at a joint ceremony.[60]

The one part of the official American presence in the Philippines with whom we had absolutely no contact was the CIA. In agreement with long-standing orders from the White House, the Peace Corps was off-limits for all intelligence activities. It is unfortunate that rumors of CIA involvement with the Peace Corps persist. I was dismayed recently to read a perceptive and moving account of one volunteer's experience in Africa during the early 1980s that ended on a note suggesting a complicity between the two organizations. The volunteer, vacationing in Barcelona, tells of a chance encounter with a self-declared CIA station chief who exclaims, "Ah, Peace Corps. Many of our agents . . . are Peace Corps volunteers." That comment finally broke the volunteer's weakening resolve, and he took the next plane to New York, fleeing the hardships and rigors of his joyless assignment.[61] To set the matter straight, there never has been any credible evidence to support such a charge, this former volunteer's account included. After thirty-five years, someone somewhere would have uncovered the evidence of such a connection if it existed.

Ironically, I sat next to the CIA station chief at country team meetings, but never once did he or any of his people approach me or any volunteer for information or assistance. Once, I was inadvertently admitted into the CIA operations room at the embassy in Manila when I sought help in deciphering a late-night telegram that seemed to indicate that a volunteer had been kidnapped or taken hostage. When the senior watch officer recognized me, he quickly took me outside to ensure that no one could misread the situation. As it turned out, the telegram was someone's idea of an amusing practical joke to play on 'Big Daddy' up in Manila. Such antics were not uncommon, and at the time I had suspected that this could be one of them. However, a cautious approach seemed called for given the nature of the message—and the harmlessness that characterized the more typical stunt. I never learned, nor did I try to find out, who the culprit was. (Should the perpetrator read this, I would enjoy hearing from him, the statute of limitations having long since expired.)

The Peace Corps was clearly part of the official American presence in the Philippines despite its occasional protestations to the contrary. It had a great deal of latitude in managing its affairs as long as there were no surprises—especially unpleasant ones—and the embassy knew what it was doing. This was easily done within the framework of the country team meetings and took no more than two hours a week to accomplish. The benefits of the association with the U.S. government outweighed whatever benefits the Peace Corps might have enjoyed as a private organization (an option many people had proposed in 1961 and some continue to propose today). It was a comfort to know that government resources were there if and when they were needed.

President Kennedy signs the Peace Corps Act 22 September 1961, with the obvious approval of Hubert Humphrey and Sargent Shriver, who stand behind him. (Peace Corps Photo Archives)

Director Joseph H. Blatchford, who took control of the Peace Corps in early 1969, never tired of selling his program wherever he went. Here he explains his philosophy to volunteer Rick Graham in Kenya. (Peace Corps Photo Archives.)

Unless otherwise noted, all photos are by the author.

In the Philippines, volunteers were inducted into the Peace Corps immediately upon arrival in-country rather than after several months of training. These volunteers worked in a government program that provided short-term loans to farmers willing to embrace new technologies.

The original Peace Corps training center near Zamboanga was as close to paradise as one could get. It was closed in 1972 as a result of budget constraints and the need for a training environment that more closely duplicated the challenging conditions of typical volunteer work sites.

This typical rural barrio home is much like the ones in which many volunteers lived.

Open-air markets took the place of supermarkets for most volunteers. The sights, sounds, and smells, initially so exotic and adventurous, soon became an ordinary part of life.

In-town transportation was provided by the tens of thousands of jeepneys that offered cheap and reliable service.

The long, tedious hours volunteers spent on the crowded, ancient buses that linked towns and cities tested the strongest resolve.

Peace Corps projects throughout the world often bogged down, both figuratively and literally, as a result of an inadequate or absent national infrastructure. Poor roads and the rainy season often defeated even the most energetic volunteer.

In an island nation, one soon became accustomed to, although not always happy with, water-borne transport. The author's second thoughts came too late to prevent his son's hazardous, but ultimately successful, crossing of the raging Cagayan River in northern Luzon.

A handful of dedicated volunteers worked among the small indigenous ethnic groups found in many remote parts of the Philippine archipelago. One of the most isolated groups, the T'boli, continues to follow traditional ways, as does this woman collecting water in a bamboo pole.

The ubiquitous carabao, a species of water buffalo, provides most of the motor power in the Asian countryside.

Dianne Stahl worked in a leprosarium in Risal Province helping patients and their families raise and market rabbits, a ready source of inexpensive protein and pelts. (Peace Corps Photo Archives.)

Vaughn and Lorenne Rundquist, here returning to their rugged site in the mountains of Mindanao, were members of the team that saved the monkey-eating eagle (in 1983 renamed the Philippine eagle) from extinction. The live chicken in Rundquist's hand is supper for a captive eagle. (Courtesy of Vaughn Rundquist.)

Under Joe Blatchford's New Directions, Americans and host country nationals shared management responsibilities. The author is shown here in 1973 with Felix Gonzales, director of the Bureau of Fisheries in the Philippines. Gonzales's agency hosted one of the most successful Peace Corps programs.

Dottie Anderson has a common reaction to her first close encounter with a mature carp, the kind used as breeding stock in the fisheries program. (Courtesy of Dottie Anderson.)

SENIOR VOLUNTEERS IN
THE PEACE CORPS

One of the most controversial aspects of New Directions was the decision to recruit older volunteers. What was once so contentious an issue is now conventional wisdom, as illustrated by this pamphlet designed specifically to attract older, experienced volunteers. (Courtesy of the Peace Corps Public Affairs Office.)

Peace Corps life was not all work and no play. These women from the nutrition education project played in the Baguio Bowl, a rough approximation of an American college football weekend, complete with pep rally, cheerleaders, and two all-female teams.

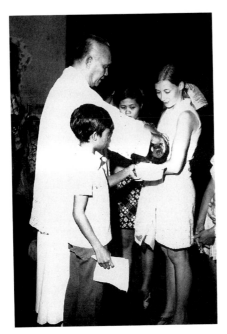

Filipinos often made volunteers an integral part of their families. Rona Roberts, like many of her American colleagues, was a sponsor at the baptism of a newly arrived member of a friend's household. (Courtesy of Rona Roberts.)

Giving birth to a child in the Philippines was the greatest compliment a volunteer couple could give their neighbors. Two Filipina matrons show their enthusiasm for Joanna Rundquist, the daughter of Vaughn and Lorenne Rundquist. (Courtesy of Vaughn Rundquist.)

Volunteers like Paul and Marilyn Chakroff found time to rekindle a college romance, fall in love all over again, and get married in a lovely outdoor ceremony. Paul is wearing a *barong tagalog*, the heavily embroidered shirt that signals a formal occasion in the Philippines.

The volunteer experience had its full share of highs and lows. Aurora Dominguez, who served nearly four years in the Philippines, was obviously enjoying one of the highs in 1975. In her expression one can see why so many look back on the Peace Corps experience as a wonderfully enriching period in their lives. (Courtesy of Marilyn Chakroff.)

John Dellenbeck, our dedicated director in the mid-1970s, later spearheaded the effort to restore independent status to the Peace Corps. In 1986 he chaired the Peace Corps's twentieth-fifth anniversary celebration.

In March 1996 the Peace Corps commemorated thirty-five years of service with a rally in Washington highlighted by a parade of the flags of countries that have hosted volunteers. (Courtesy of Mona Sturges.)

When Cultures Collide 5

The psychological and physical demands of the Peace Corps life in the Philippines—the isolation of the countryside and the frenetic pace of the large urban areas, the loss of privacy, the unaccustomed diet, the absence of amenities, and the hardships imposed by the weather—presented a real test of volunteers' fortitude and perseverance. But at least these conditions were understandable; they were within our volunteers' range of experience and expectations. A far more challenging task was the need to adapt to life in a culture different from our own. In the Philippines that difference included those concepts—so easily understood but so difficult to assimilate—embodied in the words *pakikisama, utang na loob,* and *bahala na.*

Pakikisama is the single most important concept governing relationships among Filipinos. It means that everyone in the society will do all that is necessary to keep things on an even keel. In training we constantly preached the importance of this concept, usually referring to it by the acronym SIR for 'smooth interpersonal relations.' It is a wonderful guiding principle, and it functions to keep personal relationships pleasant and nonthreatening. Unfortunately for those who do not understand its nuances, *pakikisama* has as many drawbacks as advantages. To avoid hurting someone's feelings, a Filipino might say yes when he actually has no intention of acting out that affirmative response. Rosalina Morales, one of our Filipino advisers on cultural matters, remarked, "When [we] say, 'I'll try to come,' it usually means one of three things: I can't come, but I don't want to hurt your feelings by saying no; I'd like to, but I'm not sure you really want me to come. Please insist that I do; I'll probably meet you . . . , but I'll not say yes [because] something may prevent me from coming."[1] For an American accustomed to the simple declarative sentence and wanting to know the who, what, where, and when of life, such imprecision was maddening. Juan Flavier, a Filipino physi-

101

cian and rural development specialist whose books and lectures on rural development, Philippine culture, and doing good played a crucial role in our training programs, often compared Filipino and American ways. He noted that Americans value brevity and get directly to the point whereas Filipinos admire flowery and indirect expression.[2] The Filipino willingly sacrifices clarity to be doubly certain that his pronouncements sound impressive and that no one's feelings are hurt by too blunt a statement. As a rule of thumb, local hosts assume that only about two-thirds of those accepting an invitation will actually show up, knowing full well that many affirmative responses really mean no.

Disputes in the Philippines are not to be settled in person but through the use of a go-between who can minimize any unpleasantness. As our cultural adviser explained, "The intermediary plays the role of a sympathetic listener, letting [one party] let off steam, and then helps him cool off. . . . Later, the go-between goes to the other party . . . and works hard to effect a reconciliation."[3] This indirect approach takes far longer than the more direct American approach. The advantage, however, is that it ensures that no permanent rupture develops in the relationship and that both parties are spared the embarrassment of personal confrontation and the possibility that a premature meeting would make things worse.

In the interest of avoiding injured feelings and ensuring that no one feels left out, the Filipino will go out of his way to show a personal interest even in a stranger. Americans often interpreted these expressions of interest as prying, especially when they were intrusive—Do you have a boyfriend? How much money do you make? When will you have children? The legendary Filipino hospitality comes from the same tradition. No one should ever be excluded from the group because to do so would run the risk of creating dissension. And dissension can destroy the unity that holds the group together. Flavier found barrios in which the barrio captain—a position that is similar to a town mayor, but on a smaller scale—was selected by the town fathers rather than by election. The people actually preferred this solution because they found that elections, with their competing factions, had become too divisive.[4] The community's well-being had been diminished rather than enhanced by a procedure that lies at the heart of the American democratic system. For these people it was more important to prevent discord than to practice democracy.

Among the most attractive features of *pakikisama* is the widely admired practice among Filipinos of working together cooperatively to achieve a common goal and to provide mutual aid to one another.

The Tagalog word that covers this aspect of life in the Philippines is *bayanihan*. Whether it is planting a rice field, moving a nipa hut, organizing a barrio fiesta, or building a school, everyone—young and old, male and female—joins in to do the work. To ignore the obligations imposed by *bayanihan* is to court disaster. "There is an unwritten law that if you do not reciprocate the services of others, they will avoid your needs later," Flavier reported.[5] One volunteer discovered the power of *bayanihan* one Monday morning when she visited one of the barrios in which she worked. As she wrote her parents, "One of my barrios got into high gear and built a feeding center/ nursery school over the weekend. You'll never realize how happy that made me."[6] The importance of smooth interpersonal relations and the avoidance of discord was evident throughout the society.

One Peace Corps staff member learned about local attitudes toward discord one day when he arrived a bit late at a small airport to find that his seat on the one flight a day to the southern island of Jolo in the Sulu archipelago had been assigned to someone else. In a manner that would be recognized as simply asserting his rights in an American airport, the staff member demanded in no uncertain terms to be allowed on the plane. Amidst a sudden silence around the counter an obviously embarrassed ticket agent smiled weakly and said that nothing could be done. Later that evening in the small hotel where the staff member was cooling his heels until the next day's flight, a Filipino gently rebuked him for his total disregard for *pakikisama*. It would have been permissible, the staff member learned, to write the agent's employer seeking to have him fired but not to cause him loss of face in public by shouting at him.

Carmen Guerrero Nakpil, the acerbic but perceptive Filipina writer, traces the concept of *pakikisama* to the nation's Malay roots and concludes that it has produced a culture where "to be nice, agreeable and pleasant, . . . is the general ideal." Guerrero Nakpil notes, however, that the continual pressure to repress hostile feelings and to refrain from actions that might disturb the society's surface tranquility occasionally leads to hideous acts of violence. The word *amok*, which means 'in a murderous rage,' is the Tagalog word used to describe a person whose long-repressed emotions have erupted in just such a manner.[7] Filipinos liken such behavior to that of an enraged carabao. A species of Asian water buffalo, the carabao is a hulking beast of burden that provides the brawn for Philippine agriculture. It plows the field, turns the grindstone, energizes the irrigation system, pulls the carts, and even carries its master to and from town. The animal is as docile as it is strong. It is aroused only by the most outrageous of assaults upon its dignity and good nature. But when that point is reached, the damage it can cause is enormous. Like the carabao, *pakikisama* is generally a blessing, but on occasion it can also be a curse.

Utang na loob (a debt of gratitude) is the cement that holds the extended family together in the Philippines. And in the Philippines the extended family is, indeed, extended. It includes distant blood relations for which we have no names in English, in-laws reaching out to the same degree, household helpers, and even close friends. *Utang na loob* requires that every gift, good turn, or kindness from whatever source be repaid. One is born into *utang na loob*—and owes one's parents a lifelong debt as a result. In interdependent Philippine society, interpersonal relations revolve to a large extent around granting and receiving favors.[8] Each person has those to whom favors are owed and from whom favors are expected. The hundreds of thousands of Filipinos who have emigrated from their homeland—often to the United States—bring with them the *utang na loob* of their childhood. Many observers are astonished at the large amount of money sent back to the Philippines by the expatriates, including those who have no intention of ever again taking up residence in the islands. As one of their number explained, "A good 90 percent of Filipino-Americans have to send back money. It's an obligation."[9] And these relationships never disappear: when a debt is repaid, the relationship is reversed. Roles change, but one escapes the system only through death or by being ostracized.

Debts need not be repaid by good turns of equal value because often the relationship exists between people of different economic means. A rich uncle may send a poor nephew to college, or a corporate executive may see to it that an impoverished relative is given a job. In neither situation is it likely that the recipient can reciprocate with something of equal value. Instead, a lifelong fealty is established that can be called upon even decades later. Flavier reported, "In the barrio it is an unwritten rule that a family which is better off is obligated to take care of their less fortunate relatives."[10] He sometimes discovered that this obligation had the unintended consequence of thwarting the economic and social development work he and his group were working so diligently to achieve. In one instance a particularly entrepreneurial farmer had quickly accepted the advice of an agricultural extension worker to plant a new variety of tomato seed that would produce fruit in what was normally the off-season. When he sold his crop, he made a handsome profit—enough to make a significant improvement in the standard of living he, his wife, and children could afford. Instead of that happening, however, he was approached by relatives from near and far. Each had a special reason for needing money. The farmer could not refuse them. Finally, with all the money from the tomato crop gone, he had to turn away the rest of his importuning relatives. They became angry at his refusal, charged him with failure to fulfill his duty to them, and caused him great embarrassment. The next season he avoided the problem by not planting tomatoes and thereby passed up an opportunity to improve his life.[11] (Some observers have written about similar episodes in other cultures where an *utang na loob*-like cultural tenet has affected their lives, sometimes with disastrous consequences. It may be, then, that *utang na loob* is a more universal concept than we in the Philippines thought.)[12]

The system of *utang na loob* ensures continued group loyalty and cohesiveness, but it also leads to nepotism, corruption, and the primacy of family obligations over obligations to outsiders, employers, or even the national interest. It was a surprise to learn upon arriving in Manila that many of the Filipino administrative and clerical workers in our large staff were related. Equally surprising was the discovery that many helpers employed in staff households around the country were related to the country director's housekeeper. (Because of her position, it was to her that the others came seeking favors.) In the provinces volunteers often worked alongside relatives of the local mayor, the provincial governor, or the national government's regional representative. None of this was surprising or troubling to our Philippine colleagues. *Utang na loob* was at work. Nepotism was not a practice to be condemned; it was a family obligation.

One volunteer, Byron Lee, found himself in an awkward situation as a result of *utang na loob* and his decision to ignore it. He lived with a Filipino family, and in true Filipino style he was readily accepted as a full member. His monthly payment for room and board was a significant part of the family's cash income, so he felt that he was meeting his responsibility as a member of the household. When the eldest son, previously unemployed, became an insurance agent, the volunteer's obligation was obvious to his adopted family: He must support his 'brother's' work and purchase a policy. Lee balked, explaining that he had no wife or children to benefit from an insurance policy and that in the United States children did not take out insurance policies naming their parents as beneficiaries. His refusal shocked the family. As a result the relationship cooled, and Lee decided the time had come to move into an apartment.

Twenty years later he still regretted having been a "cultural inept," incapable of finding a culturally acceptable way of handling the problem.[13]

Bahala na is a common concept among peoples who believe that their lives are shaped by forces—economic, political, or religious— beyond their control. It can be translated as 'If God wills it' or, in colloquial English, 'That's the way the cookie crumbles.' It includes a sense of resignation that what is destined to be will be, regardless of anyone's personal efforts to change the outcome. Individuals, or at least the vast majority of them in the Philippines, believe that they can do little to change their own destinies and that good fortune is more important to success than planning and individual effort. A common Tagalog expression can be translated as "Even if I don't look for my fortune, it will come if it is meant for me."[14] One authority has traced the origins of this fatalism to both *pakikisama* and *utang na loob*. Because everything is done to keep the group content, and because one owes obligations to others and in turn is owed obligations from them, everything is too intertwined to be susceptible to individual control. In these circumstances individual decision making is a waste of time because whatever is decided by one man or woman can be changed by so many "other persons, minds and whims."[15] Volunteers encountered *bahala na* most frequently on the job. When a bureaucratic mix-up delayed or prevented a project from going forward, or an error on someone's part destroyed weeks of work, it was infuriating to hear Philippine coworkers say, "*Bahala na.*" The American wanted to take action, fix blame, get back on schedule. The Filipino accepted the fact that fate had decreed that the project was not to be and went on with his life.

Sister Sylvia McClain, a nun on leave from her convent in Pittsburgh, captured the complaisant essence of *bahala na* when she wrote to friends in northern Luzon that she had discovered the prevailing attitude of those around her to be, "If I don't arrive today, I may come tomorrow or the next day. So much depends on bridges being washed out, heavy storms swelling the streams, boats staying longer in ports than the schedule calls for, plans canceled at a minute's notice" that it made no sense to pretend that one could accurately predict the outcome of virtually any plan no matter how well laid.[16]

Flavier reported that rice farmers in the barrio were not interested in learning about improved rice-growing methods during the off-season—which logic suggested would be the perfect time for it. The five-month interval between harvest and the next planting was simply too long for the farmers: Too many unpredictable things could happen during that interval that would make all the effort of learning something new of little value. But when the farmers were actually preparing to plant, they were ready to listen to new methods.[17] Long-range planning and the concept of *bahala na* did not fit comfortably side by side. Volunteers, constantly aware of both their desire to do good and the finite limits of their two-year period of service, wanted action. Today was more important than tomorrow; doing something, even imperfectly, was better than doing nothing; obstacles were for overcoming, not to be used as excuses for accepting defeat.

A volunteer working in a nutrition education program in the Visayas region wrote home, "Damn the slowness in this country."[18] She was eager to proceed with her work in the outlying barrios where a better understanding of nutrition was badly needed. Frustrated and annoyed by the unreliable public transportation system that limited her work to a single barrio a day, she decided to buy a motorcycle. But then weeks went by as she struggled to complete the necessary registration, insurance, and delivery arrangements. It was at the height of her frustration that she expressed herself so directly and, in doing so, spoke for many of her volunteer colleagues.

In his book on the Peace Corps in the Philippines, Larry Fuchs described in detail how the traditional American values of individualism, personal responsibility, and advancement based on merit clashed with *pakikisama, utang na loob,* and *bahala na.* The title of his book, *Those Peculiar Americans,* is purposely ironic to show that in the Philippines the Americans were the peculiar ones, not the Filipinos. (One of the standard ripostes from those of us in the Peace Corps to an overzealous expatriate was, 'So, you think 40 million Filipinos should change because one *Kano* [as in *Amerikano*] wants to do it differently?!')

Learning to understand and accept Philippine values on an intellectual level was an adjustment that most volunteers were able to make. The tough part was making them one's own when they contrasted so sharply with the values brought from home. Over the years one of the lessons the most perceptive of volunteers learn by living and working in another culture is just how American they are. It was fashionable in the 1970s to consider oneself liberated from the crass American values of parents and other authority figures. Yet, when put to the test, many volunteers discovered that these very same values were the ones driving their own lives. We came to appreciate that there was merit in the value system of the host country, but we also came to understand how much our own lives had been shaped by ours.

At this point it is necessary to add a word of caution concerning stereotypes, oversimplification, and exaggerated cultural differences. Any attempt to define the culture of forty million Filipinos who speak different languages and live under widely varying circumstances is a hazardous undertaking. No one set of generalizations can speak accurately for everyone. There are differences between and among particular groups of people—whether farmers or urbanites, highly educated or unlearned, rich or poor, westernized or not. In making generalizations, one is likely to understate the extent to which differences exist within the culture. An example from everyday life in the 1970s illustrates this problem. Although the *barong tagalog* was the national costume for men, most Filipino businessmen in Manila wore a coat and tie. Upper-class Filipinos noted sarcastically that only two kinds of people wore the *barong tagalog*: foreigners wanting to be seen as sensitive to the local culture and farmers from the provinces. Everyone who mattered wore western-style clothing.[19] When President Marcos declared martial law, he began a campaign to encourage the practice of Filipino traditions such as the wearing of the *barong tagalog*. He and nearly all of his key political allies wore them on a daily basis. As a result their popularity soared.

The Philippine technocrats who managed the development programs appeared to want to replace *pakikisama, utang na loob,* and *bahala na*—or at least some aspects of them—with what they considered more modern and functional values, values often at odds with those described earlier. To suggest that the culture of the Philippines is monolithic is surely wrong. Yet, every culture, if it is indeed to be seen as a culture, must have some sort of defining characteristics. Even at the risk of creating a stereotype that does not fit everyone or every situation, discussions of culture must include the use of generalizations, and it is in this sense that they are used here. Moreover, to posit certain traits as defining a particular culture is not to suggest that these same traits are lacking in other cultures. Certainly, in the United States, for example, we cherish smooth interpersonal relationships, and we take our family obligations seriously. Often we must resign ourselves to living in a world where not everything is under our control, and we also resort to *bahala na* when there is no other choice.

But at the same time we need not minimize the fact that there are substantial differences in the degree to which Americans and Filipinos pay homage to these values.[20] It is not a situation in which certain values are present and others are absent. It is, rather, a question of priorities. In this regard, Alfredo and Grace Roces wrote a book to reduce the culture shock experienced by visitors to the Philippines. They concluded that the ten values Filipinos most cherish are "family ties; being a good son; beauty and elegance; consensus and group agreement; public image and what people say; gratitude for past favors [and] acknowledging this as a debt of honor; friendliness and conviviality; diplomacy; honor; and gentle manners." The book reported that "western values such as verbal, face to face candor; rugged individualism; swift, objective action regardless of who gets hurt; personalized viewpoint; and efficiency would score low with Filipinos."[21] Americans came to the Philippines with a different set of cultural priorities, not necessarily a different set of cultural values. It was the tension between our priorities and our host's that tested our patience and resolve. We were the ones who had to adapt, and this was not an easy task.

The Peace Corps developed many techniques to prepare people to live and work in an alien culture, and we put them to good use in the Philippines. We used lectures and readings, bull sessions between newcomers and experienced volunteers, situation role-playing with Filipinos who were knowledgeable about both their own and American cultures, short-term barrio home stays that provided real-life experience, and intensive language training that was as much acculturation as it was learning. The training program was as good as any in the Peace Corps, yet we knew that virtually every volunteer (and every American staff member) would sooner or later (probably sooner) suffer a degree of culture shock that would have many of the superficial symptoms of clinical depression. (The difference between the two is that clinical depression requires chemical or psychiatric treatment, whereas culture shock can be 'cured' simply by having a good day.) One volunteer couple described their experience many years later in a newsletter sent to the supporters of the international rural development program they now head:

> By this time [i.e., after the excitement and the novelty of the new situation had worn off] nothing was right in our lives. Our zeal was gone. We hated the culture, the stench, the food, the people, the language and most of all we despised the poor. Suffering from deep culture shock, sickness and loneliness we were in sad straits. . . . It was the Christmas season. But the joy and excitement of the holidays was far from us. There was no news from home. It was hot, no snow, no Christmas

tree, no cards, no letters . . . for now we were having a grand pity party.

Like most volunteers this couple survived their personal crisis—partly as a result of a significant and surprising act of kindness from one of the poor families they thought they despised. The children of a poor family that lived in a shack near the couple's more substantial nipa hut presented them with a Christmas gift of oranges, an expensive fruit not native to the Philippines. This act of consideration and kindness shown toward two white strangers on the part of a family that was desperately poor was enough to reawaken the Americans' commitment. The culture shock that had so thoroughly devastated them immediately went into remission.[22] But the intense pain and inner turmoil of the moment remained as vivid in 1993 when they wrote about it as it had been in 1972. It was not by chance that the Peace Corps physician included culture shock in a list of "medical problems most likely to bother you and what to do about them," published in the Peace Corps/Philippines medical handbook in 1973. The "what to do" section on culture shock counseled volunteers to "take it easy and keep busy," seemingly simplistic—and certainly contradictory—medical advice, but sound nevertheless.

One of the frustrating things about culture shock is that it can strike without warning, then recede to some inner depth where its impact is negligible, only to reemerge and strike again. One volunteer from Kentucky was still dealing with it after two years in-country. As he neared the end of his tour, he needed to decide between accepting a job offer from USAID or entering law school. In a letter home his wife explained why he had delayed making the decision: "In fact the reason why the decision is not absolutely final is that we know ourselves to be victims of a recognized pattern of elation/depression that characterizes the emotions of Peace Corps volunteers. . . . It's hard to make a rational decision when we know our emotions are undependable."[23]

Even after several years of living in another culture, whether in the Philippines or in any other country, it is impossible to avoid experiencing low periods. They may come not so much because of the cultural differences, which no longer seem alien by then, but because something occurs to remind us of the fact that we are still very far from home. The catalyst might be a letter from home, an American magazine, or even a memory that springs to mind for no apparent reason. As she was beginning a fourth year of volunteer service, but in a new job at a new site, Sister Sylvia wrote, "Right now I'm very tired, a bit lonesome for you and my family and a little discouraged at the whole new set of adjustments awaiting me."[24] The challenges of living the Peace Corps life never end.

Among the material that I have had the pleasure of reading during the course of this project were several sets of letters sent home by volunteers. Excerpts from one set covering an eleven-month period toward the end of Patricia Auflick's stay illustrate perfectly the up-and-down nature of volunteer emotions:

> *March 1974:* "I'm happy and really enjoying life."
> *July 1974:* "I think I must really be getting used to this place. . . . I feel so comfortable and at ease."
> *October 1974:* "If I had [the decision to join Peace Corps] to do over again, knowing what I know, I doubt if I'd do it."
> *November 1974:* "I'm in a really good mood. . . . I guess it's because I feel like I've done something constructive."
> *January 1975:* "I don't like the culture. I think it's had a detrimental effect on me and I've reached the end of my tolerance."[25]

Auflick remained in the country for nearly a full tour. Her accounts of volunteer life reflect the joys and sorrows that were such an integral part of it. She left the Philippines when her emotional cycle was at a low point; but, as later events proved, no permanent damage had been done. Several years later she returned to the Philippines, married the mayor of the town in which she had lived and worked, and settled in to raise a family. Tragically, the mayor was assassinated by one of the rebel bands that seem to be a permanent fixture of the Philippine landscape, and in time she returned to the United States with her son.[26]

Most volunteers survived their encounters with culture shock. The intensity of the affliction varied depending on such factors as age, previous experiences, job quality, and the manner in which one dealt with loneliness and making new friends. The important point that the staff and the veteran volunteers tried to make to those experiencing the pain of cultural adjustment was that the affliction was temporary. It would go away in time. 'Just remember,' we would say, 'never make any decisions while in the midst of it, particularly decisions that are irreversible like giving up and going home.' There was light at the end of the tunnel if only one would give it time to shine through.

That a significant number of volunteers failed to complete their scheduled tours was a sad reality. Reasons varied. Some left in the first weeks of training after finding themselves unable to cope with the strangeness of a different culture and turning too quickly to the easiest remedy. Others left shortly after training ended when good jobs failed to materialize, when a real or imagined crisis came up at home, or when they ran out of those most precious of commodities in the Peace Corps world: patience and perseverance.

There was always a certain amount of official embarrassment for the Peace Corps when volunteers left early. After all, from the Philippine perspective the Americans had voted with their feet, that most obvious and hurtful method of conveying one's feelings. But of even greater concern was the waste of a unique opportunity for personal growth. Many of those who failed to complete their service probably regretted the decision later. A major staff shortcoming in the Philippines and throughout the Peace Corps world was an inability to convince these volunteers that they should not use early termination to solve their problems with work or with the culture.

Unfortunately, for a few volunteers the impact of Peace Corps service and the challenge of living in a new culture proved destructive. One young man, whose entire life had been spent on a farm in the Midwest, simply lost his grip on reality one day as dawn was breaking in Manila. When the night watchman at the Peace Corps office found him in an agitated state waiting for the office to open, he called me at home and described a situation that indicated something was seriously wrong. By the time I arrived on the scene, the volunteer had wandered off. The night watchman had been reluctant to use force to keep the American from leaving, but he had followed him into the street and was able to point out to me the direction he had taken. Within a few minutes I found him quietly waiting in line at the local Philippine Rabbit bus stop.[27] I joined the volunteer in line just as an outbound bus pulled up to take on passengers. He told me the bus was going to Iowa, and he was going home. Not knowing what else to do, I said I'd go with him, and we boarded the bus. As we talked, it became apparent that he was not fully in control. He knew who I was but thought that we were in the United States. In a vague way he knew he was acting irrationally, but he could not decide what to do about it other than go home. The bus started up and off we went. Obviously, my problem would become even more serious the further from Manila we traveled, but I did not know how to get him off the bus. Then—what at the moment seemed a miracle but in fact was a rather common occurrence—a mechanical failure brought the bus to a sputtering halt. We were ordered off and, having no other option, walked back to the office. Later in the day I accompanied the volunteer and the Peace Corps physician to the psychiatric ward of a local hospital. To my amazement I discovered that padded cells really do exist. As he was locked into one I saw in his eyes a look of utter confusion and despair. It was the darkest day of my Peace Corps career. A few days later we evacuated him to the United States under a medical escort. I never learned what became of him.

Another volunteer, a young woman working in a rural health care unit in a remote barrio, began to act strangely, but it was some time before word reached the Peace Corps staff. Her Filipino coworkers had been reticent to speak up for fear that they were overreacting to what might have been odd behavior to them but acceptable to Americans. Other volunteers in the province finally began to hear rumors. We discovered that the woman had been abusing the children at the health care center where she worked and had been ritually killing small animals and insects at her home. She, too, had retreated into a fantasy world to escape pressures that had become too great to bear. The Peace Corps physician was sent to bring her back to Manila, and after a few days of observation she returned to the United States, also accompanied by a medical escort.

Marijuana, heroin, and a host of other drugs were readily available in the Philippines, especially in Manila and Baguio, and in the areas surrounding the American military bases. A few volunteers succumbed to the temptation to the extent that by the time their problem was recognized they were in serious danger of becoming addicted. In accordance with firm policies regarding drug use, these volunteers were immediately returned to the United States. A few others used marijuana in situations that were so open and blatant that I now suspect their actions were really a desperate attempt to get out without having to go through the guilt-producing process of actively choosing early termination.

Other volunteers reacted to the stresses of volunteer life in less dramatic but still destructive ways. They became heavy drinkers; they went to bed and refused to get up; they lost all interest in personal grooming and dress; and they sought solace in the arms of many sexual partners. Unfortunately, no magic potion is available that can prevent or cure culture shock. It is one of the many hazards that come with being in the Peace Corps. There are, however, proven means of surviving it. The most important of these is to be forewarned and to recognize the symptoms when they appear. (This is much easier said than done because the condition is apparent least of all to those afflicted with it.) Another survival technique, as former volunteer Steve Shaffer points out in *One Grain of Sand*, is to rely on knowledgeable friends for guidance through the process of recovery. He was particularly fortunate in living close to two veteran volunteers who had experienced the malady themselves, and he had a Filipina friend—who later became his wife—who helped ease his passage into the Philippine world.[28] Finally—and this is perhaps the best news of all—subsequent attacks tend to be less severe.

In time volunteers became amazingly resilient and truly enjoyed the experience of overseas living. As one volunteer summed up his time in the Philippines in 1973, "After going through all the shocks and lonely feelings, you receive an understanding through patience. You start to conform to the people, their customs, their culture. You do not accept them all, but you learn to understand and you learn to live with them. You learn to see the beautiful things about their country and their way of life. The sadness you felt when you first saw how some people lived is somewhat pushed to the back of your mind. . . . The taste of the food is overcome, and you find it not all that bad. You live without all the conveniences you have been accustomed to and somehow you master [living in another culture]."[29] That sentiment would probably be accepted by most volunteers who served in the Philippines in the 1970s as, I expect, it would be by most volunteers worldwide, regardless of where or when they served.

The Challenges of Everyday Life

6

Since 1961, many writers, academics, and volunteers have attempted to describe life in the Peace Corps, generally with only partial success. Professional writers and academics have the verbal ability to describe the experience, but they lack the special sensitivity and personal knowledge that can come only by having lived the life of a volunteer. Their descriptions never reach below the surface, and they lack the authenticity needed to make them convincing. Former volunteers, on the other hand, often find that words fail them when they attempt to describe an experience that is at once deeply personal, complex, and unique. A lack of communications skills is only a small part of their problem. A larger part is that most of their listeners do not have a relevant frame of reference to hear them out. As one volunteer lamented long after her service in the Philippines had ended, "Very few people wanted to know anything at all about those two or three years of our lives. It was humbling to find out that [our] experience of a lifetime didn't matter much to people who used to be [our] closest friends."[1]

A few people have been fortunate enough to be both gifted writers and Peace Corps volunteers. Their accounts are vivid, stirring, and often uplifting. One of the best of these is *The Ponds of Kalambayi: An African Sojourn* by Mike Tidwell. Tidwell's account of his two years as a fisheries extension worker in a remote town in Zaïre during the mid-1980s earned him praise from both the Peace Corps world and general readers. He is scrupulously honest as he tells his story of accomplishment and failure, challenge and frustration, excitement and boredom, friends and enemies. Even though the setting of Tidwell's adventure was a decade later than our years in the Philippines and he was in Africa rather than in Southeast Asia, much of what he writes is pertinent to every Peace Corps experience. His story is organized around universal themes: surviving the Peace Corps training program; struggling to adapt to a new culture; learning to be productive on the job; discovering as much about oneself as about one's hosts; and learning to set aside, at least for a time, some of one's Americanness.

Another of the best of the Peace Corps books is *Living Poor: A Peace Corps Chronicle* by Moritz Thomsen, who served in Ecuador in the mid-1960s. Thomsen was a middle-aged volunteer (unlike Tidwell, who was a recent college graduate). Both men served as agricultural extension agents, but Thomsen brought twenty years of farming experience. Both men learned, as do many volunteers, that although they might be specialists—Tidwell in fisheries and Thomsen in poultry—they rarely had all of the answers; indeed, both brought the farmers whom they counseled to near disaster before they achieved modest agricultural successes. Thomsen remained in Ecuador following his Peace Corps service and completed two more books on the subjects first explored in *Living Poor* before his death in 1991.

A third book with genuine literary merit is George Packer's *Village of Waiting.* In it the author gives a vivid account of his eighteen-month struggle in the early 1980s to reconcile the seeming irrelevancy of his job as an English teacher with the crushing poverty of the small rural village in West Africa where he lived and taught. (New Directions had not been universally successful in the 1970s in bringing its programs more in line with host country needs, although Packer does indicate that his was to be the last English-teaching program in Togo.) Whereas their jobs had given Tidwell and Thomsen a strong sense of purpose that compensated for the loneliness, frustrations, and hardships they endured, Packer's job did the reverse: It magnified the impact of these three conditions of Peace Corps service. In the end, Packer fled his assignment in confusion and despair.[2]

Three other books by volunteers deserve mention: James W. Skelton's *Volunteering in Ethiopia: A Peace Corps Odyssey*; Steve Shaffer's *One Grain of Sand: A Peace Corps/Philippines Experience*; and *Peace Corps Roller Coaster,* a collection of the letters home of Dan and Lisa Hebl. Skelton's work is set in the early 1970s and highlights one of the Peace Corps's success stories: its role in the elimination of smallpox in Ethiopia. The book recounts the experiences of volunteers as they wrestle with the joys and sorrows of volunteer life. As one reviewer commented, it "brings back those times and memories of our Peace Corps days—a firsthand account of what it was really like."[3] Shaffer's book takes place in the Philippines in the late 1970s. Because much of it deals with his courtship of and marriage to his Filipina language teacher, it provides excellent insight into the family life of typical Filipinos. The book's strength, however, is also a weakness with respect to its being able to convey a representative picture of volunteer life. Because of his marriage he was instantly accepted as an integral part of a large extended family, with all of the support and companionship it included. Accordingly, Shaffer was spared some of the most difficult aspects of the Peace Corps life. The Hebl book tells the story of a young married couple teaching and coaching in Kenya during the early 1990s. As its title implies, the account highlights the constant cycle of emotional highs and lows that characterize life in the Peace Corps. In the end the frustrations—of life in a culture where being white and being female invite harassment and discrimination—overwhelm the satisfactions of humanizing the atmosphere at the hidebound rural school where they teach.

Reading books by volunteers is one way to gain some insight into the way one lives the Peace Corps life. Another is to use volunteers' experiences to develop a composite. This is the approach that I have attempted, based on the three years I spent in the Philippines as well as more recent communications with scores of volunteers from the same period. No one volunteer will have experienced everything in the composite that follows, but they should all find aspects of their own experiences there. Moreover, even though the examples used as illustrations are drawn from the Philippines, many of them could just as easily have come from other countries in the Peace Corps world. The vocational, cultural, and physical challenges transcend the specific countries in which they occur. In all instances local languages must be mastered, the scarcity of accustomed amenities must be accepted, the intestinal havoc created by unfamiliar foods and organisms must be endured, and the family and community support structures that previously provided the underpinnings of one's existence must be replaced. Every volunteer faces these challenges regardless of the country of assignment. The differences are more in degree than they are in kind. For example, learning to speak Korean or Thai is more difficult than learning to speak Spanish or French, but neither is easy. Malaysia is farther from home than Guatemala, but neither is close. There may even be greater differences between urban-based and rural-based volunteers in the same country than there are between volunteers in different countries. Although Tidwell and Thomsen served on different continents at different times, they describe a rural life with many similarities, and both tell of the discomfort they felt in their rare encounters with Third World urban life. These similarities create an instant sense of community whenever former volunteers come together, despite the fact that the experiences each had took place in a different country. Therefore, I offer the following composite picture as one that is specific to the Philippines but generally applicable to all parts of the Peace Corps world.

The Philippines is a large, populous nation whose people are spread across eleven major islands and over seven thousand smaller ones.[4] The eleven major islands are Luzon, Mindanao, Mindoro, Palawan, Panay, Negros, Bohol, Leyte, Samar, Masbate, and Cebu. During the 1970s volunteers were posted to all parts of the country in sites that ranged from the remotest of barrios to the frenetic bustle of Manila. Volunteers in rural areas—and the Philippines is largely rural—were isolated from the rest of the nation not only by physical distance but also by the unreliability of—or even the total lack of—public transportation and the absence of anything approaching a modern telephone service. Existing public transportation between towns was often erratic, crowded, and slow. One volunteer, Alvin Hower, de-scribed the typical bus that plied the rural highways—if that is not too dignified a word to describe the narrow, unpaved, potholed ar-teries that connected various areas—as consisting of "a wooden body over a truck frame [with] wooden benches, a low ceiling and [glass-less] windows."[5] To ride in one was to experience humanity in a way that gave new meaning to the expression *close-packed.*

Even when volunteers had access to private transportation, it sometimes made little difference in the degree of difficulty they en-countered in traveling around the country. Sister Sylvia described a jeep ride from the airport in Zamboanga to the Peace Corps training site in the nearby barrio of Ayala as one that produced "all kinds of anxious moments." In an account she sent to a group of Phil-ippine nuns, she wrote, "As we started out our path was blocked completely by fallen trees so the driver had to use [his] *bolo* to cut his way through." (A bolo is a sharp cutting instrument often made from one of the leaves of a car spring sharpened to a fine edge and inserted into a wooden handle. It is an all-purpose instrument that seems an extension of its owner's arm.) "When we came to [the place where we were to meet another jeep] the river had overflowed the road and was bouncing down [a cliff on the far side] into the ocean. We had to cross over the swollen river in the jeep. As [the driver] tried to steer upstream the current kept pushing the tailgate nearer and nearer [the cliff]. . . . We made it by an inch and a prayer."[6] It was hardly the type of trip that would encourage unnecessary repetitions.

One November my family and I accepted an invitation to celebrate Thanksgiving with volunteers living in the Cagayan Valley, a remote region in the north of Luzon. By the time we set out from Manila, rain had been falling furiously for nearly a week, although the weatherman promised a sunny change. Having complete faith in the ability of our four-wheel-drive Wagoneer to overcome all obstacles, we confidently headed north. Our confidence was fully justified until we found our way blocked at the usually placid Cagayan River, where a key bridge had been washed away. Unfortunately, the Wagoneer could neither fly nor swim. Ever entrepreneurial, Filipinos were on hand offering to ferry us across a now raging and swollen torrent. In the driving rain we were herded into three *bangkàs*. These long, narrow canoelike boats have an astonishingly low freeboard of two or three inches. To deal with the fast moving water, the boatmen had equipped their craft with hastily made and, it seemed to us, haphazardly attached bamboo poles to act as outriggers. It was highly improbable that these would provide sufficient stability, but it was our only option. Each *bangkà* had two paddlers at the bow and two more at the stern. Between them was room for two passengers to sit in the bottom of the boat. As I watched the first *bangkà* shove off carrying a poncho-draped son and a volunteer who had accompanied us, I had to wonder how or why I got myself into these situations. But the most unnerving part of the whole adventure was seeing people crowding both banks of the river happily awaiting what they were sure would be a few accidents—perhaps even some fatalities— to enliven an otherwise ordinary day in the province of Isabella. One could almost hear a sigh of disappointment when the last of our small flotilla reached the far shore safely.

Volunteers quickly learned that the rare presence of a telephone in a nearby household was more often a status symbol than a communications apparatus. Often the owner knew no one else who owned a phone whom he might call, so it was never used. Chances are it would not have worked anyway. The post offices in larger municipalities advertised long-distance telephone services, but usually there was a delay of several hours between the time one began the process of making a call and the time a connection was made at the other end. Even then it was not uncommon for the caller to be heard while the voice of the party at the other end was lost somewhere along the way. The most urgent of communications were sent by telegram, a system that proved reasonably reliable. Everything else went by mail—a slow and uncertain process—or was left unsaid.

Electricity was often unavailable, or sporadic at best. Even in those areas nominally considered electrified, blackouts and brown-outs in the evenings were a constant part of volunteer life. As a re-sult, many volunteers soon fell into the local habit of rising with the sun and going early to bed. Those who lived near the ocean came to appreciate the appropriateness of Kipling's "'an the dawn came up like thunder outa China crost the Bay.'"[7] Throughout the Philippines the sun rises quickly, even dramatically, between 5:30 and 6:00 and sets just as quickly and dramatically twelve hours later. The sunsets over Manila Bay are among the most glorious in the world. Visi-tors from abroad are always impressed with their startling beauty, as were we until the novelty wore off. Sad to say, by the time we left we hardly noticed them.

Houses in the barrios were clustered together in tight enclaves, surrounded by rice paddies and other farmland. Because most houses were open and airy, barrio life was lived in full view of one's neigh-bors and fellow townsmen. Little escaped public notice in the barrio, especially when the activity involved the fair-skinned, relatively tall, energetic Americans. (The Peace Corps has never attracted many African American volunteers. In the Philippines we had only a few during the 1970s. They found that their darker skin tones attracted just as much attention as did their colleagues' lighter skin tones.)

Even the volunteers posted to urban areas could not escape attention in their neighborhoods. They stood out just as starkly as their country cousins and, to make matters worse, had many more onlookers who took great delight in watching—and commenting on—their every move. Urban-based volunteers, surprisingly, often had greater difficulty adjusting to their circumstances than did their rural-based counterparts. Even though they had access to more ameni-ties, had a wider variety of entertainment options, and associated with Filipinos who were often better educated and more like them-selves, they did not have the intimate contact with Filipinos that the rural volunteers did. One volunteer teacher assigned to an urban setting complained, "I might have more easily overlooked the in-appropriateness of my job if my [site] hadn't been too urban and too western for me. People spoke English, wore western clothes, read western-style newspapers, [and] lived in wood and cement two-story homes along paved streets. Although this western veneer covered a core of a deeper Southeast Asian culture, it was all too 'normal' for me."[8] (As the Third World population has shifted increasingly to large metropolitan areas, the Peace Corps has followed. An ever-growing number of volunteers has been posted to urban settings in the 1980s and 1990s.)[9] Ironically, the urban volunteers also tended to have an occasional spasm of guilt that they were not living in the proverbial mud hut that was supposed to define the Peace Corps experience. Nor did their rural colleagues allow them to forget this fact, even as the country dwellers camped out in their city-based friends' living quarters during the periodic respite from the rigors of rural life.

Volunteers also needed to look at food in a different context. In the Philippines food was a central component of social life. Typically there were five meals a day. In addition to breakfast, lunch, and dinner Filipinos enjoyed two *meriendas*—scheduled snack times— one in midmorning and one in midafternoon. Food was used as an expression of welcome at any time of the day—a sign of acceptance and a device for bringing people together. Every volunteer shared the experience of one who reported in a letter home, "We went and visited all the houses where we would be staying [and were] served a *merienda* at each. One cannot refuse to sample the food or it is an insult, so we were all stuffed."[10] A day spent making courtesy calls on Filipino officials was guaranteed to be a day when, in the words of another volunteer, we would be "overcarbohydrated." In time we all learned to pace ourselves so that we could continue to eat at every stop. One strategy that proved effective was to put a small amount of food on a plate and then eat only half of that. Leaving some food uneaten was acceptable whereas refusing food in the first place was not.

Among ordinary Filipinos the diet consisted of large quantities of rice accompanied by smaller amounts of fish (fresh when available or dried when not), the occasional piece of pork or chicken, and, rarely, beef or carabao. Americans are constantly amazed at the prominent role played by rice in the Filipino diet. As one remarked after being in the country six weeks, "You wouldn't believe how much rice the typical Filipino eats at every meal, including breakfast, and how little of anything else."[11] In season there was a plentiful supply of fruits and vegetables, but at other times of the year it was necessary to fall back on canned goods. Variety was added to the diet by using a number of unusual, at least for many Americans, spices and flavorings: garlic, fermented fish sauce, both the milk and meat of the coconut, and a hot sauce made from vinegar, garlic, and chili peppers. Those volunteers who did their own cooking soon wrote home for a supply of familiar spices, the most popular of which were those essential for making spaghetti sauce—that cheap and familiar meal that often substituted for an otherwise constant diet of rice and fish. Others, especially single men, fell into the habit of eating in the small ubiquitous *turo-turo* restaurants. These businesses, often home-based, had no menus. Instead, a number of different preparations were set out and the customer selected by pointing to the desired dish. (In Tagalog, *turo-turo* means point-point.)

Every Peace Corps country has its share of exotic, if not actually weird, local eating habits. Mike Tidwell describes the crucial role played in Kalambayi, Zaïre, by the termite larvae of the central African savanna. He reports that "people munched the agreeable-tasting bugs by the handful. They stewed them in manioc leaves and fried them in oil. Just when food supplies had begun to reach distressing levels [as the food stocks from the previous harvest were depleted and the new crop was not yet ready], the protein-rich larvae had arrived to carry everyone into the December harvest season."[12] In the Philippines only the truly well acculturated volunteers could master their squeamishness and eat *balut*, a half-boiled, ready-to-hatch duck egg. The sight of a nearly formed duckling complete with little beak, a pair of eyes, and the beginnings of feathered wings was too much for most of us, and we politely but firmly refused the opportunity to eat one.

Steve Shaffer reports a much more common eating experience that, although not exactly to our liking, most of us did master. His first breakfast with his host family consisted of a fried egg, cooked some hours earlier and left to congeal, and a helping of leftover rice. Not wanting to complain so early in his stay, he ate it all without comment.[13] He learned, as we all did, that this was standard fare, and many a day started in this fashion. Frequently one would arrive at a breakfast consisting of one cold fried egg and a pile of rice only to find the plate and food teeming with tiny ants. I had been in the country less than a month when I learned how to handle this situation. By tapping the edge of the plate lightly but rapidly with a spoon, I could produce a vibration that ants found unbearable. Within a few seconds they would all scurry away and breakfast could begin. Ants were a constant of volunteer life in the Philippines. They existed everywhere, in every household, restaurant, and marketplace. Attitudes toward ants could be used to illustrate the differences among those volunteers who were new, midterm, or fully seasoned. The new volunteer refuses to eat rice with ants in it. The midterm volunteer carefully picks out the ants and eats the rice. The old hand "simply eats the whole thing, rice, ants and all."[14]

The most disturbing of the Filipino habits for many volunteers was the regular practice of eating dogs. Whether true or not I never learned, but all veteran volunteers swore that they knew of a couple who, as the end of their service drew near, bequeathed their pet dog to a neighbor. On their final day, the departing volunteers were treated to an elaborate *despedida*—a going-away party—only to find that their pet had become the main course. The government has reportedly now made it unlawful to eat dogs because of official complaints from dog-loving countries, but the practice undoubtedly continues in some areas.[15]

The early Peace Corps training experts knew intuitively that adaptation to the host country climate would constitute a major adjustment for the new volunteer. To deal with this aspect of volunteers' preparation, they established training sites in Puerto Rico and Hawaii to prepare volunteers for the tropics and in Arizona to prepare them for desert countries. Although their execution of the strategy was faulty (training should have been in the country of assignment, not in the United States), their intuition was correct. Weather and its effects on people are universal concerns, and in the Philippines this was no exception. During the annual wet season, drenching rain is a daily occurrence. Nothing is ever completely dry. Leather shoes turn green with mold, roads flood, bridges wash out, barrios are isolated for days and even weeks at a time, landslides wipe out roads and entire villages, and people—and animals—sicken and die. Raincoats are unsuitable in the heat, and umbrellas are unwieldy and nearly useless in a driving rain. Ponchos often offer the best hope for protection from the elements. With the rainy season come the typhoons, bringing storms of immense power and wreaking havoc on crops, buildings, and people alike. Typhoons have struck Manila with such force that ocean freighters have been flung up out of Manila Bay to come to rest along one of the city's bayside thoroughfares. In the provinces tens of thousands of nipa huts—these are open, airy dwellings built from bamboo poles and the branches of the nipa palm—are destroyed annually by the typhoons. One soon comes to accept as prudent the rural Filipino's reluctance to invest heavily in his home knowing that sooner or later an uncaring and impersonal Mother Nature will destroy it.

The constant wetness constituted a challenge to the healthiest of volunteers. Typically the rainy season was the time for colds and flu, but there were other problems as well. One volunteer couple who had desk jobs and who also made long trips to outlying areas by motorcycle wrote home, "We are plagued with skin diseases because our warm moist skin provides such a good home [for unwanted organisms.] Because we sit so much we often have particularly tender and fungus-infested bottoms."[16] Our younger son developed a weird fungal infection of the skin that began as dime-sized white blotches all over his torso. These gradually increased until some were the size of coffee saucers. I could think of no explanation other than incipient leprosy. But our good Peace Corps doctor said it was simply *tinea versicolor* (whatever that was) and no cause for concern. The blotches went away in time, along with the rainy season. Only the rice farmer, who depended on the rains at planting time, truly regretted its passing.

The annual dry season was welcomed by everyone else with great relief. Fresh fruit and vegetables became plentiful, the roads once again became passable, and the temperature and the humidity remained acceptable, especially in the early months. The months of December, January, and February could be a delight in the Philippines, although many Filipinos tended to complain about the evening chill. Old Peace Corps hands—those most likely to have adapted to the climate—often wore sweaters during the early part of the dry season, an act they would have found incomprehensible when they first arrived in the tropics. One woman wrote home to her parents after nearly two years, "The nights seem cooler than last year and we have no trouble sleeping."[17] She did not realize that it was she and the others in her group who had changed, not the weather.

But as the dry season progressed, the mercury rose and with it the humidity. A great hush began to fall over the barrios at noon—and on the open-air markets of the cities—as people sought refuge from the oppressive heat. We quickly learned to follow the warning of an anonymous denizen of the tropics that only mad dogs and Englishmen go out in the noonday sun.[18] In the early 1970s we sent prospective volunteers a suggested clothing list with this reminder: "As you've probably been told a hundred times, the Philippines is a humid, tropical country [and] one or even two changes of clothes a day is not unusual." We westerners would find ourselves dripping with perspiration after even the slightest exertion whereas our Filipino colleagues remained perfectly dry and comfortable. On many occasions, before shaking hands, I would surreptitiously dry them on a large cotton handkerchief carried for the purpose in order not to offend the person I was greeting. When I visited the American embassy, the transition from the hot steamy street to the icy air-conditioned interior was a nearly life-threatening event as the cold air attacked my drenched skin and clothing. As the dry season lingered on, the temperature and the humidity rose ever higher. We began to look forward to the first rains, which meant cooler temperatures and relief from the dust that turned to mud on sweaty arms and hands. Eventually the rains did come, hesitantly at first and then in regular downpours. The seasonal cycle had begun again.

The daily lives of the Peace Corps revolved around the same set of mundane chores that most people face. There were the routine demands of the job, the places to be and the things to do. There were the housekeeping necessities of shopping, cooking, and cleaning. There was a need for diversions and, as always, there was the constant interaction with other people. One great difference was present, however, and that was found in the environment within which these chores were to be performed. Virtually everything the volunteers knew about managing their affairs had to be relearned. The first and most obvious challenge was the need to become proficient enough in a new language to get on with the other challenges. But add to that the fact that the supermarket had been replaced by a bustling open-air market long on noise and confusion and short on familiar goods, that the public transportation system seemed to have no order or fixed routes, that western plumbing had been replaced by a hole in the floor and a bucket of cold water with dipper attached, that telephone communications were nonexistent, and that no one appreciated the urgency the volunteer felt to get on with the job. The problem was particularly acute during the early weeks at the volunteer's site, a time the Peace Corps called the settling-in period. This rather innocuous-sounding phrase described an experience that was usually one of the most highly charged and anxiety-ridden periods of volunteer life.

Complicating everything was the immediate loss of all personal privacy that inevitably accompanied Peace Corps service, especially for those living in small towns and barrios. Volunteers became, in effect, public property, owned in common by everyone. They were stared at openly; followed by packs of running, jumping, laughing children (often a lot of fun for the volunteers, too, but not day after day after day); invited to every fiesta, wedding, baptism, and funeral; and rarely given a moment of solitude. Being a warm and generous people, Filipinos could not bear the thought that *their* volunteer might be lonely. Hence someone was always hanging about. The volunteer could not go to the market or the *sari-sari* store without attracting a crowd. Several volunteers swore that their mail was read at the local post office before delivery. One volunteer reported that "lack of privacy is a condition of living in a [Philippine] community."[19] Another, while half-humorously comparing his life to that of Prometheus after the gods had taken their revenge, noted that "Prometheus, despite his torture, didn't have the entire population of Crete staring at him." He went on to describe the "thousands of eyes [that] follow you as you buy a newspaper, climb a flight of stairs, or try to flag down a jeepney."[20] One couple complained of the children who would follow them home and peer into their windows.[21]

But the most unnerving occurrence for many was always being the center of attention, the honored guest, the treasured community resource whenever they attended a public event. They would be seated in the place of honor, served first, and fussed over. Invariably at some point they would be called on to present a surprise number, a dreaded event for everyone except those volunteers with special musical or dramatic talents. All public affairs—and many private ones as well—have a formal, written program listing the scheduled speakers, presentations, and entertainments in numerical order. At one or more places in the program the notation will simply read "surprise number." When the proceedings reach that point, the master of ceremonies—without advance warning—calls on someone to perform. That person then climbs up on the platform and sings or tells jokes or displays some other talent. The Peace Corps volunteers soon learned that the odds were highly in favor of their being selected. As Patricia Auflick told her family, "I always try to think of a number before I go someplace just in case."[22] Fortunately for me, I was usually in the program as a speaker or in some other formal role, so I generally was spared this ordeal. When I was not on the agenda, I lived in mortal terror of those nearly paralyzing events.

The lack of privacy was particularly acute for married couples and women. Childless couples constantly had to answer direct questions about why they had no children. Childlessness was cause for serious community concern. Surely, the neighbors and coworkers felt, there must be something they could do to help correct the situation, even if only to ask repeatedly if there had been any change in the unfortunate wife's condition. Beyond that, as Flavier pointed out, an absence of children in the family was taken as proof by Filipinos that the husband lacked some essential male quality. Manhood is verified by producing children; in their absence the husband is suspected of being "weak," "not a real male," or a "burned out fuse."[23] In the 1970s the concept of family planning was still novel and foreign in the Philippines. (Filipinos laughingly described their preference for family planting rather than family planning.) There were often six or eight children in a family. Even having a dozen children was not particularly unusual, so a volunteer couple's decision to remain childless during the early years of marriage was considered strange.[24]

On rare occasions a volunteer wife would become pregnant and decide to give birth in the Philippines. (By the 1970s the Peace Corps had abandoned its policy of immediately returning pregnant volunteers to the United States and permitted the volunteers to decide such matters for themselves.) One volunteer couple who made the decision to remain in-country throughout the wife's pregnancy reported that the Filipinos gave the baby "rave reviews. While out walking with her, the people would rush up and want to touch her and we would sometimes have to hold her up high out of harm's way. Some of them would call out, 'Puti, puti' (white, white). They just couldn't get enough of that highly valued white skin."[25] The couple had resolved the issue of childlessness to everyone's satisfaction, but in doing so they had intensified the attention they attracted.

The unmarried woman volunteer faced the greatest problem of all. The widely reported sexual revolution of the 1960s in the United States, the newly relaxed laws governing the sexual content of American books and magazines, American films and television programs that exploited sexual themes, and a large dose of wishful thinking on the part of the local male population created an environment in the Philippines that most American women found objectionable. Simply because she was American the woman volunteer was considered by Filipino men to be an easy target. Compounding the problem was the fact that if she was white, she was also considered beautiful. The combination was nearly lethal. Dina Kageler remembered it this way: "The worst of it was the involuntary metamorphosis from a shy church-college coed into a sex goddess. It was a role for which I was totally unprepared and one which . . . sent me to my bed crying from shame, embarrassment and anger. . . . White skin, blonde hair, blue eyes—I might as well have worn a flashing red neon light on my head: 'Free Sex, Take What You Want' or 'Grab Here, She'll Love It!'"[26] Kageler wrote about the experience twenty years later in a letter under the heading "The Worst of It." She vividly remembered the extent of her despair over this aspect of living in the Philippines and remained angry that her training had done so little to prepare her for the ordeal. (Under a second heading, "The Best of It," she described the final two years of her three-year stay when she worked in Mindanao with the T'boli people, an indigenous ethnic group struggling to maintain its identity. Her memories of that experience are far happier.)

Another woman living in a small barrio, Angela Wallace, solved the problem by choosing to "almost entirely avoid male Filipinos between the ages of 16 to 60." She had encountered the prevailing attitude that "all American women are fast" and "no American [woman] can resist the amorous Filipino." She, as she counseled others to do, had worked out her own way to handle the problem: stay as far away as possible. Once having made that decision she was able to "really enjoy my small town, rural life. The quiet peacefulness of daily life is very refreshing after the rat race of American life."[27]

This unwanted attention was exacerbated by the widespread acceptance of the double standard in Philippine society. Filipino men, even married men, are permitted to roam, to indulge in extramarital affairs, and even to keep mistresses without being subject to severe community censure.[28] Not only American women judged the Filipino men harshly; Guerrero Nakpil devoted many of her popular essays at the time to poking fun at them and making them appear to be slightly ridiculous, but to little avail. Filipinas could hold important positions in business and the professions—and many of them did—but when it came to their domestic lives they were as restricted as the men were unrestricted.[29] One group of volunteers, all women, was invited to a party by the local detachment of the police constabulary. When the volunteers learned that the men's wives would not be in attendance, they all declined. They concluded that the men were simply hoping to test the reality of their image of American women as "wild, drinking and easy." One volunteer who declined the invitation, Patricia Auflick, wrote home that she was "tired of being leered at, but so far I haven't spoken my mind. . . . Boy, I'd sure surprise a few Filipinos if [I did]."[30]

Most of the Peace Corps women eventually learned to discourage unwanted sexual attention without resorting to the use of the strong language they often found on the tips of their tongues. Some, larger and more fit than the routinely short and slender Filipino, also had to learn to resist the further temptation to pummel their would-be suitors. This was fortunate because, had they given in to that very understandable impulse, it would have created another problem for them: Such unladylike behavior had no place in the decorous world of Filipino women.

One particularly fair-skinned, blonde volunteer with the swine production program found an effective way of dealing with overly aggressive males. In her job she often castrated newborn piglets as she made her rounds to the farms where she worked. She used a small scalpel, which she carried prominently displayed on a chain around her neck. It was a constant topic of conversation, and when so moved she could make the recitation of its use very funny. She took particular delight in explaining its purpose to men who had become bothersome, usually adding more clinical detail than customary for their benefit. These men understood her meaning right away and moved on.

American women also had a difficult time adjusting to the stringent standards of conduct expected of them in the provinces. Women were not to drink or smoke in public, even at parties where the host provided an ample supply of beer, spirits, and cigarettes for the men. Women were not to travel alone or to be alone with a man other than a member of the immediate family, except in the course of business. At social gatherings women usually congregated sedately by themselves in one room while the men cavorted in another. The American women who joined the men ran the risk of being the topic of gossip and rumors for months as a result of such brazen behavior. As a result, they stayed with the Filipinas and were often bored to death by the small talk about children and household matters. Given the fact that these American women had come of age in the 1960s and early 1970s, it is hardly surprising that they chafed at the restrictions. After nine months in the Philippines, Auflick informed her family, "Males in this country are unbelievably egotistical and chauvinistic. It is the way they are raised and women accept the subjugation. I'm thinking of starting a women's [seminar], but I've got to do it subtly."[31]

The loss of privacy and the special difficulties of female volunteers in particular were hardly unique to the Philippines. All the women working in traditional cultures throughout the developing world faced similar conditions. At one time or another they asked, Why can't we, just once, blend into the background and be only ourselves and ourselves alone instead of being the object of our neighbor's unending fascination?

Every volunteer also had to come to grips with the crucial matters of health, hygiene, and the dramatic reaction that changes in food and environment could have on bodily functions. When both food and environment change at once—as they have a tendency to do in the Peace Corps world—major readjustments of a type previously unthinkable are required. After a year's service in any Peace Corps country, volunteers could sit around the dinner table comparing the results of their latest stool samples; trying to top one another with stories of parasites, worms, and various kinds of amoebas; and describing the most outlandish foods they had ingested—all the time truly enjoying yet one more meal of rice and fish. Every account of Peace Corps life eventually reaches the subject of the body's plumbing system. The inbred American squeamishness about discussing such matters in public quickly gives way in the Peace Corps environment to its opposite: a compulsion to compare and contrast the workings of one's own digestive tract with those of one's colleagues.

The first scheduled event in the Philippines for volunteers was a lecture on health and hygiene. The little fifty-page medical booklet that everyone received began, "As the Greek warriors aptly put it: 'forewarned is forearmed.' Let this be a constant reminder that any known human disease or ailment knows no friend nor foe. And it strikes suddenly. . . . It pays to be vigilant and careful, especially in the preservation of one's health."[32] The booklet then describes the most common of the health risks facing volunteers in the Philippines: flu, amoebiasis, giardiasis, hookworm, hepatitis, mononucleosis, dengue fever, tuberculosis, ascariasis, malaria, tropical sprue, typhoid fever, rabies, and cholera. Other sections of the booklet deal with accidents, anemia, food and drink, fungi, and venereal disease. The list is imposing, even depressing, and purposefully so. We wanted to impress everyone with the seriousness of the subject of health. But we also knew that all of these fearsome-sounding ailments were curable, although in some cases the course of treatment was long and difficult. Therefore, every medical orientation session ended on an upbeat note with a reminder that the human body is sufficiently strong and resistant enough to fight off anything for three days, time enough for the staff to reach and bring out even the most isolated volunteer. Even as I provided this reassurance—corroborated by our physician—I wondered how true it was. Fortunately, in my time the validity of the theory was never put to the test.[33]

White women in the tropics faced a particular medical problem that, once diagnosed, was readily and effectively treated. For some reason they were far more susceptible than white men (or the local population) to a form of anemia that sapped the will and energy of even the most dedicated volunteer. Life became a drag, appetite disappeared, lethargy set in, work became a chore, and nothing seemed to make it right. Often the women concluded that it was culture shock—the symptoms were similar—and they patiently awaited recovery. When recovery did not come, they blamed themselves for a lack of personal fortitude and became even more depressed. Once diagnosed properly, however, the vitamin folic acid quickly restored everything to normal. Those of us not formally associated with the medical office immediately christened this 'miracle drug' *frolic* acid, although the medical profession found our sense of humor odd.

Men had their own special medical problems, but they were a bit more difficult to discuss in polite society. On one of his regular consultation trips to the Philippines from his headquarters in Bangkok, the Regional Peace Corps physician was asked by our rather strait-laced American ambassador what the Peace Corps's major medical problem was. When the physician replied, "Venereal disease," the ambassador frowned and changed the subject. The State Department was uncomfortable dealing with some of the earthier aspects of volunteer life. In many Peace Corps countries, sexual outlets are readily available for male volunteers through normal romantic liaisons or, as in the Philippines, through commercialized sex that is widespread, inexpensive, and dangerous. PC/W also had great difficulty in dealing with this problem. During the 1960s the Peace Corps issued directives prohibiting cohabitation; refused to supply condoms, birth control pills, or other contraceptive devices; placed brothels off-limits; and announced that sexual indiscretion was a cause for instant dismissal. (Presumably PC/W, satisfied that it had taken decisive action, then returned to sweeping back the sea.)

In the 1970s there was still some residual adherence to the standards of the 1960s, especially among those Americans who had spent most of the previous decade beyond the borders of the United States. But, for the most part, the Peace Corps was ready in 1971 to accept sexual conduct as a private matter—as long as it did not lead to public outrage—and to treat venereal disease as a medical matter, not a moral one. This was the course taken in the Philippines, although it would be wrong to give the impression that the transition from seeing sex as a moral issue to seeing it as a health issue was easy for everyone.

We were pushed in that direction by the women of Group 53, who in November 1972 wrote me: "After reading the [medical] handbook, hearing Dr. Agbayani, . . . and [knowing that] the men of the Peace Corps are provided with prophylactics and because this provides them with a measure of birth control protection in addition to protection from venereal disease, . . . [we feel] that in the interest of equality for the sexes the needs of women in this area should also be considered. . . . Therefore, we are requesting Peace Corps to provide some type of birth control measure for unmarried women. Pills or the IUD are preferable."[34]

When Dr. Agbayani made the mistake of addressing his concilia-tory letter of reply to "the Girls of Group 53," all hell broke loose. He never did really understand why the use of the word *girls* caused so much trouble, but he was willing to accept it as some strange American quirk and make amends. In the end, we apologized to the *women* of Group 53, established a no-questions-asked policy with respect to condoms, pills, and IUDs, and included women in the pre-viously male-only lectures on the hazards of venereal disease.

Illness is a great leveler. The various viruses and bacteria that make life miserable on occasion have no respect for size, shape, or gender. One strapping six-footer who grew up on a Kentucky farm spent most of his two years fighting off wave after wave of a rare in-testinal disorder. His petite, equally hardworking, and adventurous wife was barely touched. Her letters home describe the never-ending battle her husband fought against an intestinal problem that would not go away. She would regularly report that her husband was once again in Manila trying to find a cure. In the end he was cured, but it was a long time coming.[35] The entire top strata of the official Ameri-can presence in the Philippines once spent a very long week not daring to stray far from bathroom facilities. When it became known that they had suffered this mishap not because they had ventured out into the bush on some heroic mission but because they had eaten spoiled shrimp at the posh Washington's Birthday Ball, all sympathy for their plight ended. (Some hours before the ball, the hotel staff had placed the iced shrimp on the serving trays. When the electricity went out for an extended period, knocking out the air conditioning, the ice melted, the bacteria multiplied, and the tropics' own version of the quick weight-loss diet took over.)

Although health concerns were a regular part of the Peace Corps, during my time in the Philippines we were spared the agony that accompanied the loss of life. The first Peace Corps director in the country, Larry Fuchs, wrote movingly about "a boy for whom I had developed a deep affection [who] had died of an amoebic abscess of the liver" early in his tour.[36] Occasionally we would become worried, but inevitably modern medicine and the body's resilience would win out. Despite my aversion to the role of *in loco parentis*, I sometimes found myself being just that. I once stood by trying to look cheerful and unworried as a medical orderly in a poorly equipped rural hos-pital wheeled a volunteer into the operating room for an emergency appendectomy. The operation was completely successful, but as I knew from my own experience, there is nothing worse than being sick far from home and surrounded by strangers. My feigned cheerfulness was the only help I could offer. Tidwell tells a frightening story in *The Ponds of Kalambayi* of his bout with bilharzia, more commonly known in the Peace Corps as schistosomiasis, a disease that attacks the bladder and intestines. His two-day struggle to reach a medical clinic proved to be a test he barely passed.[37] Stories such as his and the emergency appendectomy, fortunately, were the exceptions; far more typical were the intestinal tract disorders, the fungi, the flu, and the infected cuts and scrapes that would eventually yield to modern medicine, even if they were mightily discomforting in the meantime.

In the Peace Corps, as in every other part of life, humor often saved the day. Volunteers developed a wonderful capacity for turning some of their worst moments into witty and wry commentaries that often made themselves the butt of the joke. One volunteer newsletter described an imaginary site-briefing given to a new staff member by the country director.

> *Country Director:* "McFurgle, Darwin would be happier than a hookworm at the central school if he could observe the life forms there. Imagine a species that lies around eating fish and lapping at fermented coconut sap and cane squeezings all day."
>
> *McFurgle:* "Sounds disgusting. Do these things frighten the volunteers there?"
>
> *Country Director:* "McFurgle, those things are the volunteers there. Good luck."[38]

Seasoned volunteers had great fun parading their self-conferred superiority over new arrivals. In the Philippines, this meant eating *balut*, hissing at waiters (that is the accepted way of calling one, although it hardly comes naturally to an American), speaking the dialect so quickly that no one can understand it, and as one third-year veteran, Alvin Hower, quaintly put it, "taking your whizzes in public." Hower took the comparison of the acculturated old-timer and the neophyte even further by pointing out that the latter can get "close enough to kill the cockroach" whereas the old timer "lets it eat out of his hand."

One group of volunteers—all women—decided to turn the tables on their Filipino cross-cultural instructors by staging a classic American football weekend, which they christened the Baguio Bowl. Football is totally alien to the Filipino psyche; it is rough, competitive, boisterous, and certainly not ladylike. The scheduled events included a pep rally complete with a bonfire, a homecoming king and queen, two teams (all female), cheerleaders (played by the Filipina instructors dressed in pleated skirts and bobbysocks), and a marching band. In the midst of the game, the offensive team came out of the huddle, but instead of running a play they broke into a riotous version of a fast-paced cha-cha. The only major logistical problem the group encountered in preparing for the Baguio Bowl was finding a football. First they put their qualms aside—it was considered bad form to have anything to do with the military—and asked Clark Air Force Base to lend them one. Unfortunately, it was spring, and the military was playing baseball, not football. In desperation they cabled the Philippines desk officer in Washington seeking help. Within a few days a brand-new football arrived in Manila via diplomatic pouch. It may have been the only time in sports history that a game ball arrived in a sack surrounded by packages and envelopes marked CONFIDENTIAL, SECRET, TOP SECRET, and FOR AMBASSADOR'S EYES ONLY. Sometimes the urge to be American, to escape the confines of someone else's culture, can be overwhelming. The Baguio Bowl was the perfect outlet. As Patricia Auflick told her family, "It was a kind of insanity that drew us all together."[39]

On occasion the staff found itself to be the target of volunteer humor. One postcard mailed to the Manila office read, "Urgent— dozens of volunteers sighted at happy hour, refusing to report to assignments. . . hobnobbing with tourists and fat cat Americans and generally just not taking cues from the culture. Please airdrop fifty copies of Doctor to the Barrios. . . . Urgent, send fast. Can't talk now, hostesses closing in."[40]

Volunteers often reveled in sending a lady of the night knocking on a traveling staff member's hotel room door claiming that some nice Americans in the bar had sent her up. In those cases someone always confessed amidst great laughter the next morning at breakfast. James Skelton tells the story of a volunteer in Ethiopia who was under great pressure from a new director to shave his beard and cut his hair. When the volunteer finally did so, he angrily mailed the shorn locks to the director, an action about which he had serious second thoughts the next morning. As it turned out, the director had a sense of humor and all was well.[41] Volunteer humor was often earthy, sometimes tinged with bitterness, or so 'in' that bystanders missed the point entirely. But it saved the day more than once.

Living the Peace Corps life in the Philippines required a willingness to adapt to a new culture, to experience weather patterns that were entirely different from those left behind, to adapt to new foods, to lose a certain degree of one's privacy, and to elevate health concerns to a level never necessary before or since. In addition, it meant learning to manage the humdrum but necessary details of ordinary life in a foreign language and in situations that were often simultaneously exotic and stressful, and it meant rethinking one's own values, aspirations, and relationships. As Maureen Waters wrote in 1974 just as she was about to extend her tour of duty for a third year on the island of Bohol: "Sure I have wanted to scream in frustration, bang heads together, [even] leave—but I wouldn't trade these two years for anything. . . . It was hard at first and it's still not easy to adapt to all the cultural differences . . . but there are so many opportunities here to grow and go with the country, I can't help getting excited about all of the things one can get into with a little patience and willingness to bend."[42]

Those who have lived the Peace Corps life are marked by the experience permanently. Nothing is ever truly foreign again, and differences between groups of people the world over become far less important than the similarities that also exist. Whether in the Philippines or in other countries where the volunteers have worked, the result is the same: personal growth of a kind and quality that no other experience can duplicate. Such growth does not come easily; some of the scars that can come with it remain for years, and regrettably some people are harmed by the experience. But for the vast majority, it produces a sense of achievement, satisfaction, and good fortune that endures. A Philippines volunteer, Mark A. Van Steenwyk, was expressing this thought in 1976 when he wrote that the Peace Corps offered "an encounter with the realities of life, a growth process which enables the individual to discover for himself his own weaknesses and capabilities."[43] To that we all say Amen.

New Directions at Work

7

Almost everyone who joins the Peace Corps does so with the hope of doing meaningful work. A Philippine fisheries volunteer from the 1970s recalled that his experience had been important "first of all for what it was meant to be—a chance to impart skills, ideas, knowledge, and a bit of western culture to others while simultaneously educating myself to all the new and different things [the Philippines] had to offer."[1] Another volunteer from the same era wrote, "I felt I needed to accomplish something and worked very hard to achieve my goal."[2] Being productive was central to volunteer motivations. A volunteer whose service began on an uncertain note as he dealt with sickness, a work assignment "that wasn't there," and the temptation to give up and go home was saved when he began to make a contribution. He recalled, "Finally, I got straightened out and working . . . and things were great."[3] There were a few volunteers—one should not pretend otherwise—who had joined for other reasons: to find themselves, to escape—or at least delay—military service, to avoid unpleasantness of some sort at home, or to see the world. But those were a small minority. Most were determined to make their service count for something, and the question of whether it did or not was never far from their conscious thoughts. Jane Raney, an older woman who has written insightful and moving poetry based on her Philippine experience, put it this way:

> Some days when awakened by the dogs and
>   roosters, the tikis and the goats,
> I lie abed and think contentedly
> What a lot I have done in only four months . . .
>   Adjusted to a foreign life,
>   No longer lonely, no longer missing
>   My own chair, my own bed.
>   Each day I am coping
>   With a new set of variables.

> Each day the sun is hot and bright,
> Now I am used to sweating.
> However, some days when awakened by the dogs and
> roosters, the tikis and the goats,
> I sit up straight and ask,
> What am I doing here?
> How little the world is changed by my daily
> Going out and coming in.
> Does it make a whit of difference
> That I am struggling to learn a new language?
> To appreciate ways strange to me?
> To introduce ways strange to others?[4]

She, like so many others, wanted her service to "make a whit of difference." The challenge was not only adjusting to a foreign way of life. She also needed to give something to her new neighbors, to "introduce ways strange to others" in the hope that something good would come out of it. And she had to accept the fact that she probably would never be certain whether she had succeeded or not.

Cynics and skeptics have great fun lampooning the utopian, egotistical, and self-deluding aspects of so grand an idea—that one person's effort can cause change—in a world filled with problems that have frustrated the efforts of the largest and richest nations and institutions. But these naysayers are wrong. Bill Moyers said it best when he described the appeal of Peace Corps service as "a bell, sounding in countless individual hearts [saying], 'You matter. You can signify. You can make a difference.'" Moyers understood that the appeal of volunteer service was felt most strongly by those who by nature were idealistic, adventurous, and perhaps a bit more optimistic than the more pragmatic and realistic of their friends and colleagues. "Romantic?" he asked. "Yes, there was romance to it. But . . . the best volunteers waged hand-to-hand combat with cynicism, and won."[5] When the volunteers of the 1970s came along, they did so confident of their ability to contribute something meaningful to their host countries. There might have been some loss of the unwavering faith the earliest volunteers had in the essential rightness of the American way, but they nevertheless maintained the faith that their contribution could be of value. The only real questions concerned the what, where, and how of doing it. And, of course, those questions led directly to one of the most important debates ever to take place in the organization: whether the promotion of social and economic development (Goal One) or the promotion of understanding among people (Goals Two and Three) should be paramount.

In the early years the Peace Corps ranks were filled by new college graduates, most of whom had liberal arts degrees. It was an article of faith that this type of person was the most likely to possess the qualifications that were essential for service: a sense of mission, desire, and flexibility. The recruitment of volunteers was centered on college campuses (those without college degrees were discouraged from applying); agency rules and regulations (for example, those concerning sexual conduct, the limitations placed on vacation destinations, and the requirement that country directors approve volunteer marriages) were designed for young people not yet to be fully trusted with their own futures. Liberal arts degrees, youth, a jack-of-all-trades approach to volunteer jobs, and a deep sense of wanting to do good were the cherished principles on which the Peace Corps was built. Amateurism—as difficult as it is to understand in the present age of specialization—was seen as a strength, not as a weakness.

The struggle to break free from this legacy was at its most intense during the early 1970s. Blatchford's New Directions was seen by traditionalists to be striking at the very soul of the agency. His proposals were decried as wrongheaded, mean-spirited, and destructive. His rhetoric was rejected as nothing more than a smoke screen designed to hide an attempt to eviscerate a beloved remnant of a shattered Camelot. The participants in that struggle twenty years and more after it took place still find it hard to speak well of one another.

Fortunately, the battle over strategic direction was confined primarily to Washington. There the partisanship was most outspoken, the name-calling most shrill, and constructive dialogue least likely to occur. PC/P was spared the worst aspects of the debate because the two sides had little chance to mix. In 1969 nearly all of the volunteers and in-country staff were products of the earlier philosophy. As their tours ended, they were leaving the country just as the New Directions volunteers started to arrive. Therefore, in a matter of a year to eighteen months the composition of the volunteer contingent and the staff shifted heavily to the New Directions strategy. The constant rotation of volunteers and staff into and out of a country—often an administrative nightmare—became a blessing. The shift to placing greater emphasis on Goal One was far less painful in the Philippines than in PC/W.

Nevertheless, critics were more than happy to express their doubts about the new importance placed on jobs and results. One volunteer, Christopher Newhall, whose four-year tour in the Philippines spanned the old and the new, counseled incoming volunteers to be skeptical of "Joe Blatchford of the Nixon administration [and his plan] that we should be first and foremost skilled technicians who can teach and/or catalyze some practical aspect of the development process." He worried that "goodwill for goodwill's sake seems to have been forgotten" and forcefully concluded, "Who you are as a person is more important than what you achieve on the job."[6]

Another volunteer, Tony Hart, complained that the new emphasis on *doing* something was placing an unwelcome burden of guilt on volunteers who experienced trouble with their jobs. He wrote, "When I do meet down-and-out volunteers or when I'm down-and-out myself the source of the feelings almost invariably seem[s] to come from frustration in [the] work, which in turn leads to viewing the whole of [the] time in Peace Corps as a failure. If the job is going bad the whole thing is going bad, and that's not right." Although there was no conscious effort to create a sense of guilt as volunteers struggled to make their jobs meaningful (and almost without exception they had that struggle), the accusation is probably correct. The staff did place great emphasis on job performance and counseled volunteers to use job performance as a means of making a difference, becoming part of the local community, and overcoming culture shock. The alternative—making the job secondary to the experience of living with and relating to Filipinos—was the equivalent of settling for half a loaf when the whole loaf was within reach. Hart explained, "I view my situation [in the Philippines] as composed of (1) my living experience and (2) my working experience. My living experience would include going around drinking Tanduay [a local brand of rum] and San Miguel [the local bottled beer] and talking with people, throwing stones at the obnoxious roosters and dogs, feeling neat when I hear the young women sigh and giggle as I walk by. . . . Now, in comparing the [living experience with the job experience], I see [the former] as overwhelming[ly] the more valuable part of my stay in Peace Corps. Maybe I'd rate it 9 to 1, living experience over working."[7] In the interest of full disclosure, the staff included his comments and those of Newhall in a packet of material sent to prospective volunteers. Needless to say, additional comments were included that extolled the virtues and satisfactions of solid job performance.[8]

Ron George expressed his ambivalence over the tension between the two aspects of the mission twenty years later as he tried to assess his own tour in the Philippines. He wrote to me in 1993, "My experience . . . was both frustrating and rewarding . . . [because] I took too many Protestant work ethics with me." He had come to realize, he said, that his Filipino neighbors and colleagues had only "wanted me to have a good time, enjoy their culture and the experience, and share a little of America with them." The teachers with whom he worked were not particularly interested in the new reading program he was attempting to introduce. His sense of disappointment remained a quarter century later as he reminisced about his Peace Corps years. But in typical American fashion he was still trying to figure out how he could have been more effective. In his 1993 letter he said that he had finally concluded that if he had first won the support of the school system superintendent his success rate would have been much higher. It was obvious that after so long a time his mind was still on the job!

The three volunteers cited above who criticized New Directions were in education programs. They had each encountered a situation in which their presence was seen by the local educational establishment either as an accommodation of a superior's request to accept a volunteer or as a matter of habit because the school system had 'always' had a volunteer. Tony Hart was taken aback on his arrival, he wrote in 1975, when his supervisor asked, "What will you be doing while here at the central school?" Hart's response, "I kind of thought you'd tell me," created an awkward situation that "had not yet been overcome."[9] Obviously, the Peace Corps staff had not done its job. But beyond that, the fact remains that volunteers were not viewed by the Department of Education as valuable resources to be used to accomplish something important. Each of the three education projects had violated one of the fundamental principles of New Directions programming. None of them dovetailed with the country's own perception of its development needs. Little wonder, then, that volunteers assigned to jobs that lacked a clear and direct relationship to national goals looked to the nonjob aspects of Peace Corps life to find meaning. The fact that all three made the effort to find true meaning—and did indeed find it—speaks well for them and their understanding of the multifaceted mission of the Peace Corps. Unfortunately, the situation also points up the unnecessary complications that arise when the job becomes merely a cover for *being somewhere* rather than an opportunity for *doing something.* It should be noted that the lukewarm assessment of education programs in the Philippines is not to be taken as a condemnation of educational programs throughout the agency. As discussed below, there have been—and still are—situations in host countries where one or another aspect of education is considered to be crucial to the nation's development and where volunteer participation is highly desirable and well supported.

New Directions unquestionably tipped the balance in favor of jobs, both in terms of the rhetoric employed and in the way Peace Corps programs were revamped around the world. The first question asked of host countries was, What do you want to accomplish? Then, What kind of skills or special training does it take to do that? Only then were the conditions in which the volunteers would serve considered in order to ensure that there would be genuine contact with local people. In essence, this was a reversal of the underlying premise established in the early Peace Corps. New Directions took for granted that volunteers could become part of their local communities if they were working in jobs that were important, instead of assuming that they could find something important to do if they became part of the community. Again, it is essential to understand that New Directions did not entail an abandonment of the personal nature of the Peace Corps. This component continued to be a key part of the formula that makes the organization such a wonderful expression of America. But it is also true that New Directions elevated the job aspects of volunteer service to a higher level than they had been assigned previously. (The increased emphasis on jobs, which was deemed so revolutionary in the early 1970s, has become standard practice at the Peace Corps. An official publication announced in 1995 that "becoming a Peace Corps Volunteer today can be a challenge . . . but it is possible to be selected if you develop the skills and experience needed for an assignment.")[10]

New Directions recognized that the Peace Corps could make a difference in various ways. The primary requirements were that the projects be designed in cooperation with host country officials (or in some instances with private institutions), that they address identified national priorities, and that prospective volunteers either have the skills needed to do the job or be able to acquire them through training. Beyond these the programs could go in many directions.

In Korea, for example, the nation's priorities differed markedly from those in the Philippines. When it first invited the Peace Corps to work in the country in 1966, Korea was already on the verge of leaving the ranks of the undeveloped. It had a highly effective education system and a sound economic development plan, and it knew exactly what type of volunteer could help in the move forward: teachers of English. As Donald Hess, an early director in Korea, explained to me in January 1995, "Korea had to buy its raw materials in the world marketplace where English was used. [The Koreans converted] those materials based on an increasingly highly skilled society whose technical skills were largely acquired in the English medium. Then [the Koreans] took the finished product back into the world marketplace where again English was the most common language." He reported that his complete conversion to the Peace Corps's English teaching program occurred when he "realized that at the two medical schools in Korea there was but one textbook written in Korean[;] all others were in English." Clearly, if the country's development plan was to succeed, an ever-larger proportion of its population had to learn English. Under such circumstances Peace Corps volunteers possessing only liberal arts degrees and a few months of training could legitimately be considered skilled volunteers. After all, they had more than twenty years of experience in their field, speaking English. At first PC/W had some difficulty in reconciling Korea's English program with New Directions rhetoric, but in time they did. So did a congressional survey team when it concluded that "by providing Koreans with the means for self-advancement, [the Peace Corps's English program had] made a major impact in contributing toward Korean self-sufficiency."[11] Although English language programs in the Philippines were seen by both Filipinos and volunteers as make-work programs at best and totally irrelevant at worst, in Korea they were essential and everyone knew it.

In Malaysia yet another situation existed. English is a second language, widely taught in the school system—Malaysia was an English colony for more than a century—and the government quickly lost interest in basic-level Peace Corps English teachers. The congressional team found that "the Malaysian government ha[d] ruled generalist volunteers unacceptable for assignment there; as a result, the volunteers—as a group—represent[ed] a highly diversified set of skills and backgrounds and forms of expertise." Moreover, the survey continued, the volunteers—most with master's degrees and some with doctorates—constituted "an impressive example of New Directions programming . . . balanced by a judicious diversification of individual assignments to various fields of activity."[12]

Malaysia in 1972 fit the New Directions mold in another aspect as well. It was home to twenty volunteer families, including fifty-seven children. The congressional team's conclusion with respect to families could not have been more complimentary if it had been written by Peace Corps's own public affairs department. The survey reported that one such family was "a distinct asset—not merely a tolerable burden. Through associations cultivated by his wife and children, both on and off campus, the volunteer [had] substantially broadened his own range of contacts with Malaysians, which originally had been almost exclusively professional in nature."[13] Critics of New Directions had predicted that the decision to permit families to serve together abroad would destroy the cross-cultural component of Peace Corps. In actual fact, this component was enhanced by the presence of families, not diminished, a lesson also learned in the Philippines. The teenage daughter of a volunteer couple wrote to other families considering the Peace Corps, "I'm studying in my town, I call it my town because . . . I belong here, and I truly fit among my [Filipino] classmates. The school is the center of most activity for my brothers, sister, and me."[14]

Before leaving the congressional report behind, it is interesting to note one other matter with respect to Malaysia, New Directions, and Peace Corps during the Nixon/Ford years. The country director in Malaysia whose work was so highly praised was Edward J. Slevin, a Californian who had been active in Republican politics. Predictably, he was the target of considerable snide and petulant criticism from those leveling charges of partisan politics at Blatchford. Yet Slevin proved to be as good a country director as the Peace Corps has ever had. It was not his Republican credentials that made him so; it was his commitment to the mission and his leadership abilities. (During the 1980s Slevin returned to the Peace Corps and served another term as a country director, this time in the Philippines.)

It would be wrong to assume from these examples about the successes of New Directions that the new strategy was quickly and uniformly adopted throughout the Peace Corps. Unfortunately, that was not always the case. In some countries the patterns that had been established during the 1960s were too firmly set to break easily. Sometimes the host government would not change; at other times the difficulty lay with the in-country Peace Corps. (As has been pointed out, individual country programs had considerable autonomy, and if a country director was willing to endure some sharply worded cables and letters from PC/W, change could be delayed almost indefinitely.)

This problem was particularly acute in West Africa where, the same congressional investigative staff concluded, the "New Directions concept [was] essentially inoperative." The problem, according to the House report, resulted from two factors: The numbers game had made a reappearance in the region, and in-country staff resources had been spread too thin.[15] In time, however, as George Packer writes in *The Village of Waiting*, the irrelevant English programs in West African countries were ended as New Directions thinking lost its controversial nature and became simply the way things were done.

As discussed in chapter 4, the Peace Corps program in the Philippines took on a fresh look as it adopted the development philosophy inherent in New Directions, made alliances with additional government entities, and began elevating the idea of *doing something* to a position equal to if not actually above the idea of *being someplace*. The new approach brought a new vocabulary into being that included such terms as *institution building, multiplier effect, appropriate technology, binationalism, host country contribution,* and the widely abused, misunderstood, and unfortunate term *nonmatrixed spouse*. Like all jargon, these words made discussion of the development effort easier and more focused. Each encompassed a complex set of underlying principles. By using these bits of shorthand, participants could forgo lengthy discussions on principles and move directly to the details of a specific project. Yet for the uninitiated, their meaning was not obvious, and newcomers often found themselves lost.

Institution building, for example, reflected the new concern for strengthening the governmental institutions that delivered economic and social services to the people of the Philippines. This meant that volunteers' potential contributions would be judged not only by their own direct efforts but also by whether the work could strengthen an existing delivery system. James Skelton's *Volunteering in Ethiopia* describes his own participation in an institution-building program. He developed an accounting system that permitted a smallpox eradication team to track its resources, analyze its activities, and develop future plans. Skelton's work was far less exciting and direct than that of his Ethiopian and volunteer colleagues who did the actual work of detection and vaccination in the rugged Ethiopian countryside. But his contribution made the entire program more effective. Once the accounting system was implemented, Skelton's presence was no longer necessary; the system had a life of its own apart from the presence of a specific individual.[16]

The adoption of this approach in the Philippines required a greater change in operations than might appear at first glance. Previously, the volunteers had been placed in local settings—for example, at a barrio primary school or at a local high school or college—where their intended impact was to be site-specific. The new approach had much larger implications. Volunteers were to be an integral part of national efforts to foster development. The volunteers' contributions were to be felt both locally—at a rural health clinic, for example—and nationally through their collective impact on the *system*—in this example, the nationwide system for delivering health care to rural communities.

The Philippines government had to accomplish two goals. First, it needed to deliver a higher quality of service at the local level;

second, it needed to improve the larger delivery system itself so that it could function more effectively. The goal was to ensure the existence of a permanent entity that would last and become increasingly more proficient in delivering needed services. Early in my stay, when I was acutely aware of the charge that Peace Corps was nothing more than an agent of cultural imperialism, I worried that participation in institution building could turn out to be just that—the imposition of American values on another country. When the secretary of the Department of Agriculture and Natural Resources, Arturo Tanco, expressed his hope that volunteers could demonstrate the vaunted American work ethic to their Filipino colleagues, I protested that doing so could be seen as cultural imperialism. The virtues of hard work, discipline, and a respect for orderly progress toward predetermined goals were too American, too western, I explained, and we had to be sensitive to the local culture. "Nonsense," he snapped. "Those are the values of a developed country, and we need them."

The idea of using volunteers in an institution-building exercise was a far cry from the original concept of volunteers living at the local level, discovering a need, and then working to fill that need. Not surprisingly, some volunteers and staff members believed that the new approach was faulty. The tension between Goal One and Goals Two and Three was readily apparent, especially whenever the stark reality of the obstacles hindering the building of institutions forced itself upon us. As one volunteer wrote in 1976, "Volunteers for whom goodwill is of primary importance seem to be more comfortable [in the Philippines]. Their time is invested in personal relationships and their effectiveness on the job is almost a natural consequence of these relationships."[17] Other volunteers needed a more tangible sense of making a contribution. Discovering that her job required little in the way of real work, one woman described her feelings as "a combination of suppressed rage, deep disappointment, [and] fear that I had made a really bad decision" in joining the Peace Corps. A second job turned out much better. Twenty years later she recalled with pride the role she had played in building an institution that "had nine employees when I began my work. When I finished my service in 1975, there were about 250 employees. When . . . I returned [to visit] in 1978 the project had new headquarters and 550 employees."[18] She had truly been involved in institution building.

The importance of institution building was driven home in the Philippines by the experience of one woman working in a rural health unit. She had tried without success to convince a mother to take her severely malnourished child to the local hospital. The woman refused because in her town people only went to the hospital to die. The health delivery system was considered so ineffectual that it was thought to be a threat to one's well-being rather than a source of it. The mother recognized her baby's need but not the role the hospital could play in meeting that need. Three days later the baby was dead.[19]

The *multiplier effect* referred to the insistence (or, perhaps more accurately, the hope) that each volunteer's work would both deliver a service to a specific client base and upgrade the quality of the work performed by the volunteer's Filipino counterparts. Volunteers assigned to agricultural extension programs, for example, delivered services directly to farmers and also introduced the concept of agricultural *extension* to their colleagues in the Department of Agriculture and Natural Resources. Filipino employees of the department in the provinces were accustomed to waiting in their offices for farmers to come to them, rather than actively seeking out the farmers and persuading them to adopt modern methods. One volunteer, if successful, could convert an entire office of deskbound bureaucrats into active extension agents—the best means, experts agreed, for transferring new technology from experimental stations to the farm.

After a year with the Bureau of Agricultural Extension as a nutrition education worker, a volunteer concluded, "Any impact I make within BAE must be with the [Filipino] technicians [i.e., those who visit the farms] and their supervisors. They are the people who will remain in the job for the rest of their lives. . . . I will be here only two years." She had come to realize that even though the satisfaction of personally providing a service was great, the greater contribution was in strengthening the system.[20]

Appropriate technology embraced the idea that solutions to social and economic problems needed to take into account local conditions.[21] For example, the developed world has always looked for laborsaving devices that could perform jobs faster, cheaper, and better than human workers. But this mind-set is totally inappropriate where there is high unemployment. Westerners often scoff at the sight of a multitude of Third World workers spending a week or two doing what one large piece of earthmoving equipment could do in an afternoon. They totally miss the point, however, that the 'Caterpillar solution' would deprive these workers and their families of a livelihood, thereby creating a far greater problem than that created by taking a bit longer to complete a job. The same situation existed in the agricultural sector. The use of modern herbicides, initially thought to be a key ingredient of the Green Revolution, resulted in putting many agricultural workers out of a job because they were no longer required for weed-control tasks, as did the introduction of small farm machinery such as the Rototiller.[22] Similarly, the investment of substantial capital in a medical or scientific research institute, or some other high-tech enterprise, is an extremely poor use of a Third World country's budget for health services. When three-fourths of the deaths that occur in the developing world are the result of communicable and preventable diseases, it makes no sense to spend money on high technology.[23] Far better to spend it on the foundations of a good health care system: sanitary methods of human waste disposal, vaccinations, and the provision of potable drinking water. The Marcos regime was especially guilty of wasting resources on inappropriate projects. It built a heart research center, a kidney treatment facility, and a lung disease institute that were the envy of other Asian countries but that did little to address the nation's health problems. A UNICEF study looked into the building program and concluded, "Too little was spent on saving the lives of poor people, and too much on saving the lives of the rich."[24]

Binationalism, one of the key principles of the New Directions philosophy, recognized that the Peace Corps was a guest in the host country, that program decisions should be jointly made, and that wherever possible differences in opinion should be resolved in the host country's favor. The basic direction of a country's social and economic development effort was a matter for it to decide. Once decided, Peace Corps and the host country needed to integrate volunteers into the plan. This approach contrasted sharply with the one that put hundreds of volunteers into nonjobs in education without giving any real thought to what was appropriate or necessary.

Binationalism recognized that the assessment of needs and opportunities is best made by those who are directly involved. Outsiders rarely have the special insights that lead to practical solutions to another's problems, as the long history of colonialism clearly shows. Flavier, very much a Filipino in touch with the people of the barrios, found that even he had to take his direction from those who lived in the provinces. Discovering a high incidence of neonatal tetanus in a remote barrio, he took prompt, decisive action—or at least he thought he did—and showed the local people how to use stainless steel scissors to cut the umbilical cord instead of the sharpened piece of bamboo they traditionally used. Flush with pride, he said to himself, "Why . . . we will modernize the world concept of the people before we are through." Six months later he returned to find tetanus still a problem, the scissors ignored, and the bamboo still in use. Eventually the local people told him that there were strong cultural taboos against using anything not indigenous to the barrio in childbirth, and they could not switch to something as 'foreign' as scissors. Rethinking his recommendation—so textbook correct, yet so inappropriate in this barrio—he came upon the right solution: sterilize the piece of bamboo![25] The problem was solved.

The Peace Corps's publicly stated commitment to binationalism was a departure from the prevailing notion that development assistance meant bringing American solutions to Third World problems. As an economist recently put it, "Development [was] something done *to* or *for* its putative beneficiaries, not *by* them."[26] But, as Blatchford wrote in 1970, "The transfer of technology has to start with a desire to receive and use it, which in turn requires that someone see the problem through the eyes of the recipient."[27] This required a change in perspective which, as Flavier learned, often led to solutions that were remarkably different from what one expected. The people involved must be equal partners in the decision-making process, and the Peace Corps had to make a firm commitment to the principle of listening, as well as talking.

Paired with binationalism was the concept of *host country contribution*, or the extent to which the host country supported the Peace Corps in its work. If a program was truly important to the Philippines, the government was expected to provide some support for it. PC/W wanted to see such support expressed in monetary terms: either in cash or in kind, the latter being goods and services provided by the Philippine government that offset expenses the Peace Corps would otherwise have incurred for training, volunteer support, or administrative and logistical matters. But for staff members managing the program, a far more important measure of host country contribution was the level of interest demonstrated by the leadership. Inevitably, especially in the first year of a project's existence, there was a clash of egos, interests, and objectives between volunteers and host country bureaucracies, which intensified the farther down the bureaucratic chain one went. Aspects of a program that were readily agreed to by staff and the secretary of a department often became matters of major dispute at the working level. No bureaucracy changes easily, and given the institution-building aspects of the volunteer programs, bureaucratic change was often a key objective. When the inevitable happened, when egos clashed, when local Filipino supervisors wanted to ignore departmental directives, when volunteers found themselves purposely isolated from the activities of the office to which they were assigned, corrective action depended on the intercession of senior officials.

The first swine production project was nearly torn apart by such a problem, and only through decisive action by departmental leadership was it saved. The program called for volunteers to be used as agricultural extension agents in the Bureau of Animal Industry (BAI). The volunteers (identified as Group 43) arrived in mid-1971 already possessing some agricultural skills. They received the normal language and cultural training as well as specialized instruction in tropical swine production. On assignment they were to bring the newest technology to local farmers and help them increase production levels. (The traditional methods used by many Philippine farmers required two or three times as long to raise a hog to market size as did modern breeding and feeding practices.) The BAI agreed to provide motorcycles for the volunteers, to give them office space and administrative support, and to integrate them into its extension service.

Within a few months it became clear that Peace Corps and the BAI had a major problem. The Filipinos at the local offices found the volunteers too demanding, too impatient, and too critical of the way the local extension agents were performing their jobs. The Americans were unquestionably seen as meddlers, not as constructive change agents. The volunteers, for their part, complained that their extension agent colleagues rarely left the office, that they lacked even rudimentary skills, that they charged farmers a fee for providing services that were meant to be free, and that BAI supervisors had no interest in carrying out the secretary's swine production program. The secretary, angry at both the Peace Corps and his own bureau, summoned everyone involved to a three-day confrontation to settle all the outstanding issues. He faulted his own people for their failures in program execution, and he faulted the volunteers for their unreasonableness and insensitivity. Then he demanded that they work together right then to develop a plan that would put the program back on track. Much to everyone's surprise, a good plan was developed and later approved by the secretary. In the end both the DANR and the Peace Corps agreed that a substantially better program emerged along with a reenergized BAI.

Given the aggravations endured by the volunteers and their Filipino counterparts during this difficult period and the fact that less than 50 percent of the group completed their two-year service commitment, it is easy to understand why this program could be cited as evidence to refute New Directions' emphasis on placing volunteers in host country institutional settings. But in doing so a far more important point is missed. The Peace Corps is not just the sum of individual volunteer experiences, as many mistakenly believe. It is also an institution that can grow and change and become better at carrying out its mission. The experience of Group 43, although painful, was one of those catalysts that create change and promote growth. It showed the Peace Corps and the DANR that making modifications in a traditional system is not accomplished easily or quickly. It reminded everyone that skills alone do not make an effective volunteer; patience, tolerance, and perseverance are also essential. And it proved conclusively that top-level host country government support is critical if a program is to succeed. As a bipartisan congressional evaluation team from the United States declared after a trip to the Philippines during which it reviewed the Group 43 project, "The process of integrating Peace Corps volunteers into the regular government system . . . has not been accomplished without some pain and disruption, but the effort has been necessary."[28]

This kind of host country support was greatly appreciated, far more than the monetary or in-kind contributions PC/W took pleasure in publicizing. It showed that the host country and its representatives were willing to put themselves on the line, to work on program problems that were far from easy to solve, and to make midcourse corrections when it became apparent that initial plans had been faulty.

The term *nonmatrixed spouse* was a mystery to anyone outside the staff. Even the women (and the occasional man) to whom it applied were bewildered by it, until they began to grasp its meaning—and then they were furious. As the Peace Corps worked to recruit volunteers with specific skills, it had eased the policy on accepting married couples or families. Previously, families (defined as married couples with at least one minor child) were completely denied an opportunity to serve. Couples were accepted only if both members had the skills needed to qualify for the program. When most projects called for generalists with college degrees, this stipulation caused little difficulty because both spouses usually met the standard.

With the coming of New Directions these policies changed. Families were accepted, as were couples—even if only one spouse met the program qualifications. The result was the presence of a number of volunteers who were not formally part of any program. These were mainly the wives of men who had the necessary skills to be placed on the 'matrix,' the term used for the list of qualified volunteers for a project. Someone, somewhere, decided that the unqualified volunteer, therefore, would be called a nonmatrixed spouse. As Rona Roberts remembered long after her ordeal was over, "Unfamiliar with the ways of bureaucracies, or with the way bureaucratic processes get further tangled when two countries' bureaucracies are involved, the real meaning of 'nonmatrixed' did not become clear to me until a few days after my arrival in Manila. . . . All summer I [had been calling] the Washington office to learn about my assignment [and was promised] a great job."[29] When she learned that little or nothing had been done to prepare a job for her—and her qualifications were the equal of or better than her husband's—she was devastated. Rebecca Okie wrote to incoming nonmatrixed spouses, "Being a NMS means that you probably won't have a technical training program. . . . Peace Corps/Philippines won't have time to worry about whether your work is productive or not. You have to worry about that yourself and it gets to be quite a burden. . . . You'll literally have to go begging for a job . . . but most [government agencies] only want an American for status and display. . . . [Filipinos] will look at you as an accessory to your spouse (if you're a wife that means you can keep house, get a manicure, have babies and speak at women's clubs). An NMS has to be prepared to have her or his self-image and self-confidence badly shaken."[30] The difficulties that the nonmatrixed spouses faced were especially galling because their motivation and commitment were of the highest order, and the prospect of having a nonjob was unacceptable. The staff did not manage this problem well, partly because it was already fully challenged by its efforts to redirect the program and partly by an institutional carryover from an earlier time when volunteers were expected to keep quiet, do as they were told, or be sent home. It is to their lasting credit that most of the nonmatrixed spouses did find their own way and did make lasting contributions to the Philippines, to the Peace Corps—and, one hopes, to themselves. (Washington attacked the problem by changing the terminology from nonmatrixed spouse to *volunteers in special placement*. Of course, little changed as a result.)

The rather complex concepts underlying this specialized vocabulary represented the bedrock of Peace Corps's attempt to develop sound, productive jobs for volunteers. The agency was a vehicle for providing trained manpower for the government programs that delivered social and economic services to the people. The Philippines already had an adequate supply of senior administrators in positions of leadership who, in turn, were supplemented by experts from USAID, the World Bank, the major American private philanthropic institutions, and many other national and international organizations. What was lacking was a sufficient supply of trained and properly motivated people at the delivery end of the system where the plans made at the departmental level were to be translated into action. It was this gap—what a contemporary development expert called a "manpower link"—that the Peace Corps was asked to help fill.[31]

The volunteer role was twofold: the delivery of services to individual Filipinos and the redirection of the delivery system itself toward more effective methods. As one veteran volunteer, Barry North, wrote to potential volunteers, "Setting good work examples should be a project for [Peace Corps volunteers] all by itself. Government agencies tend to be fair[ly] to partly corrupt[;] they call it backsliding [under martial law]. . . . In most cases what an individual working for the government does in one day could be done in a half day or less." One of the major causes of the near-disaster that struck Group 43 (the swine production project in the BAI) was the intensely negative reaction on the part of the volunteers to the work habits of the bureau's employees and the similar reaction on the part of the Filipinos to the volunteers' heavy-handedness. That specific problem was resolved, or at least reduced to manageable proportions, when the secretary of the department directed in the most forceful manner that bureau personnel be more open to the new work ethic he wanted to instill and that the volunteers jettison their sense of self-conferred superiority and learn to work within the cultural norms of the country. In the words of Barry North, "As long as a [volunteer] has to depend on others for cooperation and help (which of course will be most of the time), he or she will have to learn to slow down the work pace to that of his or her Filipino partners. Try not to let this frustrate or discourage you. As stated before, setting good work examples ought to be a project all its own, and working at a steady constant pace, though probably a bit slower than what you are used to, is one way of doing it."[32]

By putting volunteers directly into the government's bureaucratic system, the amount of cultural adjustment needed was increased because of the differences between the Filipino and American attitudes toward work. One volunteer working in a rural health unit described the way he learned about this difference: "In the clinic, I groped for that working identity every American depends on and many Filipinos simply cannot understand. I wanted to solve every problem and told everyone exactly that. I tried to become a member of the 'rural health team' boldly attacking every problem because I thought a work identity must be universal. . . . Gradually I came to see how absurd and compulsive I looked, like Don Quixote attacking windmills."[33]

New Directions' programming did not make life easier for volunteers, host country officials, or government workers—or for the Peace Corps staff. It introduced complicating factors that could not be ignored. Volunteers were placed in government bureaucracies that were, virtually by definition, deficient in fundamental ways. Job performance standards were raised, thus raising host country expectations, and whenever actual performance failed to meet the new standards and expectations, embarrassment and frustration resulted on all sides. Planning done at the national level rarely took into account the full nature of working conditions at the local level, and the volunteer was left facing the consequences. Clearly, programming that placed higher priority on the cross-cultural elements of the Peace Corps mission—as it did before New Directions—was easier on both staff and volunteer than the new policy. But it was also clear that neither the host country nor the volunteers were satisfied with an approach that gave higher priority to simply *being* there. As the 1973 congressional report on the Peace Corps in Asia concluded, "The adjustment toward full integration [with host country bureaucratic structures and priorities] has . . . become an unavoidable feature of the Peace Corps in the 1970s. For unless the developing nations come to regard the Peace Corps as a valuable resource—and one that they can control and *use* [emphasis in the original] to implement their own policies—the program will become superfluous. In terms of the future . . . the Peace Corps will either make this transition successfully or it will cease to be relevant."[34]

Volunteers handled the frustrations of working in an imperfect bureaucratic system in several ways. Some simply ignored the bureaucratic structure and dealt only with clients—be they farmers, young mothers, malnourished children, or students. One woman despaired of ever being productive, at least to the extent she wished to be, as an English teacher in the school system. She took the opportunity to turn a summer project working with the T'boli people in a remote part of Mindanao into a full-time assignment where her work was entirely on a person-to-person basis. Some months after she had abandoned the school system she presented the staff with a *fait accompli* and asked for its blessing.[35] She received it, but not without some grumbling on the part of the staff member who had to explain the situation to the people at the Department of Education.

Other volunteers talked themselves into believing that it was not the job that was important but the personal relationships in the community. Tony Hart admitted, "I consider my work just an excuse to be here." In his mind he was not abusing his position as a volunteer or failing to make an effort. It was just his way of ensuring that "frustration in [his] work [did not lead] to viewing the *whole* of [his] time in Peace Corps as failure."[36] Still others gave up the struggle and went home. This last method of dealing with the problem was invariably accompanied by much soul-searching, anguish, and guilt. No one favored it, yet far too many chose it when the burden of Peace Corps service became too great. If the Peace Corps has a major shortcoming, it is its inability to reduce the percentage of volunteers who leave before the end of their tours. An accurate count of early terminations over the entire history of the Peace Corps is not available, although estimates of 40 percent exist.[37] A failure rate this high should not be acceptable.

But most volunteers accepted the challenges of working within a bureaucracy. They knew that long-term progress depended on the presence of a strong service delivery system, and they were willing to contribute toward that reality, even if the day might not come until long after their departure. The one thing they wanted most was a meaningful job, wherever it might be found. The most calamitous situation was to arrive at one's site unexpected, as one volunteer did: "No one had known about my coming. No one knew who I was, what I was, or why I was."[38] Another common complaint emerged after a volunteer whose job seemed to start off well discovered "that the people I worked with accommodated me because it is somehow prestigious to have an American in the office."[39] Few volunteers want to spend their two years of service bolstering the ego of some bureaucrat. Other problems concerned the inflexible bureaucracy, supervisors who did not believe in the work they directed, coworkers who spent official working hours moonlighting at a second job, and the discovery that the technical skills one had did not match the ones needed at the site. Volunteers often had to scale back their original (usually unrealistic) goals and settle for those that were more manageable but still worthwhile. For one volunteer in a rural health unit, it meant accepting that although he had "some impact on some of the manifold health problems besetting these people, [he] had to realize that [he was] not Tom Dooley."[40] (The famous physician and his hospital ship *Hope* brought modern medical care to many of the world's destitute. His endeavors symbolized for many what it meant to help make the world a better place.)

Another volunteer, one of the original members of the swine production program, said after eighteen months in the country, "I came to the Philippines with big ideas about changing the world overnight, but it didn't happen. I have found, since the time I've been here, that sometimes the little changes are the most rewarding. . . . [My Filipino coworkers now] think that extension work is an important part of agriculture. That's not changing the world, but in my [barrio] if you go to the [agricultural] office and ask what extension is, you'll get an answer."[41]

Concerns about health, safety, living conditions, martial law, or even Peace Corps policies were far fewer and less intensely felt than were those related to jobs. The most important part of the staff job was to ensure that volunteers had satisfying and productive work. When those conditions were met, everything else fell into place. Volunteers who were working and productive had higher levels of personal satisfaction, were less likely to be ill, were more closely connected with their communities, contributed more to the Philippines, and personally benefited more from the experience. One volunteer who survived the difficult start of the swine program recalled after his service ended, "I can remember spending days on end as my work schedule tightened visiting farmers, attending meetings, and developing . . . an endless number of proposals, plans and feasibility studies [to develop a livestock cooperative]. . . . Perhaps we were lucky . . . . [But] the cooperative was established. . . . [Seeing it finished] was more than reward enough. . . . I will always be grateful that I was one of the lucky ones."[42] Every volunteer wanted that sense of accomplishment; unfortunately, not all of them achieved it. One reason was the very nature of work in the Third World with its inadequate resources, inefficient and corrupt governments, and nonexistent infrastructures. Another was a staff failure to meet its goal of making every volunteer job a good one, even though that goal was probably unrealistic. In any event, too often volunteers were left to their own devices with results that damaged morale, credibility, and the organization's contribution. Still, the need to *do something* overwhelmed the need to be somewhere.

Life along the Potomac

8

The Peace Corps in the Philippines liked to think of itself as an independent force for good, working with Filipinos to hasten that country's passage along the road to development. In many respects it was just that. A large degree of autonomy was enjoyed and considerable latitude was available to achieve goals in ways that made the most sense. Simultaneously part of, yet apart from, the official American presence in the country, PC/P operated under the loosest possible embassy reins. There was, however, a larger reality: The Peace Corps was firmly and irrevocably headquartered in Washington.

In the 1960s and 1970s PC/W was a small organization by Washington standards. A few hundred men and women—not the thousands of people in the more typical federal bureaucracy—were located in the center of the city close to the White House. There they performed the lofty—as well as the mundane—chores that enabled the Peace Corps to function. During its first fifteen years PC/W was in a continual process of change. Every new director reshuffled the organizational chart. In Shriver's time, change was almost constant as the Peace Corps learned how to manage its far-flung empire. Vaughn reshaped the haphazard organization he had inherited from Shriver along more traditional bureaucratic lines during a period of intense turmoil and uncertainty. Blatchford, in one of his first executive actions, brought in an outside management consulting firm and with its help effected a massive organizational overhaul. The pattern of change accelerated after Blatchford's departure as five Peace Corps directors and an acting director followed one another in rapid succession over as many years. Each had his or her own ideas about what constituted an effective organization, and it sometimes seemed as if the ink had not yet dried on the latest announcement of pending reorganization before another new director arrived and started the process all over again. Whether any of these reorganizations made a substantial difference in the agency's effectiveness or its efficiency is debatable. Those in the field looked upon the constant reorganizations with bemusement. Titles changed, as did reporting relationships, but little else did. (It should be noted at this point that these comments apply only to changes within the Peace Corps itself, not to the changes that resulted from the creation of ACTION, a well-meant but badly flawed idea to consolidate government-sponsored volunteer activity in one super agency—but more on that later.)

The basic functions around which PC/W is organized remained constant. The most visible and important of these was the leadership provided by the Peace Corps director. By the force of character, public persona, dynamism, and personal identification with the overall mission, the director had an immediate and palpable impact on the organization as a whole, especially in Washington where the director's presence was experienced on a daily basis. The first three directors—Shriver, Vaughn, and Blatchford—became Washington notables. Shriver and Blatchford did so because each had a media-attracting personality and each took decisive—and at times controversial—actions at the Peace Corps. Vaughn did so because he faced the beginnings of the antiwar protests in the Peace Corps, the arrival of volunteers determined to have a voice in Peace Corps governance, and the loss of the nation's uncritical acceptance of the organization. All three men were, in the words of today's sports writers, impact players. Unfortunately, it was to be seven years and a half dozen incumbents later before a director was once again in a position to exercise the kind of leadership that these three did. Some who held the position in the interim were in office so briefly that the Peace Corps's institutional memory hardly recalls their names. One is hard-pressed at the Peace Corps Archives to find files relating to the tenures of directors Kevin O'Donnell, Don Hess, Nick Craw, acting director Alfredo Perez, or Carolyn Payton, President Carter's first Peace Corps director. Even John Dellenback, who had the longest tenure during those years, has a file that is absurdly slim compared with those dedicated to Shriver, Vaughn, and Blatchford. The others were so stymied by being part of ACTION that the leadership they could have provided was dissipated in internal struggles with the parent agency.

The director's real work was almost wholly centered in Washington, although directors typically seized every opportunity for field visits in order to escape the burdens of Washington and to rekindle the flame of service that is so easily smothered by an extended stay in the nation's capital. The director had a fully developed staff to deal with congressional liaison, public affairs, and administration. One group tended to the needs of congressmen and senators— the men and women who control the purse strings in Washington. Another wrote speeches, publicized the good works of the Peace Corps, and kept the organization in the public's eye. The third group prepared budget requests, controlled finances, obtained passports, purchased equipment, arranged transportation, and did the many essential things that were rarely noticed or appreciated except in their absence.

The recruitment and selection of future volunteers was also controlled out of the Washington office. Except during the earliest days, when applications from prospective volunteers poured into Washington by the tens of thousands, the Peace Corps has actively recruited people for service abroad. When the numbers game was being played most intensely, recruitment activities were needed to generate the large pool of applicants from which the needed trainees would remain after the rigorous selection process winnowed out those deemed unfit to serve. With the advent of New Directions, active recruiting efforts served the additional purposes of sustaining public awareness of the Peace Corps's continued existence and finding people with the skills needed to fill the more precisely tailored programs being developed. To carry this out, recruitment offices were established throughout the United States, often on or close to major university campuses, staffed by former volunteers, with the purpose of accomplishing two somewhat contradictory tasks: selling the value of the Peace Corps experience and simultaneously screening potential volunteers to ensure that only those with appropriate motivations and skills actually applied for service. The recruiting apparatus was the largest of the agency's domestic organizations, although its size was obscured by the fact that it was dispersed throughout the country with only its management staff resident in Washington.

Rounding out the organization in PC/W was the hierarchial structure designed to link Washington with the overseas posts. The Peace Corps divided its world into regions. All of the country programs in South and Central America and the Caribbean, for example, were organizationally included in the Latin America Region. (The fact that several of the countries were former British colonies and spoke English or Portuguese rather than Spanish was a complication with which the Peace Corps learned to live.) The countries in sub-Saharan Africa formed the Africa Region. During the 1970s all of the remaining programs, including the program in the Philippines, were tossed together into a somewhat artificial region called the North Africa, Near East, Asia, and Pacific Region, or NANEAP. Each region was headed by a regional director who reported to the Peace Corps director and was, in turn, assisted by desk officers. These latter officials were responsible for coordinating activities between specific countries and the Washington establishment. Desk officers were generally former volunteers who could speak with some authority on the programs and conditions in their country of responsibility.

The creation of the regional organizational framework—an aspect of the Peace Corps from its earliest days—was a bureaucratic necessity but a somewhat confusing one. The director obviously could not carry out his responsibilities in Washington with the administration, the Congress, and the public and, at the same time, be in personal touch with scores of country directors. Some sort of intermediary contact was required to provide a Washington 'ear' for the overseas programs and to provide a conduit for Washington policy and directives to reach the field. The regions served this purpose. But there was not necessarily much common ground among the country programs grouped into each region. To take an extreme but not invalid example, there was no reason to expect that the program in Yemen would have anything in common with the program in Fiji, both part of the NANEAP Region. Yemen is in a remote corner of the Arabian Desert, and Fiji in the far reaches of the Pacific Ocean. Their cultures are dramatically different, and living conditions in one bear no resemblance to those in the other. Moreover, with the director in Washington setting overall policy for the entire organization and the individual country directors being given—especially under New Directions—wide latitude in implementing the policy, there was a real question as to what the regional director's role was. As a country director I had paid little attention to the two regional directors under whom I had served (perhaps to their consternation). As a regional director, therefore, I was torn between pushing my own ideas—about which I felt strongly—and recognizing how inappropriate such actions seemed to country directors. I never did resolve that inherent contradiction but tended to uphold the primacy of the country director in the decision-making process.

The mood at PC/W during the 1970s can best be described as one of joyless determination. Every issue became a crisis. Desk officers juggled a dozen demands from the field with a dozen more from the Washington bureaucracy. The Peace Corps was besieged by members of Congress, the press, and the sometimes irrational demands of administration and ACTION colleagues. Regional directors spent too much of their time interviewing the prospective staff members required to meet the need for new blood due to the now faithfully enforced five-year rule, meeting with various Washington-based people pursuing agendas not necessarily related to the well-being of the Peace Corps, and defending solid country programs that met host country needs even if they did appear on the surface to be inconsistent with the agency's publicly stated mission.

All of this frenetic and Washington-centered activity made PC/W a somewhat disconcerting place for a country director to visit. If pressed, even the most modest of the men and women who held country director positions would finally confess that their own special view of the Peace Corps was the correct one. *They* represented the real Peace Corps, *they* and *their* volunteers were on the cutting edge of bringing development to the Third World, and *they* had the knowledge and experience that PC/W needed. Therefore, it came as a shock for country directors to visit the Washington headquarters and discover that they were often considered intruders. For the visiting country director it was reminiscent of the scene from *The Caine Mutiny* when the junior officers of the *Caine* went to the fleet flagship to request that their inept captain be relieved of command. The certainty with which the *Caine*'s younger officers had begun their trip to the flagship evaporated in the midst of the purposeful activity of the admiral's staff. The resolve of the *Caine* delegation vanished; they slipped quietly away, their crucial message undelivered.

In Washington country directors could be found wandering the halls looking lost and out of place. What had been so abundantly clear in the field became confused and uncertain in the face of Washington's orthodoxy. Strong and heartfelt recommendations became mild questions with little follow-up. Reports written with great care were slipped back into briefcases rather than delivered. And soon phone calls would go out to the international airlines to make plans for an early departure. How much of value was lost by the gulf that separated the field from Washington will never be known. But just as Larry Fuchs, the first country director in the Philippines, had discovered a decade earlier, field realities that did not match preconceived notions were unwelcome in Washington.[1] During his time, part of the reason for this was that none of the Washington people had field experience. Ten years later, when many of the people on the PC/W staff were former volunteers or staff in the field, that excuse was gone. But the underlying problem remained. Perhaps it is the nature of headquarters organizations the world over to be self-centered, myopic, and unresponsive. But, even if this is so, it still came as a shock to find that such a state existed in the Peace Corps, an organization that prided itself on being more in tune with its basic mission than typical bureaucracies. In the end, it was a sad fact of life that visitors from the field felt less at home in Washington than they did when visiting a Third World ministry halfway around the globe.

For all the complaints about an unresponsive home office—and when I conducted my first country directors' meeting as regional director, I was also accused of being uncaring—PC/W had to be successful in carrying out its primary purposes or the Peace Corps would have disappeared. First on that list of primary purposes was the establishment of a well-conceived and articulated strategic direction within the framework of the organization's mission as set out in the Peace Corps Act. It was in this area that Blatchford, with New Directions, made his greatest contribution. At a time when redirection was crucial, it came from the top, where leadership of this sort must always come.

A second area where the fate of the Peace Corps was in PC/W's hands was in the matter of recruiting prospective volunteers. This activity became even more important with the advent of New Directions and its emphasis on providing skilled (rather than generalist) volunteers who possessed at least a basic level of skill in an appropriate area. Field personnel often gave too little credit to the recruiters in Washington upon whom the overall success of Peace Corps ultimately depended. Similarly, congressional investigators sometimes piously concluded, for example, that "the agricultural sector throughout West Africa could usefully absorb more PCV's with farm backgrounds or agricultural training. . . . To date, however, the Peace Corps ha[s] not been successful in recruiting volunteers for such service to the extent desirable—possibly because of a lack of concentrated effort."[2] Whether the specific criticism leveled against the recruiters—in this case, lack of effort—is justified is beyond the scope of this book, although I suspect based on my experience in the Philippines that it is not. Nevertheless, the truth is that the Peace Corps in the field treated the recruiters as second-class citizens, especially once the effort became an ACTION responsibility. Recruiters were to do as they were told and be quick—and quiet—about it. One incident that illustrates this point took place in the early 1970s when Nicholas Craw, an energetic and capable head of the Office of Citizen Placement (OCP), as ACTION's recruiting arm was called, tried to improve morale and team spirit among his people. One morning, at his instigation, every member of OCP came to work sporting campaign-style buttons that read, "OCP is #1."

Almost to a person Peace Corps people reacted in indignation: Who did they think they were? Everyone knew that Peace Corps was #1. OCP's attempt to motivate its own personnel was interpreted by the Peace Corps—as ever prickly and defensive when it came to even unintended criticism—as a threat to its standing, not as an attempt to strengthen the recruiting apparatus on which it depended.

The third area in which PC/W's work was crucial was in the matter of funding. By the early 1970s congressional enthusiasm had waned and with it had gone the almost automatic approval of the organization's budget request. There was nothing those in the field could do to influence the funding process other than to ensure that all visitors from Washington, especially Congressional representatives or their staffs, received a favorable impression of Peace Corps work. Beyond that the field could only hope for the best while finding ways to hold down costs and make do with less as the availability of funds became ever more uncertain.

All of the important budget work took place in Washington in a decidedly unfriendly environment. After reaching a peak of $114 million in 1966, the appropriation began a gradual decline, partly as a result of a drop in the number of volunteers in the field and partly as a result of a loss of public and congressional support.[3] In late 1971 and early 1972 the budget problem reached crisis proportions. PC/W faced its most important financial challenge and, to its lasting credit, rose to the challenge. Using a gutsy brand of brinkmanship, and the unwavering support of several key Republican senators, Blatchford and his team turned back a determined effort by Peace Corps's old enemy, Otto Passman, to destroy the agency.

Finally, PC/W served the field as a wonderful and always available whipping boy, someone to blame when something went wrong. Difficult decisions with respect to staff dismissals, the rejection of inappropriate host country program requests, even the refusal of unwanted embassy advice could be blamed on PC/W policy. In hindsight, admittedly, this negative response to PC/W was unjustified and uncharitable. After all, these people provided the support without which field activity simply could not have existed. Yet field personnel were reluctant to accept that fact and rarely gave PC/W the credit it deserved. Actually, the reaction of the field staff to PC/W was similar to the volunteers' reaction to the in-country staff. Neither wanted to accept what should have been obvious: Both field staff and volunteers needed the support of their respective bureaucratic hierarchies if they were to be successful themselves.

Yet the larger truth remained: The goals of the Peace Corps were achieved, or not achieved, only when volunteers in the Third World

came together in common cause with local citizens. Without that interaction, the Peace Corps was little more than an abstraction. Those
who attempt to assess the Peace Corps and its work would do well to
remember this. Too often they concentrate on what is said and done
in Washington, leading to conclusions that are distorted by the hothouse atmosphere of the capital. A major row, for example, between
the current management and the keepers of the Peace Corps flame
(and a typical event throughout the early 1970s) makes for good
news copy but hardly reflects the reality of the Peace Corps where
it counts most: in the Third World. Similarly, bitter disputes between
the Peace Corps and ACTION, another common feature of the 1970s,
made life difficult for people working in Washington. But it had
little effect abroad where the connection with ACTION was either
unknown or ignored. The point to remember is that the Peace Corps
can be understood best by looking at the field operations; looking
elsewhere will inevitably lead to distortion.

The creation of ACTION by the Nixon administration in 1971, with
Blatchford as its director, was greeted with a surprising amount of bipartisan support, in view of the fact that all of the proposed major
components of the new organization cherished their independent, or
near-independent, status. The idea underlying the new super agency
was greeted warmly. People accepted that there was a "growing need
for broad-based citizen participation . . . to successfully solve the
many economic and social problems facing the nation."[4] In keeping
with the honored American tradition of self-help, ordinary Americans were asked to pledge their time and talents to help alleviate
society's ills. The government's role was to provide some organization, coordination, and money to facilitate the process. ACTION was
the entity through which that role was to be carried out. Government-sponsored programs that relied on volunteers already existed
in several departments and agencies. The most prominent of these
were the Peace Corps, an autonomous arm of the State Department,
and Volunteers in Service to America (VISTA), part of the Office of
Economic Opportunity. These two programs, one international, the
other domestic, would form the core of the new agency. They were
joined by the Service Corps of Retired Executives (SCORE) and the
Active Corps of Executives (ACE), both from the Small Business
Administration, and Foster Grandparents and the Retired Senior
Volunteer Program (RSVP), both from the Department of Health,
Education, and Welfare. Together the six programs formed ACTION.
President Nixon had first proposed this reorganization in a speech
delivered at the University of Nebraska in January 1971. On that

occasion the president pledged an all-out effort to bridge the generation gap by bringing together Americans of all ages to volunteer their talents in the service of the nation's and the world's less fortunate people.[5] The plan to create ACTION was also hailed by its backers as the Nixon administration's first step in its massive plan to reorganize the executive branch of the federal government to eliminate duplication, increase cooperation and coordination among programs with similar objectives, and bring the acknowledged efficiency and effectiveness of the private sector into the realm of government. In this respect ACTION was to be a demonstration project through which the administration could prove the wisdom of its overall reorganization of the federal bureaucracy. The response was all that the administration could have hoped for: The House of Representatives approved the measure 224 votes to 131, and the Senate approved it 54 to 29.[6] Even some longtime Peace Corps stalwarts welcomed the creation of ACTION, despite the implicit loss of their own agency's prized independence, because they felt that ACTION would provide the cover the Peace Corps needed to escape the wrath of the suspected Peace Corps haters in the Nixon administration.[7]

Certainly there were those who objected to the formation of ACTION, or more precisely to the loss of independence entailed in becoming part of it, but their objections failed to carry much weight. Sargent Shriver, having fought so hard for independence, predictably found much to criticize. He told a Senate subcommittee, "Not one additional person will volunteer in the future because of government bureaucratic reorganization. Probably nothing is of less interest to potential volunteers. . . . [They] will never rally around an organization chart." Senator Harrison Williams said, "We do not need a program [i.e., ACTION] focusing on the concerns of volunteers; rather we need programs which continue to stress the plight of the poor and disadvantaged." VISTA volunteers were among the most vocal of the opponents. They feared that "President Nixon was pushing the merger as a means of abolishing [VISTA]." Present and former VISTA volunteers packed the congressional hearings on ACTION and distributed statements roundly condemning the proposal. They charged that the larger ACTION bureaucracy would hamper their ability to initiate creative projects to combat poverty and destroy entrenched self-serving power bases at the local level; that lumping together programs that enlisted the young as volunteers with programs that used the services of older Americans was a thinly disguised attempt to dilute the revolutionary fervor of the young; and that "their own pioneering efforts in community action at home [would] be eclipsed by the 'more glamorous' and 'more highly publicized' activities of the Peace Corps volunteers overseas." The employee union representing VISTA fought the formation of ACTION (and opposed the nomination of Blatchford as its head) charging that the creation of such an agency was in reality an effort to cripple the union's ability to promote worker rights. As a precondition for its support it demanded recognition as the new agency's sole bargaining agent for all employees. In the end, however, ACTION's opponents failed to generate any significant enthusiasm for their position. As former Peace Corps Latin America Region director Frank Mankiewicz said at the time, "I don't think that [the creation of ACTION] is an issue that people want to fight about."[8]

On 1 July 1971, as the *New York Times* reported, President Nixon "signed into being his new volunteer agency called Action [*sic*] and said it was particularly fitting that it should begin operations the day after the 18-year-old vote became a reality."[9] (Nixon linked the two events because he saw both as evidence of his administration's promotion of fuller involvement of the young in the nation's business.)

ACTION had three operating units: International Operations (IO), Domestic Operations (DO), and the Office of Citizen Placement (OCP). Each was headed by an associate director of ACTION. International Operations consisted of what was formerly the Peace Corps, minus its recruiting and selection function and a variety of staff units (e.g., the general counsel's office and the public affairs office became ACTION units). Other than that, the international organization remained essentially the same. The sixty country programs remained divided into three regions, and each region had the usual complement of desk officers and support staff. The overseas programs were initially untouched by the creation of ACTION, whose existence was rarely mentioned. In fact, few if any country directors took the trouble to explain the change to host country counterparts, and certainly volunteers did not consider themselves to be ACTION volunteers. For the Peace Corps abroad, the creation of ACTION was a nonevent.

There was resentment in Washington, however. When the headquarters staff was ordered to abandon its Peace Corps letterheads, titles, and other identifying marks in favor of ACTION, the discontent was widespread. The title Peace Corps Director, for example, was replaced by Associate Director, International Operations, ACTION, hardly a title to catch a headline writer's eye or to impress one's family and friends. An attempt after Blatchford's departure to force a name change at the overseas posts was ignored, much to ACTION's annoyance. John Dellenback, the Peace Corps director from 1975 to early 1977, had to struggle to obtain permission from the director of ACTION to use stationery with the Peace Corps logo and to sign his letters as Peace Corps Director. He was successful in his quest, but permission was given only with respect to correspondence with other countries or while traveling abroad. The Peace Corps reaction to all of this was perfectly summed up by Sargent Shriver's oft quoted complaint that "Peace Corps isn't even listed in the telephone book anymore."[10]

It was to be some years before the magnitude of the mistake the administration had made in creating ACTION became clear. As a Republican congressman from Oregon, Dellenback had originally supported the consolidation. He explained in 1986, "I helped write the legislation that created ACTION . . . [but] when I became Peace Corps director I changed my mind and concluded that we . . . had made a legislative mistake. . . . I became absolutely convinced of the uniqueness of the Peace Corps mission."[11] Years of experience had shown that the benefits of combining volunteer agencies was more apparent than real. The principles on which ACTION was founded—the elimination of duplication, the efficiencies of scale, the concentration of resources, the bringing together of the generations, and the transfer of skills, people, and experiences among the various participants—simply were not sufficient to overcome the scheme's basic flaw. The missions and organizational cultures of the participating agencies were different, and the effort to bring them together in one bureaucratic family was doomed from the start. The ACTION critic in the Senate who had initially objected to making volunteer concerns the agency's organizing principle rather than the issues of poverty on the one hand and underdevelopment on the other proved to be correct. It was not the volunteer who was important but the volunteer's work. And in time experience showed that this work was different depending on which program the volunteer participated in.

Nowhere is this statement more true than in the contrasting objectives of the Peace Corps and VISTA, the former being concerned with Third World development and the latter with domestic anti-poverty work. Peace Corps, especially under New Directions, had a strong social and economic development bent combined, of course, with important cross-cultural objectives. Volunteers participated in public and private development projects in Third World countries while experiencing the life of the host country and bringing a more balanced sense of American life to their hosts. The volunteers worked to create additional resources in the host countries by helping to introduce better agricultural practices, small business development programs, and cooperative community endeavors. They helped to introduce new concepts of sanitation, nutrition, and preventive health care to eliminate the all too prevalent sources of sickness and premature death. When their efforts were successful, the entire community benefited because typically all but a tiny portion of Third World populations suffered the adverse effects of underdevelopment.

This *development* work of the Peace Corps is fundamentally different in nature from the *antipoverty* work of VISTA. In the Third World, the vast majority of the people suffer from the economic inadequacies of their countries. An absolute shortage of resources is the problem, not the *distribution* of resources, as in the United States. The poor in the Third World are not a neglected, downtrodden, or despised minority. They are the majority. Development work takes place within the existing social structures; it enlists the efforts of the local leadership as well as that of the ordinary people. Local power structures are as eager for the benefits of development as the rest of the populace are. This is not to say that class differences are absent in the Third World. They certainly exist and can be obstacles to progress. But the larger point is that the vested interest of the leadership is often not sufficient to cause them to block development because in doing so they would also deny themselves its benefits.

In VISTA the volunteers work among minority populations (minority in the sense of numbers, not necessarily in the sense of race, gender, or age). VISTA constituencies often feel, and at times actually are, isolated from the mainstream; they are living in poverty in a society where most people have enough. Local power structures ignore or consciously exploit them, and their lives often seem bereft of the cultural support structures that add so much meaning to the lives of people in the Third World. In this latter respect a sociologist from the University of Kentucky once expressed to a class of graduate students her puzzlement over the difference she found between the ordinary people of Malaysia and the poor of Appalachia. Neither group had much in the way of material goods or access to adequate social services, but the Malaysians found great joy in their lives and the poor of Appalachia did not. Those of us who lived in the Philippines were similarly puzzled by the relative happiness of average Filipinos whose material possessions seemed so meager, especially compared with those of the average American. There is a major difference in the way that inhabitants of the Third World view life and the way some segments of the poor in the United States do.

Add to this the further difference between working in the United States and working in one of scores of foreign countries and one can begin to see why there was so little overlap in interests, programs, problems, and solutions between VISTA and Peace Corps. One was not more difficult than the other, nor was one more important than the other. They were just different. Weeks and even months could pass in ACTION without meaningful contact between Peace Corps and VISTA. The remarkable thing was that ACTION management never recognized that such a state of affairs indicated something was seriously amiss.

Complicating the already major problem caused by the poor strategic fit of the several ACTION programs was the inescapable fact that the managements of ACTION and the Peace Corps were destined to clash—especially once Blatchford, who had credibility in both camps, left the agency following Nixon's reelection in November 1972.[12] Even its most loyal admirers will admit that the Peace Corps's collective personality has a rather exclusionist underpinning: It snobbishly considers its understanding of the Third World to be more valid than anyone else's; it is internationalist to the core and rejects anything that puts domestic concerns first; it responds with acute hostility to criticism from outside its own ranks (although within the organization Peace Corps bashing is a favorite pastime); and it is suspicious of and inhospitable to people forced upon it from outside.

Little wonder then that Nixon's appointment of Michael P. Balzano to be head of ACTION in early 1973 was greeted with dismay. Balzano, a young Ph.D. with a tendency to flaunt his working-class background, had made his mark with a doctoral dissertation describing VISTA as a "mass confusion of philosophies."[13] The conservative tone of his thesis brought him to the attention of the Nixon White House, which hired him as an assistant to Charles Colson, soon to become enmeshed in the Watergate scandal.[14] Balzano had no discernible international experience and was rumored not even to possess a passport at the time of his nomination. He publicly vowed to bring change to ACTION, even if it took "bringing tanks right up to the agency's front door" to get it done. The Peace Corps chose to take his hyperbole literally. It never forgave him for the use of the military metaphor—after all, the Peace Corps was about peace, not war. He, in turn, never forgave Peace Corps for the reception it accorded him.

Balzano's primary interest was in the domestic activities of ACTION, principally VISTA, about which he was well informed. The Peace Corps was delighted by this turn of events because it permitted the agency to continue on its own course. When Balzano did turn his attention to the international side of ACTION, he encountered the same coolness and grudging acceptance that had greeted his arrival. Country directors referred to him as *Dr.* Balzano, not so much because they had never met him as to indicate that he was not part of the group. At one country directors' meeting in Thailand in 1974, instead of appearing in person as scheduled, Balzano sent a videotaped message. The message itself was perfectly appropriate to the meeting and its participants, but the country directors remained unmoved. He would continue to be *Dr.* Balzano to them. (Shriver had always been Sarge, Vaughn was Jack, and Blatchford was Joe.) Balzano had a keen sense of what was happening around him and bitterly resented Peace Corps's attitude. Try as he might he never did win their acceptance during his four years as the head of ACTION.

Peace Corps paid for its effrontery by having to suffer through a period of rapid turnover in directors. Balzano quickly replaced Donald Hess, the director who had replaced Kevin O'Donnell (Blatchford's successor) with Nicolas Craw, previously the head of ACTION's volunteer recruiting and placement arm. Craw was a young, colorful, and articulate director. He was a racing enthusiast who reportedly transported his race car by jet to races around the world. Although that particular jet-setter image might belie the Peace Corps's carefully cultivated image of seriousness and world service, Craw was an energetic leader who quickly aligned himself with its priorities and objectives rather than those of ACTION. Not surprisingly, given Balzano's drive to bring the Peace Corps under the ACTION umbrella in spirit as well as in fact, Craw's tenure lasted just a year, after which he was dumped unceremoniously and without warning. Craw was replaced by an acting director, Alfredo Perez, a Peace Corps veteran who brought to the position a thorough understanding of the organization. But with virtually no political or administration connections he lacked the power base needed to get a formal appointment. As is always the case when a position is filled by an 'acting' official, the most that could be accomplished was a continuation of the status quo. Perez did an admirable job for six months in keeping the Washington staff focused and functioning.

By early 1975, however, after a failed attempt by Balzano to win approval for a person of his own choosing, President Ford had appointed John Dellenback to head the Peace Corps. Dellenback, who had lost his Oregon congressional seat in the 1974 election, was sufficiently well connected to his former colleagues in the House and to key Ford administration officials that he could fend off the worst of Balzano's attempted intrusions into the operation of the Peace Corps. He was a man of great civility, in sharp contrast to Balzano's confrontational outspokenness, and the two rarely communicated with any real degree of understanding. Dellenback clearly had the best interests of the Peace Corps at heart. He provided genuine and needed leadership and continued to do so for many years after his official tour came to an end following the 1976 presidential election. (He was an initial organizer and prime mover behind the effort to separate Peace Corps from ACTION. In 1986 he was chairman of the Peace Corps's 25th Anniversary Foundation, the sponsor of a massive three-day celebration.)

Although one should not put all of the blame for the chaos in Washington on the personality clash between Balzano and the Peace Corps, there was certainly more than a little of this at work. But the fundamental flaw remained in the concept of ACTION as an umbrella organization for all of the nation's government-sponsored volunteer programs. The incompatibility of the various programs grouped together under ACTION, especially evidenced in the differences between the domestic and international programs, continued to be apparent. President Carter's ACTION director, Sam Brown, was as liberal as Balzano was conservative, yet he also found himself at loggerheads with the Peace Corps. Brown fired his Peace Corps director, a woman with solid credentials, after a long-running public feud about the appropriate role of the Peace Corps. Its root cause, apparently, was Brown's failure to understand the differences between VISTA's antipoverty mission, with which he himself identified, and the Peace Corps's development and cross-cultural mission.[15]

The matter of the irreconcilable differences between ACTION and the Peace Corps was finally resolved when Carter's second Peace Corps director, Richard Celeste, negotiated an understanding with the White House in 1978. Celeste was another in the long line of directors who instantly recognized the inappropriateness of the ACTION connection. Fortunately, he had sufficient political clout to take a major first step toward restoring Peace Corps independence. Under Celeste the agency was given considerable autonomy to direct its own affairs, although strictly speaking it remained under the ACTION umbrella. This understanding proved to be the first step in a series of executive actions that eventually led to the restoration of Peace Corps independence in 1981.

With the benefit of hindsight, it is clear the creation of ACTION was a disaster. ACTION was meant to demonstrate the Nixon administration's determination to reorganize the government along rational lines. Its main purpose was not really to bring a variety of seemingly similar volunteer programs together but to show that the administration could "group, coordinate and consolidate agencies and functions of the government, as nearly as may be, according to major purposes."[16] ACTION's primary value to the administration was as a demonstration project that would pave the way for the larger, more sweeping changes in the federal bureaucracy planned for the future. Unfortunately, the planners overlooked two factors that in the end would undo it: The activities they had grouped together were fundamentally dissimilar, and the Peace Corps's resistance to subjugation would be long-lasting, nonpartisan, and powerful. The first factor was immediately apparent to most of those who worked in the Washington office; the second factor was longer in developing, but in time it grew into a well-organized, determined lobby so strong that the obvious solution could no longer be ignored. (This discussion of ACTION should not be interpreted as a condemnation of the programs that made up Domestic Operations, or of the volunteers and staff who carried out anti-poverty projects in the United States. Those activities accomplished much that was commendable and are deserving of their own separate analysis.)

No sooner had the Peace Corps begun the unpleasant process of merging itself into ACTION during the fall of 1971 than a budget crisis of a magnitude never before experienced threatened to destroy its credibility, effectiveness, and future. The crisis was partly the unintended consequence of growing congressional disillusionment over American foreign aid and partly the result of the specific intent of a small group of powerful congressmen and senators to deliver the Peace Corps a body blow from which it might never recover. The struggle for survival tested the Blatchford team's resolve as nothing else did. In the end, however, after the dust had settled, it became clear that the Peace Corps had the broad public and political support necessary for it to become a permanent part of the American foreign affairs presence. It had won the decisive battle in its struggle for survival, although the outcome had remained in doubt for many long months.

The process by which the federal government funds its various activities is an arcane one that at one time or another tests the patience of everyone involved. The process begins with a request from the administration to the Congress for a specified amount of money to fund a specified program during the approaching fiscal year. Each house of the Congress then considers the request and, after due deliberation, *authorizes* an amount of money for the program, an amount that can be less than, equal to, or more than the administration's request. If the two houses of Congress authorize different amounts, as often happens, a committee representing both groups develops a compromise. The authorization, however, merely establishes a ceiling for the amount of money that can be spent; it does not actually provide any funds. Each house must then reconsider the administration's budget request and *appropriate* funds that can actually be spent. Once again differences in the House and Senate appropriations are resolved by a joint committee. The final appropriation is then sent to the president for his acceptance or rejection.

But this budget process usually requires many months before it is completed. Often the fiscal year for which the money is required is already under way—sometimes months under way—when the funds are finally appropriated. In such circumstances, the Congress passes what is called a continuing resolution, which permits government entities to spend at the level approved for the previous year, the level requested for the coming year, or at some other specified level, until an appropriation is approved for the current year. During the entire process, it is important to note, the critical debates and decisions take place at the committee level, not on the House or Senate floors. The House and Senate members who chair the authorization and appropriations committees have immense power to shape the outcome of the budget process. Only the courageous or the foolhardy will take these powerful congressmen on in a public fight. But, as the Peace Corps discovered at the end of 1971, sometimes survival demands that such a fight be fought.

The Peace Corps began the 1972 fiscal year on 1 July 1971, spending at the requested level of $82 million (itself an $8 million reduction from the previous year's budget of $90 million) as a result of a continuing resolution necessitated by congressional failure to approve a foreign aid bill.[17] The delay in the foreign aid bill was not caused by any major concern about the Peace Corps; it was a result of the high level of dissatisfaction in Congress over American foreign policy and the lack of any clear consensus on its future direction. The Peace Corps found itself in the midst of a major policy dispute, but only because its appropriation was part of the total foreign aid package. As one Washington observer who decried the "foreign aid mess in Congress" lamented, the Peace Corps was "a small morsel caught in a legislative stew not of its own making."[18] Unfortunately, however, its powerful enemies took advantage of the situation. After several months operating at a level of $82 million, the Peace Corps was shocked to find that Congress authorized only $77.7 million. This obviously meant financial trouble because the agency had to recover from the earlier overspending that resulted from operating at the $82 million level for several months and factor in a further $4.3 million reduction. ACTION director Blatchford and Peace Corps director O'Donnell ordered immediate budget cuts in headquarters staff and administrative expenses to deal with the monetary shortfall. But the problems had only just begun. The ever-hostile Otto Passman chaired an important congressional committee and managed to reduce even further the Peace Corps spending authority under a second continuing resolution. Instead of the earlier spending level of $77.7 million, already a painful reduction from the requested $82 million, Passman engineered passage of a resolution authorizing only $72 million. At this point the fight for survival began in earnest.

In January Blatchford and O'Donnell mobilized ACTION's formidable public affairs apparatus to spread word that the Peace Corps was in trouble. The threatened budget cuts coming so late in the fiscal year would, they maintained, require "recalling nearly 4,000 of the 8,000 volunteers in service, . . . [w]ithdrawing from 15 of the 55 countries, . . . [c]ancelling the training plans and postponing or cancelling the projects of 2,400 volunteers [currently] scheduled [and] reducing staff both at home and abroad for the second time [in the] year."[19] The media and popular response was all that could have been hoped for. Newspaper reports and editorials from around the country declared, "Don't Cut the Peace Corps," "An Unwise Economy," "Peace Corps in Jeopardy," "Lingering Death for the Peace Corps," "Congress Letting Peace Corps Down," "Bankrupt Peace Corps Would Mar U.S. Image," "Peace Corps in Trouble," and "Peace Corps Loss Would Be Tragic."[20] A political cartoon in the *New Republic* showed an overfed American eagle labeled "Military Budget" at the bedside of a gravely ill dove labeled "Peace Corps." The eagle says plaintively, "Poor little guy. . . . How could anybody starve in this land of plenty?"[21]

In early March 1972 Passman grudgingly accepted an additional $2.6 million for the Peace Corps if President Nixon would agree to transfer these funds from other programs in the foreign aid budget. This Nixon quickly did.[22] Passman's attempt to scuttle the Peace Corps had failed, although only by the slimmest of margins. He continued to be a thorn in our side, but never again could he threaten the

"Poor little guy . . . How could anybody starve in this land of plenty?"

Mauldin cartoon © 1995 by the *Chicago Sun-Times.*
Reprinted with permission.

organization's very existence. In fact, the following year—fiscal year 1973—the Peace Corps budget was raised to $81 million, and it continued to increase for a number of years thereafter.

Although neither he nor anyone else knew it at the time, the great budget battle of 1972 was to be Blatchford's last major contribution. Within a few months the presidential election campaign was under way, and Blatchford did his part as a loyal member of the Republican administration. As one journalist reported shortly after Nixon's landslide victory, "Blatchford himself has been one of the most loyal of the President's three dozen 'surrogates' or stand-ins, uncomplainingly speaking to some of the most obscure organizations in America." His political actions predictably drew complaints from people both within and outside the Peace Corps, especially because Blatchford's campaign efforts were designed specifically to blunt the belated addition of Sargent Shriver to the Democratic slate. (Shriver was the hastily recruited replacement for Senator Thomas Eagleton, who had withdrawn himself as the vice presidential candidate as a result of the uproar that followed the discovery that Eagleton had once been treated for depression.) Democratic senator Alan Cranston, from Blatchford's home state of California, even called for a Department of Justice investigation into the possible illegal use of ACTION employees during the campaign. Of course, as many quickly noted, Cranston's actions reflected the senator's own concern that Blatchford might run against him for his Senate seat in 1974, and he wanted to discredit Blatchford in advance of such an eventuality.[23] (The high-sounding pronouncements of Washington movers and shakers are often not exactly what they seem to be on the surface, and one accepts them at face value at one's peril.)

After his overwhelming victory Nixon, in a move that rattled many members of his first administration, called for the resignation of all of his appointees. Blatchford recalls turning to a colleague at a postelection meeting where the resignations were demanded and saying, "But I thought we won."[24] Whether he would have been reappointed remains a moot point; Blatchford accompanied his pro forma resignation in the fall of 1972 with a letter explaining that his was a real one. There is reason to suspect, however, that he would not have been on the list of those being reappointed. Political observers often noted during Nixon's first term that Blatchford was an enigma to many of his colleagues. He was a Republican, but he held ideas that often seemed liberal, at least to some in the White House. He had resisted administration pressure to bust heads when his offices were taken over by the Committee of Returned Volunteers in 1969. H. R. Haldeman suggested that the president considered Blatchford "soft" in dealing with dissent.[25] Speeches that contained such statements as "The shame and terror of the Vietnamese war are bound to dampen our national ego for years to come" were unlikely to win him friends among the hawks that dominated administration foreign policy.[26] And being described as "one of the most idealistic men in the Nixon administration" would hardly be considered a compliment among a group of self-described pragmatists. Whatever the outcome might have been, Blatchford forestalled it by taking himself out of the game. In the perverse way that is Washington, the fact that he was viewed with suspicion by both liberal and conservative extremists suggests that he was probably on the right track. Certainly his pivotal role in making New Directions an essential part of the Peace Corps and his victory in the 1972 budget battle warrant the gratitude of

today's 150,000 Peace Corps alumni. One cannot say as much for
his role in the creation of ACTION, but in the context of Washington and its often unfathomable ways, being right on two out of three
major issues—as someone once declared—ain't all bad.

The Washington-based partisan struggle over New Directions,
the creation of ACTION, and the budget crisis of 1972 all took place
while I was in the Philippines. From my standpoint, the remarkable thing about these three issues was not the intensity and dramatic nature of the battles that accompanied them but how little
they actually affected the day-to-day activities of the Peace Corps
abroad. Although New Directions was one of the most important
innovations in the organization's history, its implementation in
the Philippines was more a matter of learning how to make it work
than it was a call for strategic analysis and debate. The creation of
ACTION was of little consequence from the distant vantage point of
Manila. We never used the name, knew nothing about the domestic
side of the agency's work (and cared less), and considered ourselves
only and wholly Peace Corps.

Similarly, for those serving in the Philippines and other countries in the far reaches of the Pacific, the budget crisis of 1972 was
not directly relevant. Other than the constant pressure from Washington to reduce overhead costs—appropriate pressure because there
existed relatively painless opportunities for expense reductions—
we were immune from the financial crisis that was so unnerving
for Peace Corps programs in countries closer to the United States.[27]
In the winter of 1971-72 every Peace Corps site where the cost of
repatriating volunteers (i.e., the cost of a plane ticket home) was less
than the cost of keeping them in the field found itself in danger
of being sharply curtailed or closed down. Peace Corps/Philippines
was spared this uncertainty because the reverse situation prevailed
there: It cost more to fly volunteers home than it did to keep them
in-country.

We were also spared the worst consequences of the rapid turnover
in directors that was becoming the norm in Washington. Fortunately for the program as a whole, much of the leadership role had
been transferred to the field as a result of New Directions, and those
abroad willing to provide their own leadership could look on the continuing Washington turmoil with a degree of detachment as well
as astonishment. For me personally, however, the role of distant observer evaporated in a hurry when I became part of the Washington
establishment in the summer of 1974.

By late spring 1974, approaching the end of three years in the Philippines, I asked for a Washington assignment. My contribution in the Philippines having been made, I wanted to bring what I had learned to the larger organization. Discussions with then director Nick Craw of the possibility of a transfer to Washington resulted in agreement that a regional director slot would be appropriate and that the Africa Region was the one. Several weeks before my departure from the Philippines, the Department of Agriculture and Natural Resources honored the Peace Corps for its work in food production, nutrition education, and rural health services. At the award ceremony I summed up in an acceptance speech what I had learned: "Progress, if it is genuine and measurable, comes about as a result of many, many small contributions. There is no such thing as a 'Great Leap Forward.' Progress comes only as a result of a multitude of people each contributing some small portion of the work needed. The sum total of these small contributions can lead to progress, but progress cannot be attained without them. . . . Each of us counts, and each contribution is important. Peace Corps in the Philippines is proud to be . . . making some of the contributions which will eventually lead to the solution of the world's food production problem."[28] That was the lesson I wanted to take to Washington, a Washington that in my naïveté I was certain was eagerly awaiting the opportunity to welcome and embrace my message. Little did I know that my time at PC/W would be spent in a different fashion as I came to grips with the Washington mind-set, which cherishes form over substance, personal prerogative over organizational mission, and appearances over reality.

In the best tradition of the Peace Corps, my family and I decided to take the long way home. (Volunteers and overseas staff invariably use their passage home to visit as many parts of the world as their financial and time constraints will permit. In many instances people have spent six months to a year in making the homeward journey, as did my daughter when she completed her volunteer service in Malaysia in the 1980s.) We left Manila in a tropical downpour that made our trip to the bustling international airport—in the same Wagoneer that had brought us into town thirty-four months earlier—as much an exercise in fording newly created streams and negotiating huge potholes as it was in highway driving. The extent of the changes that we had all undergone during our stay in the Philippines was indicated by the fact that we looked upon the chaotic conditions of our departure as normal and unremarkable. Despite my doubts three years earlier, we had indeed become as much at home with life in the

Philippines as those Peace Corps staff members whose savoir faire I had so admired in 1971.

My eagerness to get on with the job, however, soon overwhelmed my desire for travel and responsibilities as a parent and husband. Halfway through our planned trip I hastily made arrangements to fly back to Washington, leaving my wife and children to continue the trip without me. I may have had a sense of urgency about taking up my new position, but the Peace Corps did not. When I arrived in Washington, the Philippine desk officer told me that assignment to the Africa Region had been ruled out. She had learned via the Peace Corps grapevine that someone had belatedly concluded that the region should be headed by a black American, a decision that automatically canceled my candidacy. I was in full agreement with the decision and in fact had been puzzled by the original plan. I was upset, however, by the way the decision reached me. Surely, someone in authority could have told me directly. Such was not to be. I wandered the halls like a man without a country. My paycheck continued while I did nothing. A few weeks passed, during which I took another vacation, spent long empty days in the office, and began thinking of a return to teaching and graduate study. But finally, on the very day that I had planned to resign and get on with my life, I was told that my selection as regional director of NANEAP had been approved. (Delayed, no doubt, by the slow-moving wheels of the Washington bureaucracy, but in all likelihood also by the growing estrangement between Balzano and Craw, who was my primary sponsor.)

The view from the Peace Corps windows on Connecticut Avenue was as compelling in 1974 as it had been three and a half years earlier. The White House was still there in all of its glory, as was the Capitol beyond. But instead of facing a desk with that impressive view in the background, I was now in my own office sitting behind the desk looking out through my open door into the innards of Peace Corps/Washington. And, as it turned out, the switch from looking outside to looking in was both symbolically and operationally appropriate. The next two years was a period of intense introspection as the Peace Corps assessed the impact of New Directions on its mission and adjusted its operating policies accordingly.

No significant change in strategy is ever perfect at its inception, and New Directions was no exception. It was time to evaluate what had been accomplished and to determine what yet remained to be done. In this process of evaluation the five-year rule proved its merit. Virtually everyone who had developed New Directions had departed by mid-1974, and no one had a personal stake in protecting its authorship. (As critics have noted, the American political process often makes people defend original positions long after the evidence shows them to be no longer tenable, thereby making change exceedingly difficult.)[29] Because of the five-year rule, the Peace Corps was now in a position to examine the evidence and move in whatever direction it indicated.

Those of us who had supported and implemented New Directions had also seen both its strengths and its weaknesses. We were eager to build on the former and to correct the latter. The strength and the overall soundness of New Directions needs no further discussion here. But a serious weakness had to be addressed. The rhetoric of New Directions had inadvertently led to some unrealistic expectations with respect to skills.

Originally the new policy had made it clear that skilled volunteers—those with actual work experience or an appropriate academic degree relevant to their volunteer work—were expected to represent only about 30 percent of the total Peace Corps. Shortly after New Directions was launched, a Peace Corps recruiter in the Pacific Northwest said that the new rules meant "the backbone of the Peace Corps [had] always been, and [would] continue to be the generalist." Nine months later a former volunteer and current Washington staff member wrote that a critic of New Directions had "left the impression that the eventual goal was to . . . drive out all the young volunteers. In fact, Director Blatchford had projected an eventual 70-30 mix of generalists to specialists, meaning that the vast majority [would] always be young liberal arts graduates."[30]

Unfortunately, the agency's publicity efforts gave the impression that the proportion of skilled volunteers was much higher. Hundreds of news releases praised the "Union Plumber [Who Brought] His Skills to Costa Rica"; the "66-year-old Milwaukee author, teacher and lecturer" who had been adopted by a West African village; the "former conservation aide with the Wisconsin Department of Natural Resources" who was helping to preserve and develop parkland in Niger; the "pretty blonde who graduated many years ago from the Salida Hospital in Colorado" and was on her way to Botswana; and dozens of others whose skill levels were undeniably high but whose presence in the Peace Corps was more the exception than the rule. Articles written by Peace Corps staff and speeches given by agency officials also repeatedly emphasized the presence of skilled volunteers: "The Peace Corps has changed: Skilled farmers are in demand." "In the last two years the Peace Corps has changed. . . . We have three times as many agricultural graduates as we ever had. We have urban planners, architects, engineers, and businessmen." "The Peace Corps is geared to seeking volunteers with specific skills now." "The Peace Corps is confident it is more technically efficient for its second decade of activity."[31] All of this led people to think that the Peace Corps was far more skilled than in fact it was.

At the same time country directors were developing programs that were more in line with host country development needs. They were abandoning the classroom and moving into agriculture, nutrition education, public health, business development, and any of a host of activities that directly benefited developing countries. Predictably, this created a demand for skilled rather than generalist volunteers that far exceeded the number of such people who could be recruited. One of the major concerns expressed by country directors at my first regional country directors meeting was the shortfall in program fill rates. (By fill rate they meant the percentage of requested positions actually filled when training began.) It was not at all unusual to find fill rates of 50 percent or less in programs that required volunteers with specialized agricultural degrees or master's degrees in business administration, home economics, or public administration. New Directions had corrected a real problem at the end of the 1960s, but its momentum had carried it too far in the other direction. Now the organization found itself in the position of not being able to meet the promises its rhetoric implied. The skilled volunteers simply were not available in sufficient quantity to meet host country demand.

What was needed, according to the recommendations of a review committee from the National Academy of Science, was a continuation of the Peace Corps's "distinctive character as a volunteer program supplying middle-level manpower to help other countries and to promote international understanding," but with the addition that it be done within the context of the agency's abilities and resources.[32] This suggestion was in line with the Peace Corps's own internal evaluation of the situation. A report written by the NANEAP Region country desk officers recommended that in-country staff become more active "advocates of an informed perspective responsive to both the country's needs and Peace Corps's ability to meet those needs."[33] By this they meant that the Peace Corps needed to take the initiative in helping host countries use the volunteers more effectively. Staff needed to explain how properly trained generalist volunteers leavened by the presence of a small number of skilled volunteers could meet genuine development needs. As had been learned in the

Philippines—and elsewhere as well—ample opportunities presented themselves for this type of work in public health, nutrition education, some areas of agriculture, and in precisely targeted community development work. To do this the organization needed to become more proficient at program development, better at training volunteers, and most of all, more realistic in its promises. In all of this reassessment there was the occasional voice saying, 'I told you so,' but for the most part the recognition that volunteers must *do something* as well as *be somewhere* went unchallenged. The effort to raise the importance of volunteer jobs to a higher level had been successful; what was once a matter of intense debate was now conventional wisdom.

No quantitative data existed that showed—or even suggested—that the agency or its volunteers had lost any of the commitment to Goal Two and Goal Three during the years when New Directions was at its most intense. The very nature of the Peace Corps, its legacy from the 1960s, the aura that surrounded it, and the reasons people joined it all worked to reinforce its mission in intercultural relations and understanding. Nevertheless, some staff members continued to worry that there had been a weakening in this area of volunteer effectiveness. One former volunteer and cross-cultural training specialist concluded that there had been a serious erosion in volunteer commitment as a direct result of the increased emphasis on job skills. He felt that volunteers in the mid-1970s were less likely to work through the inevitable periods of discouragement that were part of the experience, that they were unable to deal with the situation when it became clear that initial job expectations were not going to be fulfilled, and that a high proportion of resignations was a direct result of volunteers who failed to understand that the interpersonal aspects were fully as valuable as were jobs. In the end he concluded that "it was the relative shift away from total dependence on the AB generalist" that caused the largest part of the problem.[34] (His conclusion regarding the sanctity of the AB, or bachelor of arts, generalist has always been a puzzle, because there is no evidence that those who chose a more specialized education are by that fact rendered inflexible, uncaring, unmotivated, and misanthropic.)

The NANEAP country desk officers dealt with the cross-cultural issue more constructively. In their March 1975 report to me, they said that "although the sine qua non of Peace Corps programs must remain the provision of trained manpower to those areas of the world requesting such aid, the continued validity of Goals two and three should be re-asserted." The desk officers were particularly worried that Congress and the American people had forgotten that Peace Corps's "peculiar success as a program of American foreign assistance . . . derives not from the provision of manpower alone but rather particularly from the manner and spirit of that provision." In other words, they stressed that the Peace Corps not be evaluated only on job accomplishments. Remember, they said, that the promotion of global understanding carries equal weight. They put aside the generalist vs. specialist question and concentrated on the main point, that of ensuring that Goal Two and Goal Three receive appropriate and necessary emphasis.

The resurgence of these goals as important objectives was greatly enhanced by President Ford's appointment of John Dellenback as PC/W director in 1975. Dellenback was a man with great faith in human nature and in the efficacy of activities that brought people from all walks of life into contact with one another. He took the 'provision of trained manpower' as a given and shifted the emphasis to putting as many volunteers into as many jobs and as many countries as possible. As he said on one occasion, "The Peace Corps comes as close as a government agency can to living out genuine concern for others. It conducts the United States' most effective foreign relations. It is our nation's best instrument for giving to some of our brightest and best the opportunity to put their lives on the line in meaningful service to others."[35]

During my fifth year with the Peace Corps I was Dellenback's deputy, and as such was given the assignment of preparing a rationale for allocating scarce resources, should financial constraints make it necessary to eliminate some programs. (The development of such a rationale had become de rigueur in the mid-1970s, and every federal agency needed one to show its seriousness of purpose.) My proposal was a reasonably straightforward one that used a variety of criteria to rank countries in inverse order of their relative economic and social development. (To a remarkable degree the use of infant mortality data alone would have led to the same conclusions as the more complicated formula because the health of society's youngest members best indicates the quality of life of the whole. Where infant deaths are high one can safely assume that development is low. In those situations where the infant death rate is high—and going higher—one can assume that the situation is desperate.) Dellenback accepted my proposal but carefully tucked it away lest someone, sometime, use it as an example of how the Peace Corps could survive with less. He wanted to put management emphasis on growth, not on reduction, however rationally implemented that reduction might be carried out. His approach was not a return to the discredited numbers game of the 1960s; rather, it reflected his belief that the Peace Corps was an expression of the American ideal at its finest and that the more volunteers there were in the program the more effectively that ideal would be expressed.

Dellenback's arrival as Peace Corps director marked the end of the conscious use of the phrase *New Directions.* By then the objectives of the initiative had been accomplished: the New Directions philosophy had been absorbed into the organization. No longer were volunteer jobs to be left to chance. No longer were volunteers put in the field simply so that they could be someplace. The need for volunteers to do something had become an integral part of the Peace Corps formula. As the National Academy of Science had recommended in its study, the organization "should make continuing use of expert advisory panels for program sectors with a high technical component [and] broaden its contacts with relevant technical and professional bodies as well as organizations engaged in development assistance" to insure its continued relevance to the development process.

The Peace Corps had survived the sometimes difficult transition from the time when a high level of idealism, flexibility, and commitment was considered enough for volunteer service to the time when these cherished qualities needed to be buttressed by one other: an ability to do a job that would contribute to host country development. Possibly this transition would have occurred in the natural course of events as the organization matured. It is equally possible, however, that the Peace Corps would have disappeared as a result of the growing disenchantment surrounding it at the end of the 1960s. New Directions—and all of its component parts—reversed that disenchantment and provided the Peace Corps with a new lease on life. That new lease, although many have forgotten its origins, continues as America's premier volunteer agency moves toward the end of its fourth decade of service.

The high sense of purpose, the excitement, and the camaraderie that distinguished Peace Corps/Washington in its early years had sadly diminished by the time I reached the capital in 1974. Long before that time the truly important work had been shifted to the field, leaving in its place the routine necessities of bureaucratic life. Although some of the efforts in Washington were devoted to making appropriate adjustments to important strategies, far more time was spent on matters that were at best tangential to the mission. By far the most discouraging and enervating of these was the constant and insidious struggle between ACTION and the Peace Corps. ·

From the time of Blatchford's departure from ACTION in 1972 until the Peace Corps was granted a substantial amount of autonomy in 1979, the two organizations coexisted in a state akin to that of a cold war. A major part of the problem was the fundamentally different mission of ACTION's two major components, the Peace Corps and VISTA. Similarities between the two that seemed to exist were in reality not there. When this basic flaw was compounded by the appointment of people to head ACTION whose primary interests and natural inclinations were domestically oriented—as was Nixon's second ACTION director—conflict between Peace Corps and ACTION was ensured.

ACTION under Mike Balzano was lacking in any understanding of the Peace Corps mission, its operating philosophies, and its traditions. Personnel in the Washington office were constantly interposing themselves between ACTION directives and the field operations. One of the reasons that Balzano dismissed two Peace Corps directors and barely tolerated two others was that none of them could—or probably more accurately wanted to—bring the organization into the ACTION fold. Balzano was occasionally accused by his detractors of being paranoid, especially concerning his strong suspicion that Peace Corps management was purposefully thwarting his every move. On that specific issue, however, he was correct. ACTION directives were often so diluted by the time they reached the field—if, indeed, they ever got there—that their original intent could no longer be recognized.

Here again, the five-year rule proved its worth (although not from ACTION's standpoint). None of those in the management were career employees; indeed, no one working for the Peace Corps was a career employee. None feared for their jobs, which were destined to expire in a matter of a few months or a year or two in any event. Thus, the members of the staff were remarkably free to follow their own consciences. If that meant subverting ACTION's hold on the Peace Corps, so be it. In fact, at times the Peace Corps gained some grim satisfaction as it saw the level of frustration among ACTION management grow to outrageous proportions at their inability to dictate policies to the Peace Corps.

On one occasion I was given a thinly veiled order to hire a minor political operative from the 1972 election campaign as director for the Philippines. The man was totally unsuited for the position. I knew that my own objections would be insufficient to halt the nomination, so I arranged for the nominee to pay a visit to the State Department where some of my friends from the embassy in Manila had been assigned. His visit was made under the guise of giving him the opportunity to learn something about the Philippines. As expected, those at the State Department were dismayed at the prospect of his appointment and gave me permission to add their objections to my own in blocking the nomination. The candidate disappeared. On another occasion, Dellenback, whose political ties were strong enough to ignore Balzano when he chose, simply arranged with his former colleagues in the House to include provisions in the Peace Corps legislation that he wanted and that ACTION management had refused to request.

The cost of doing daily battle with ACTION was both dispiriting and, in the end, painful for me personally. As my fifth year of service came to a close, Dellenback asked if I would extend my tour for the additional year permitted under certain conditions by the revised Peace Corps Act. I agreed, although with some reluctance because the joys and satisfactions of service were greatly diluted in Washington. For me it was more an obligation than an opportunity—my own personal version of *utang na loob*. I quickly learned, however, that I need not have wasted any time worrying: My extension was not to be. My administrative assistant learned from a well-placed source in Balzano's office that hell would freeze over before he would approve my extension. Once again, the grapevine proved a reliable source of information, and I went about the task of finding a new job.

Twenty Years Later 9

The Peace Corps is now a strong, respected, and permanent part of American foreign policy. Volunteers serve in over ninety countries, thirty more than in the 1970s.[1] More than seven thousand volunteers and trainees are in the field, a number that has been slowly but steadily rising since 1991. Support for the program in Congress is quiet but solid. As Joan Timoney, a recent director of congressional relations for the agency, said in 1995, "Of all the federal agencies one could represent on Capitol Hill, I'd choose Peace Corps any day." Part of the reason she was so enthusiastic is that she is a former volunteer, as are a majority of the staff serving both in Washington and abroad. Equally important, however, was the fact that she could count on the growing number of former volunteers and staff members serving in the House and Senate. After naming the ten sitting members of Congress with Peace Corps backgrounds, she concluded, "Not a bad alumni association!"[2]

The strength of this coalition was demonstrated when Senator Mitch McConnell of Kentucky, the chairman of the Senate Appropriations Subcommittee with responsibility for foreign aid, recommended as part of a major restructuring of the country's foreign policy apparatus that the Peace Corps be merged into the State Department. No sooner had McConnell's plan been made public than the Peace Corps world reacted with alarm, remembering the consequences of an earlier forced institutional marriage. The Peace Corps contingent in the House, which included three Democrats and three Republicans, signed a joint letter urging McConnell to keep the Peace Corps independent. Senator Christopher Dodd, a former volunteer, Senator Paul Coverdell, a former Peace Corps director under President Bush, Senator Jay Rockefeller, a staff member in the 1960s, and Senator Arlen Specter, a former member of the Peace Corps advisory council, led the fight in the Senate. The Peace Corps constituency was simply not prepared to give up its independence a second time after the long struggle to regain it ended successfully in 1982. In the end McConnell bowed to pressure, citing the "considerable experience and strong views" of his petitioners, and he removed the Peace Corps from his proposal.[3]

The agency has benefited from a period of leadership stability—in sharp contrast to the revolving door syndrome that characterized so much of the 1970s. Director Loret Ruppe held the position throughout the eight years of the Reagan administration and won widespread admiration for her ability to provide consistent, sensible, and long-term guidance for the program. Although the other directors of the last fifteen years have generally served terms of only two or three years, their tenures have been relatively free from the internal and unproductive partisan strife that characterized PC/W earlier.[4] In 1993 the organization reached a long-sought milestone: Carol Bellamy became the first former volunteer to serve as director. Bellamy went to Guatemala as a volunteer in 1963. She returned to the United States to become an effective and respected government official at the state and national levels and a Wall Street financier before becoming Peace Corps director. She was proud to describe the agency as "one of the country's greatest success stories."[5] (Bellamy resigned in April 1995 to become head of UNICEF.)

The five-year rule remains in place. Staff members still must leave at the end of that period. But a worrisome practice has sprung up that negates some of the rule's purpose. Former staff members are permitted to return after being away for a period at least equal to the time they served. This means that a former staff member who has served five years can return for another tour of duty after being away for five years. Given the rewards and satisfactions of Peace Corps staff service, it is hardly surprising that a number of people have chosen to return. In recent years two of my former positions—country director in the Philippines and NANEAP regional director—have been filled by people who were staff members with me in the 1970s. The presence of these 'retreads,' as they are called within the agency, is a mixed blessing. On the positive side they provide more of an institutional memory than otherwise would exist, and they ensure the presence of a core of seasoned and knowledgeable administrators. On the negative side their employment creates a semipermanent bureaucracy—with all the pitfalls which that term implies—and an inside-the-beltway mentality that could eventually lead to the type of problems the five-year rule was meant to preclude. (The Peace Corps explains that Ruppe's tenure of eight years—which few, if any, people complained about at the time as being a violation of the five-year rule—was permissible because she was a presidential appointee and not, strictly speaking, a Peace Corps employee.)

The Peace Corps is a far more professional organization today than it was in the 1970s when the need for a more disciplined and focused approach was just beginning to be recognized. The amateurism that was so admired in the 1960s is nowhere to be found. For example, the written material developed for recruitment purposes is precisely targeted, attractively produced, and skillfully worded. It makes Peace Corps service appealing to the desire of prospective volunteers to do good, while—in a sharp departure from what would have been permitted earlier—also appealing to their interest in self-advancement. A typical recruiting pamphlet for a health and nutrition program promises that "you [can] have a direct impact on the people whose lives you share" while gaining experience that "will be highly regarded by any employer who values resourcefulness, inner strength and initiative."[6] The contrast between this dual approach and the one used to find the first volunteers in 1961 is obvious. Previously, any candidate who admitted to wanting to benefit personally from the experience would have been rejected immediately as being insufficiently selfless. Today the complex nature of the reasons that motivate people to do good is better understood and used to advantage.

The agency's professionalism is also apparent in the kinds of technical support provided volunteers in the field. New Directions, by its very nature, required a substantial increase in the amount and quality of the technical support provided, and the organization took great pride in the advances that were made in this area. But compared with the resources provided now, those early efforts were just a beginning. The Office of Information Collection and Exchange— whose roots go back to the late 1970s—publishes over two hundred technical manuals, reprints, and training materials that provide practical 'how to' information. It also maintains an inventory of over eleven hundred items published by other sources. The titles range from the specific (e.g., *Pesticide Safety for Farmworkers* and *Understanding Soil Conservation Techniques*) to the general (e.g., *Community Health and Sanitation*). These materials are available to volunteers either directly from Washington or through another innovation, the in-country resource centers located at Peace Corps offices around the world. These centers contain a wealth of technical and country-specific material tailor-made to assist volunteers in their work. Here they can find a set of microfiche that contains the texts of more than one thousand books describing appropriate technologies for development projects in the Third World.[7] It is almost embarrassing to compare these resource centers with the so-called libraries of twenty-five years ago. The one that existed in the Philippines in 1971 was in reality only a motley collection of paperbacks that provided volunteers with reading material for their spare time. It was abandoned without remorse during the budget crisis of 1971-72.

Although professionalism has risen in the organization, Peace Corps has also slipped further from the public's view. It rarely receives the credit or notice that its nearly four decades of good work merits. Many people are surprised to learn that it still exists. In the 1970s the agency's visibility had already greatly diminished compared with that of the nascent 1960s. Today, it is almost invisible. Between 1992 and 1994 the Peace Corps had an annual average of 3.6 listings in the *New York Times Index*. Between 1972 and 1974 the average was 17.7. In the halcyon days of the early 1960s the average was 103.7.[8] In 1995 the nomination of a new director and the accompanying Senate confirmation hearings were hardly noticed by the press outside Washington. *Time* gave it six lines, and the *New York Times* buried the announcement deep within its interior.[9] Although the present director's fame—if that is not too strong a word to describe a condition of near anonymity—pales compared with that of Shriver's time, the role is still crucial to the agency's well-being. The burden of building and sustaining administration and congressional support rests on the director's shoulders, and the Peace Corps community is intensely interested in the outcome of the appointive process for this position. Alumni and active Peace Corps people alike were delighted when rumors surfaced that former senator and Peace Corps founding father Harris Wofford would succeed Carol Bellamy. When that prospect dimmed (President Clinton was working on other plans for Wofford), there was another flurry of activity to find a candidate with a strong Peace Corps background. Eventually Mark Gearan, an outsider, was selected—which may prove to be a blessing in disguise. The agency has often had to fight the temptation to look to the past for guidance, and new blood at the top may help offset the weight of tradition when the next turning point is reached.[10]

There is still some ambivalence about the Peace Corps in official Washington circles. No one is against it—although a few are wary of becoming too closely identified with it. Recently Anthony Lake, President Clinton's national security adviser, bristled at the memory of once having been thought a man well suited to head the Peace Corps. "It was awful," he remembered when people suggested in

1976 that he should "run [Carter's] Peace Corps." Lake wanted to be known for his toughness and pragmatism, à la Henry Kissinger, and not as "this squishy softy" in the Peace Corps.[11] Lake's prominent colleague in international affairs, Richard Holbrooke, rarely mentioned that he had been a country director in Tunisia. Despite the immense media coverage he received while working on the peace treaty among the states of the former Yugoslavia, his Peace Corps connection was never mentioned. Instead, the reports stressed his hard-boiled, aggressive style of operation and the great success he had achieved earlier on Wall Street. Others included Senator McConnell who, despite being married to Elaine Chao, a former Peace Corps director, considered the agency too unimportant to fight over. If some of his Senate colleagues wanted to change a part of his carefully constructed reorganization plan for foreign aid (folding Peace Corps into the State Department), he was prepared to switch rather than fight. He did not want a matter of little consequence to interfere with the prospects for the more significant aspects of his proposal.

The debate over the relative importance of goals has disappeared. There is no ongoing effort to redress the balance in one way or another. Both aspects of the Peace Corps—the furnishing of trained manpower and the bringing together of Americans and ordinary citizens of other countries—are too deeply ingrained now to require or stimulate a debate. But in the context of this study of New Directions and its legacy, what emerges in looking at the Peace Corps of the 1990s is how thoroughly embedded the concept of *doing something* has become. Nowhere is this more clearly demonstrated than in the recruiting material, which poses such questions as, Are you a recent college graduate in Health Education, Nursing, Occupational or Physical Therapy, Nutrition or other health-related field? Are you a professional already working in a health-related field? Are you a recent college graduate in an agriculture-related field? Are you an experienced farmer or rancher? Even the recruiting literature used to attract English teachers—a job once considered a natural for any English-speaking college graduate—cautions that "this program is highly competitive. You will increase your likelihood of being selected if you have significant tutoring or teaching experience, certification to teach English or a foreign language and/or the ability to speak a second language."

Because of the continuing emphasis on skills in the years since New Directions, the profile of the average volunteer has changed. A remarkable 40 percent of volunteers in mid-1995 had one or more years of genuine work experience before joining the Peace Corps. The average age has risen to thirty, compared with twenty-seven in the mid-1970s and twenty-four in the mid-1960s.[12] Rather than lambasting the efforts to attract older volunteers—as happened in the early 1970s—even the most traditional of Peace Corps supporters now proudly endorse the presence of nearly a thousand volunteers and trainees over the age of forty.[13] No one would dare suggest that these people are too hidebound, too inflexible, or too politically conservative to make good volunteers.

The Peace Corps determined in the 1980s that the benefits derived from recruiting families with children and couples in which only one member met the skills requirements were outweighed by the financial and administrative burdens that accompanied them. One can accept that the problems of the non-matrix spouse made that aspect of the program expendable, but the loss of the families is to be regretted. They did so much to make the volunteer contingent truly representative of the United States that their present absence is a decided negative.

The program emphasis of the present Peace Corps also continues to reflect the principle of providing the assistance that host countries specifically request. Education remains the largest single program sector at about one-third of the volunteer force. The placement of today's far more skilled volunteers, however, is different from what it had been. Unlike the volunteers of the 1960s, who were assigned to hundreds of nonjobs in the Philippines and in other countries as well, the education volunteers of the 1990s are typically placed in demanding professional positions that are integrated fully into the host country's development plan.

More than a quarter of the volunteers work in the agricultural and health sectors that represented such an important part of New Directions programming. The remaining volunteers work in program sectors that reflect today's overriding concerns and were either absent in previous decades or were small and experimental in nature: ecology and the environment, small- and microbusiness development, the full integration of women into host country societies, and youth development.[14]

The seriousness and intensity with which the Peace Corps carries out these programs is suggested by the extent of the technical support it provides volunteers. But, in addition, they are being held to "rigorous qualifications and stricter performance standards [that] make volunteers much more accountable for the jobs they are doing."[15] The term *accountability* has become a part of the Peace Corps vocabulary in a way that was only dreamed about in the 1970s.

A former 1970s PC/P volunteer who joined the senior staff in PC/W during the 1990s summarized the major change as being the presence of "a greater sense of accountability" today among both volunteers and staff, at home and abroad.[16]

The generalist volunteer remains an important part of the Peace Corps. The organization defines a generalist as a recent college graduate with a degree in the sciences, social sciences, or the humanities and no relevant full-time work experience. These are the people who volunteer in the largest number but for whom there are now the fewest positions. In the 1991 recruiting pamphlet *Liberal Arts*, aimed at generalists, the Peace Corps states that "while it is true that many . . . host countries are requesting volunteers with special skills or technical degrees, each year there are still hundreds of requests for people just like you." Most of the generalists who apply are not selected; those that are usually possess one or more of what the recruiters call 'eligibility enhancements.' These include extensive tutoring experience; demonstrated leadership skills; college-level French, Spanish, or Arabic; or a relevant hobby (e.g., gardening that has been reinforced by working on a farm or at a nursery). The generalist recruiting program looks for those applicants who have some special skill or trait that can provide the foundation on which to build a 'skilled' volunteer. Gone are the days when a significant part of the Peace Corps family actively promoted the concept that generalists per se make the best volunteers. The possession of a skill, or evidence that a latent or undeveloped skill is present, is the single most important criterion. Motivation, desire, and flexibility are still essential, but alone they are no longer enough.

One other change at the Peace Corps—one that the author finds sad but is of little consequence in the larger scheme of things—is that PC/W has moved. The Peace Corps offices no longer have that grand view of the White House. Instead, the offices now look out on "K" Street, the favorite address of Washington lobbyists. The modern office block that houses the agency is indistinguishable from the dozens of other buildings in the heart of downtown Washington. It is impossible to imagine this building being taken over by a horde of angry CRV members. Nor can one imagine Blatchford parking his motorcycle in the huge lobby that doubles as a mini-shopping mall; it is too large, too sleek, and too crowded with people who are obviously not Peace Corps types. (As any of the 150,000 alumni can confirm, there is something special about this breed that allows them instantly to recognize one another.) Tight security measures have been installed throughout the part of the building that houses the

Peace Corps. One must be personally escorted through permanently locked doors. The delightful informality of the old building on Connecticut Avenue is sadly missing. Ironically, the director's office is located in a direct line of sight from Blatchford's own law offices around the corner. He delights in calling incumbent directors and surprising them with his uncannily correct comments on their office decor, visitors, or attire.[17]

If the Peace Corps of the mid-1990s is strong and secure, the same cannot be said for the Third World. Regularly the media carry stories of the grinding poverty, high death rate, and forlorn future that still characterize the countries in which many volunteers work. The secretary general of the United Nations declared in 1995, "More than one billion people live in absolute poverty, literally on the brink of starvation."[18] The World Bank has reported that "eleven million children die unnecessarily each year, as well as 7 million adults."[19] The information highway is a prominent topic of conversation in the developed world, but "about 2 billion of the world's 5.7 billion people have no access to electric power" making any such conversation among them unlikely and even absurd. More than one billion people do not have safe drinking water, and nearly two billion lack sanitary waste treatment.[20] Fifty years after its founding as an institution in the "poverty-reduction business," as its new president described the World Bank in 1995, there is still much to be accomplished.[21]

But these depressing statistics mask a situation that is far more complex. Some countries that were members of the Third World in the 1960s have made substantial economic progress in the past three decades, whereas others have fallen behind—if not in absolute terms, then certainly in relative terms. Korea, Malaysia, and Thailand, along with countries in Latin America and North Africa, have emerged from the Third World ranks to become what some term middle-income countries. They and their peoples have escaped the dead-end world of the undeveloped and are making genuine economic progress.

Others—like Nigeria, Pakistan, and Egypt—that were once running even with Korea, Malaysia, and Thailand have not kept pace.[22] They remain firmly anchored in the Third World. As a recent United Nations report declared, "What emerges [from an analysis of the daily lives of people in the developing world] is an arresting picture of unprecedented human progress and unspeakable human misery, of humanity's advances on several fronts mixed with humanity's retreat on several others, of a breathtaking globalization of prosperity side by side with a depressing globalization of poverty."[23] The promise of Rostow's 'take-off point' theory has failed to materialize; the road leading to social and economic development in poorer countries has turned out to be long and arduous. As the director-general of UNESCO said in 1994, "It is true that it has taken us several decades to grasp the complexity of [the development] process, whose social, cultural, and indeed spiritual features we cannot go on blithely ignoring. . . . Development must first of all make it possible to spark off the full potential of the human beings who are both the prime movers in [development] and its ultimate beneficiaries."[24] Earlier a director of USAID reached a similar conclusion when he said, "Although development is more than simply the sum of incremental changes [among ordinary people], these changes are necessary if development is to take place at all."[25] Their point was that if development does not touch the lives of the people, it does not deserve to be called development.

The development theorists have finally realized that the process must deliver benefits to the masses; if the lives of this segment of the population do not improve, then true and lasting development will not occur. Rostow's big mistake may have been just that; he knew that food sufficiency was an essential first step, but he did not understand how important it was that ordinary people participate and share in the benefits. As one economist recently noted, "The poor [were] the objects of the development process, not its subjects."[26] That view no longer holds.

The Peace Corps has responded to the changes in the Third World by withdrawing from those countries that have made substantial economic progress in order to concentrate its resources on those where the need remains great. Volunteers are no longer assigned to a number of countries in Latin America, the Pacific Rim, and the Gulf states, which at one time had large Peace Corps programs.[27] Moreover, the organization announced in June 1996 that it would end its work in a dozen more countries over the next eighteen months.[28] In 1995 the largest group of volunteers was assigned to thirty-three countries in sub-Saharan Africa, an area described as "drained by decades of civil war, economic mismanagement, ethnic strife, dictatorship and exploitation . . . [and] long overdue for a social, political and economic renaissance." Another large contingent of volunteers serves in Central America, where "the spread of democratic institutions and the remarkable potential for economic growth" holds special promise. The remaining volunteers serve in a multitude of countries around the world where the opportunity to make a contribution remains solid.[29]

The Peace Corps has responded to the dramatic change in the way the experts look at the development process by continuing to do what it has always done: "Help people at the grassroots level in needy communities to build a better life," as Carol Bellamy told the House Subcommittee of Foreign Operations in March 1995. Today's development experts at the United Nations, the World Bank, and many other international assistance institutions are now extolling the virtues of programs "that particularly benefit the poor . . . [and] support education, nutrition, family planning, and the role of women."[30] The major development agencies have turned to establishing microloan programs to provide start-up capital to the world's poorest people. They have learned that a loan of $100 or $200 is sufficient to start a small business, provide a family with an adequate standard of living, and, in the aggregate, stimulate an economy that has been moribund.[31] They came late to the discovery of what the Peace Corps has always known and practiced: It is the ordinary people who need help, and success depends upon serving their interests. Despite the differences in methodologies between the Peace Corps programs of the 1960s and the 1970s, in both decades the ultimate objective was the same. Similarly, although the programs of the 1990s are far more technically accomplished than those of the earlier generation, the volunteers still work to achieve the time-tested goals set out in the Peace Corps Act of 1961.

The most striking change that has occurred in the Peace Corps, and a more dramatic change would be hard to imagine, is that it has moved beyond the confines of the Third World. In the past half dozen years volunteers have been invited to work in nearly twenty countries that once were part of the Soviet Union or were linked with it behind the Iron Curtain. They are now in the Baltic States, Poland, Hungary, the Czech Republic, and Rumania, as well as the former Soviet states of Ukraine, Uzbekistan, Turkmenistan, Kazakhstan, and the Slovak Republic. Even Russia is now a Peace Corps host country. Volunteers have become an important part of the American effort to help these countries in their difficult and hitherto unimaginable transition to democracy and free market economics. (More than $10 million of the 1995 Peace Corps budget came from funds originally earmarked by Congress for assistance to the Newly Independent States—rare official acknowledgment of the agency's importance to this effort.)[32] Volunteers in these countries teach English—now more than ever the language of diplomacy, international business, and cultural exchange—at secondary schools and universities. They also help groups of fledgling business men and women become proficient in English so that they can function beyond their national borders. Volunteers with business and economics backgrounds work with midlevel managers to develop skills never needed in a planned economy. A volunteer couple working in Kazakhstan discovered that "it's not know-how people need most but help in developing confidence to move forward . . . [because] in the past all steps were ordered by the government."[33] Volunteers are helping to remove the results of decades of neglect and mismanagement of land, air, and water resources in the former communist countries. They have become a prized commodity in eastern Europe and central Asia. The president of a former republic of the Soviet Union was heard to say, "A hundred volunteers is wonderful, but it is not enough. I would like to see thousands here."[34]

Not everyone welcomed the suggestion that the Peace Corps send volunteers to serve the nation's former enemies. Some questioned the appropriateness of putting the Peace Corps in countries that had once been part of a coalition strong and wealthy enough to challenge the United States for world leadership. Others worried that diverting resources to the former countries of the Soviet Union meant that the real Peace Corps world—the Third World—would suffer. Still others charged that the former communist countries had placed their bet and lost. Let them pay the price for their folly.[35]

In the end, cooler heads prevailed. Today these countries are recognized as ideally suited for volunteers pursuing traditional Peace Corps goals. They clearly want the "men and women of the United States" to help meet their needs for "trained manpower" as they wrestle with the mysteries of democracy and the free market. Both sides of the old divide have a vital interest in ensuring that there is "a better understanding of the American people on the part of the peoples served and a better understanding of other peoples on the part of the American people" after nearly a half century of cold war and its accompanying fear and suspicion.[36] This is not to say that getting programs up and running in former Soviet Bloc countries was easy. The Peace Corps admits, with just a small amount of sugarcoating, that it encountered "its initial share of frustrations" as it worked to overcome bureaucratic snarls, suspicious former communist officials still fighting the cold war, traditional cultures that viewed all change with deep antipathy, and the harshness of long winters on the steppes—a climatic change that three decades in the tropics had done little to prepare it for.[37] But, as the first Peace Corps/Philippines country director could have told them, those who start programs are in for a "complex and painful learning experience," and the pioneer's life is "lived from crisis to crisis."[38]

Volunteer lifestyles in many respects have changed little. The men and women face the same challenges and experience the same joys and hardships that their predecessors did. They work to master one or more of the one hundred languages being taught;[39] live at an economic level consistent with that of their host country counterparts; struggle to make their jobs meaningful and productive; and discover that they have resilience and adaptability far beyond what they might have suspected. Mike Tidwell's memoir, *The Ponds of Kalambayi*, tells of a lifestyle that was every bit as rugged and demanding in the late 1980s as it was in the early 1960s. Andrew Lilienthal, a volunteer in the early 1990s, even discovered that his lifestyle was more like the storied ones of old than his parents' had actually been. "What I didn't realize," he reported, "was that more than twenty-five years [after my parents served,] my Peace Corps assignment would be a lot tougher than theirs." He had to meet more "rigorous qualifications and stricter performance standards" than his parents and was sent to a village "miles from electricity, telephone service, plumbing or public transportation. . . . He did his own cooking and housekeeping while teaching subsistence farmers about soil conservation, natural fertilizers and crop preservation." His parents, on the other hand, had worked as professionals in government ministries in the capital of Ethiopia and enjoyed all the amenities of a modern city.[40] (Lilienthal's parents, Phil and Lynn, were not only exemplary volunteers in Ethiopia but also excellent staff members in the Philippines with the author, and in Thailand and PC/W as well.)

In early 1994 a volunteer working in the former Soviet state of Kazakhstan recited a tale that would be familiar to virtually every one of the organization's 150,000 alumni: "In September [when our group first arrived] we came to the office every day with a list of a dozen things we wanted to accomplish. At the end of the day, we'd gotten one thing done. Now we [still] have a list, but no timetable."[41]

Despite the similarities, there are significant differences that distinguish present volunteer lifestyles from those of their predecessors. Perhaps the most obvious ones involve communications. The fax and satellite television have shrunk the world in a way few of us could have imagined a decade or two ago. Many volunteer sites that would have been isolated earlier are now in touch with the world. Mail that took long weeks to cross oceans, traverse unpaved provincial roads, and survive Third World postal systems before finally reaching the volunteer's hands now comes instantaneously by fax. Fans around the globe watch international soccer matches, NBA basketball, and the World Series in real time, itself an unknown concept when the Peace Corps was young. Students in central Asia discuss the relative merits of Michael Jordan and Shaquille O'Neal, Madonna and Whitney Houston.[42] One senior official at PC/W commented that the advance in communication technology has proved to be a mixed blessing. Too often projects bog down in an information overload because so much is so readily available. Decisions and actions are delayed while just one more piece of information is requested and mulled over, a process far removed from the ad hoc nature of many of the program decisions made in the Philippines in the 1970s.[43]

Another difference is that today many volunteers are already experienced international travelers. By contrast, in 1971 most had never been out of the United States and more than a handful had never been on an airplane. One former volunteer who had joined in 1966 said, "I was caught up in the spirit of this great adventure. . . . I wanted to travel and live in a foreign country. I had never done any of those things." When it came time for his own son to volunteer in the 1990s, the younger man had already "lived in Europe, traveled to Africa, [and] been around the world."[44] Today's volunteers are more mature, realistic, and seasoned than those of an earlier generation, and the organization benefits as a result.

A third difference involves the whole question of sex in the age of AIDS. From the earliest days, despite PC/W efforts to the contrary, those volunteers who chose to do so could have a rich and varied sex life in many if not most countries. The monetary costs of visiting the red-light districts of the Third World were small. Female volunteers found themselves pursued by a legion of would-be suitors. The disapproving looks of fellow volunteers and host country colleagues, to the extent there were any, could be ignored. The principal danger was that one might contract a venereal disease, but the medical office had a large supply of medicines that would quickly defeat all but the most persistent of these. The situation has changed in ways no one could have predicted. The announcement on the back cover of the fall 1994 issue of the *Peace Corps Times* makes the point dramatically. It is a fervent plea for volunteers to use condoms, twenty of which are illustrated in a variety of pastel colors. Each one is labeled with a colorful slang expression used somewhere in the world to designate an item once kept hidden away in seedy drugstores behind the pharmacist's counter. (Among the most memorable names, none of them familiar to the author, were *love glove, sombrero, pocket pal, gummie,* and *umbrella.*) The text reads, "It doesn't matter what you call it. Use it. Available from your Peace Corps medical office." AIDS is present in all Peace Corps countries and runs rampant in Africa and East Asia. A few volunteers have contracted AIDS, and others now test positive for the HIV antibodies. The potential for a health crisis of major proportions exists, and it adds an unwelcome element of real danger the likes of which neither the earlier volunteers nor the leadership had to face.[45]

It is now abundantly clear that the Peace Corps has confounded the pessimists of a quarter century ago who delighted in predicting its end. In 1971 the headline in a New England newspaper reporting an interview with three former volunteers from the 1960s read, "Peace Corps's Demise Predicted." As one volunteer said, "If the Peace Corps doesn't go international [e.g., by becoming part of the United Nations], it's finished, or at least it should be."[46] Senator William Fulbright, chairman of the Foreign Relations Committee, scheduled hearings in the early 1970s to consider abolishing the Peace Corps because, as he said, it was "an idea whose time is past."[47] In 1972 Thomas J. Scanlon, who served in Chile in the early 1960s, told a congressional committee, "I am convinced that unless the Peace Corps is established on an entirely different basis than its present one, it is simply not going to survive."[48] Sargent Shriver was driven to declare, "Things have gotten so it makes me sad to even talk about the Peace Corps."[49] All of this at precisely the time the Peace Corps was becoming more relevant to the concerns of scores of host countries—and to the United States—as well as more proficient than ever before in carrying out its mission. This discrepancy between what was really happening to the Peace Corps and what some people thought was happening is a good example of the danger in putting too much faith in the accuracy of the Washington perspective. If all one knew about the Peace Corps at that time was what was being said and done in the capital, and if one listened only to the doomsayers, the end would have seemed mighty near.

Lost among all of the pessimism and self-serving declarations were the solid results being accomplished abroad and the occasional voice of reason. David Riesman, an academic with a long advisory relationship with the Peace Corps, cautioned in 1972: "The decline and fall of the Peace Corps is in the eyes of the beholder. . . . The Peace Corps has not really changed that much and it certainly hasn't changed for the worst. . . . It's less erratic, too, and many of the problems that were concealed under the life of spontaneity, glamour, and enthusiasm of the Shriver days have been wrestled with more seriously since."[50] Instead of an agency headed for extinction in the early

1970s the opposite was happening: The Peace Corps was becoming stronger and healthier; its continued existence was being ensured.

Although the two decades that have passed since 1976 have been generally good ones for the Peace Corps, the same is not true for the Philippines or for the volunteer program there. The early promise of the Marcos years disappeared in a sea of graft, mismanagement, and corruption. What had seemed an acceptable bargain in 1972—the acceptance of authoritarian rule in return for peace, security, and development—became instead a one-sided deal that enriched a few and further impoverished the many. The final years of the Marcos rule were marked by unparalleled corruption, greed, incompetence, and an ostentatious display of wealth and poor taste. Imelda Marcos, who amassed substantial political power in her own right, spearheaded the efforts to build unneeded luxury hotels, high-tech medical facilities that did nothing to solve the nation's health problems, a huge international convention center, and a nuclear power generating plant that has never produced a single kilowatt of power. And—to gain a place for herself and her children in the glittering world of the international jet set—she feted the rich and famous at elaborate festivities at home and abroad.[51] The net result was, predictably, disastrous. While Marcos and his small band of supporters enriched themselves to an extent that is almost incomprehensible (the Marcoses alone are estimated to have channeled $10 billion of public funds, bribes, and profits from ethically questionable business deals into their personal bank accounts), the country and its people came to the brink of ruination. One historian concluded, "By the end of the Marcos era . . . the Philippine nation was bankrupt. Inflation was rampant . . . [and] the number of families below the poverty line had grown from 50 percent to 60 percent."[52] Another observer concluded that "the new rice technology bought valuable time for the Philippines. . . . [It] provid[ed] a breathing space during which the country could have address[ed] crucial underlying issues. . . . The tragedy is that the opportunity was squandered."[53]

Marcos stubbornly held on to power through the early 1980s, despite failing health, growing opposition from many sectors of society, a resurgence of revolutionary activity by leftist guerrillas, and the appearance for the first time of harsh criticism for his government in the U.S. Congress. It appeared as if only death, rumored to be imminent, could dislodge him from office. In August 1983, however, the government made a mistake that in the end led to Marcos's fall from power and exile to the United States. Marcos, thinking himself secure in his hold on the country, announced a partial return to democracy that permitted the formation of political parties other than his own. Benigno Aquino, a longtime political foe of the president, decided to return from exile. No sooner had he stepped off the plane that carried him back to Manila than he was shot in the head and killed. The high-handedness of the attempt to deal with the public's suspicion that there had been government involvement—which included transparently false cover stories, sham trials of several high-ranking military officers, and the 'capture' and subsequent murder of an alleged perpetrator—fed a growing popular disaffection for the government. Marcos compounded his problem in 1985. He again misjudged his popularity and announced a snap election, ostensibly to give the people a chance to express their will but in reality to give himself another six years in office. (He planned to control the ballot count as he had in the past and had no doubt what the results would be.)

The entire world watched with wonder and admiration as the woman in the yellow dress—Corazon Aquino, the slain martyr's widow who had adopted the color yellow as her signature trademark—toppled a previously unassailable dictator of twenty years' standing and claimed the presidency in February 1986. The drama was played out in front of the world's television cameras as ordinary citizens, fearless nuns, and masses of students faced down the military's tanks. (The fact that the United States had at long last decided that Marcos was more liability than asset helped hasten his doom, but it was not the deciding factor.) Marcos and his wife fled the country to exile in Hawaii, where the former president died in 1989.[54]

If only the story had ended on this high note. But the Aquino presidency failed to live up to its early promise. Seven attempted military coups shook the government during Aquino's single term in office—although it must be said that some of them had a comic opera aspect. (One disgruntled army colonel announced his coup from a suite at a luxury hotel and then sat back to see what would happened. When nothing did, he checked out and went home.)[55] On the left of the political spectrum the New People's Army (NPA) grew ever larger and bolder. And it was common knowledge that some of Aquino's relatives were profiting handsomely from her incumbency. At the end of her tenure, the country was frequently described as the sick man of Asia.

Worsening the already grave situation facing the country was the steady deterioration of relations with the United States. Many Filipinos remembered with anger the long and supportive relationship between Marcos and a series of American presidents. The banks most loudly demanding repayment of ill-conceived loans—and in the process making the nation's economic plight still worse—were American, a fact that did not escape public notice.[56] The continuing presence of tens of thousands of American troops on Philippine soil grew ever more unpopular. As one Filipino critic declared, "You do not put a dollar tag on dignity."[57]

In this atmosphere the negotiations for a new bases treaty were started. After long months of fruitless negotiations, the two sides were still far apart over the amount of rent the United States would pay. But two events proved decisive in hastening the end of the American military presence: a natural disaster and the disintegration of the Soviet Union. The volcano at Mt. Pinatubo, located a few miles from Clark Air Force Base, had been sending off ominous signals for some weeks in 1991. The team of American experts studying the signals for clues as to what might happen included a former Philippine volunteer who had become fascinated with volcanoes while serving near Mt. Mayon, another of the country's many volcanoes. In a February 1995 letter to me, Chris Newhall recalled with pride that the team correctly forecast a violent eruption. As a result, Newhall wrote, "Ten thousand Aetas [an indigenous group that made its home on the mountain] were displaced, but alive, [as were] a smaller but still significant number of Americans and lowland Filipinos." The eruption left the surrounding area, including the American base, barren and buried under many feet of lava. Regardless of how the two sides looked at the issue, the question of further negotiations on an American future for Clark proved moot; the base was useless.

With Clark gone, the American negotiators cut their already inadequate financial offer nearly in half, much to the chagrin of their Filipino counterparts. When the Philippine Senate rejected the proposed treaty—perhaps as a further negotiating ploy—the Americans said, in effect, 'Never mind; we don't need Subic either. We're going home.' Goodwill between the two countries sank to an eighty-year low, and the once cherished relationship turned sour.

The Peace Corps also found itself an unwitting cause of the growing tensions between the two governments. During the Marcos regime, including the dramatic time of its collapse, the organization had continued to work effectively. The Aquino revolution, however, was greeted with great acclaim from the Peace Corps. President Aquino returned the compliment by attending a ceremony in Manila celebrating the Peace Corps's twenty-fifth anniversary of service in her country.[58]

But in June 1990 in the midst of the negotiations over the bases, the United States unilaterally and abruptly withdrew the entire volunteer contingent from the islands. Aquino protested that the pullout was "unneeded and embarrassing," and Secretary of Defense Fidel Ramos expressed his opinion that the move was "rather hasty."[59] One of the Filipino staff members from the 1970s recalled that "the evacuation of all PCVs was swift and unannounced. One day they were there and the next they were all in Manila on their way out. It caused quite a stir to put it mildly. . . . It [will] take a long time [to get over]."[60] Press reports at the time suggested that the decision had been made in Washington, against the advice of the American officials in Manila, and was linked in some way to the bases negotiations. (The implication was that the pullout was meant to send a message to the Philippines that the United States was quite willing to curtail aid if Filipino negotiators did not soften their demands.)[61]

As is always the case in Philippine-American relations, there is another side to the story. American intelligence reports suggested that the NPA had targeted volunteers in their effort to unnerve the American-backed Aquino government.[62] Several Americans had already been killed in recent months in the Philippines—presumably by the NPA—which tended to give the intelligence reports added weight. When it was discovered a week following the pullout that a volunteer who had missed the evacuation had actually been kidnapped by the NPA, the American position became far more compelling. Skeptics, however, pointed out that Washington had made its decision before it knew of the kidnapping and that a similar incident involving an aid worker from Japan had not caused the Japanese to withdraw. Both the volunteer and the Japanese aid worker were released unharmed several weeks later, but the hard feelings continued.

When Aquino's presidency ended—she kept her promise to serve only one term—Fidel Ramos was elected to replace her. As one of seven candidates, Ramos was elected to office by a scant 23.5 percent of the voters. Nevertheless, he has managed to develop a strong and united following during the first half of his term. In addition, there are encouraging signs that suggest, just possibly, that the long-suffering Filipino people are finally benefiting from decent government. *The Economist* magazine reviewed his progress in mid-1995 under the headline, "Ramos Rampant." The accompanying article reported, "In the past year the Philippines has gone a long way towards shedding its reputation as the sick man of South-East Asia."[63]

The rupture between the United States and the Philippines has begun to heal. In 1992 the Peace Corps returned to the country with a small group of volunteers. In 1994 President Clinton visited the archipelago to pay homage to the American and Filipino troops who died there during World War II. President Ramos, himself a graduate of West Point, welcomed his American counterpart with warmth and good cheer.

Despite the promising signs, acute problems remain. Poverty levels remain woefully high, even by Third World standards. Nearly 65 percent of Filipinos in rural areas are living below the government's poverty line, as are about 50 percent of urban dwellers. The population has soared from 40 million in 1970 to a projected 75 million by the year 2000, although the birthrate has fallen from 3.8 to a still intolerable 2.8.[64] One of the principal advocates of family planning in the 1990s is Juan Flavier, previously Ramos's secretary of health and now a senator. Corruption continues to be a persistent, perpetual, and pernicious bane on the body politic. And one can add to all this Mother Nature's continued assault on the islands in the form of typhoons, floods, earthquakes, landslides, volcanic eruptions, periodic droughts, and nearly every other weapon in her arsenal. In 1995 the typhoon season was so severe that those who christen typhoons with alphabetically selected names found themselves needing to start over. Typhoon Angela, the twenty-seventh typhoon of the year, killed more than five hundred Filipinos when it swept across the island of Luzon in November.[65]

But perhaps the most worrisome problem is the similarity of Ramos's development plans to those made a quarter century ago: He has pledged to use improvements in agriculture as the engine to drive the economy.[66] How could so many years pass with so little accomplishment? Why is the country still facing the same problems and proposing the same solutions? One answer, of course, is that the extent of Marcos's plundering and mismanagement was such that it precluded any significant progress. Another is the absence of any sense of urgency in dealing with the country's population crisis. (Flavier has been dubbed "Dr. Condom" by an unsympathetic press and is regularly condemned by the hierarchy of the Catholic Church.)[67] Skepticism about the future of the Philippines—and, by extension, the entire Third World—is hard to shake. There have been too few successes and far too many failures.

But just at this point another seldom mentioned benefit of the Peace Corps five-year rule comes into play. Just when the old hands are beginning to lose heart, they are replaced by newcomers undaunted by the doubts and anxieties that experience in the Third World inevitably produces. There is renewed optimism, a positive attitude, and a determination to succeed that reenergizes the entire effort. The struggle to bring a better life to the world's needy goes on. Even if the results are hard to measure and slow in coming, the greater tragedy would be to cease trying.

In fall 1995, *Three/One/Sixty-One,* a publication of the National Peace Corps Association, asked rhetorically, "What Do Ted Kennedy, Jesse Helms, Paul Coverdell and Sargent Shriver Have in Common?" The answer: All supported Mark Gearan, President Clinton's nominee as Carol Bellamy's successor as head of the Peace Corps. Two traditional liberal Democrats with strong ties to the early Peace Corps (Kennedy and Shriver), a former director from the late 1980s and currently the Republican senator from Georgia (Coverdell), and the Senate's ranking curmudgeon and foe of all things international (Helms) had joined in common cause to support both the nominee and the organization. The questions that had marked the early days of the Peace Corps, the rancor that accompanied New Directions, the prophets of doom, and those vowing to abolish the organization of the 1970s are all part of the past. Even the federal budget battle of 1995 left the Peace Corps relatively unscathed compared with the life-threatening action taken against other government agencies. Some of those with similar well-intentioned, hard-to-evaluate, and controversial missions—like the National Endowment for the Arts, the National Endowment for the Humanities, the Corporation for Public Broadcasting, and the Departments of Education and Energy—suffered cuts of as much as 40 percent amid talk that they would be abolished entirely, whereas the Peace Corps appropriation for fiscal year 1996 was cut by only 10 percent.[68]

Thirty-five years of the Peace Corps have convinced even the most critical of doubters that the agency's mission is valid, its work useful, and its benefits—to both the scores of host countries and to the United States—plentiful. But there is still work to be done. The Peace Corps's story, as Gearan expressed it, is "an untold story" in the 1990s.[69] Most Americans today would be hard-pressed to describe its mission, the way it works, and the record of its successes. Except for the early years, which have been covered in a dozen or more books, the history of the Peace Corps is known only by a few people who have made it their business to stay abreast of developments. Karen Schwarz made a good start in telling the whole story, even though some of her conclusions need to be examined further. The volunteers who have written about their own experiences in both fictional and nonfictional forms have undeservedly found only small audiences. And many aspects of the larger story of the institution, with all of their political, international, and human interest components remain untold. Now, however, the archival material and large potential audience is sufficient to warrant a renewed and sustained exploration. The analysis in these pages of New Directions and its impact is just one of many important topics that await the attention of historians and social scientists.

Another shortcoming is that too few of the many lessons that can be learned from the Peace Corps experience have in fact been learned. There has been only a modest effort to examine the total history and draw from it new insights into, for example, what motivates people to do good, how development occurs in the Third World, and what lasting impact the organization has had on its members and their country. Part of the reason for this situation lies in the very nature of the Peace Corps as an action-oriented, rather than analytical, entity. The immediacy of the issues, both in the field and in PC/W, is such that little time or opportunity remains for the thoughtful consideration of long-term concerns. Moreover, the five-year rule, in many ways a blessing, makes it difficult for the agency to accumulate a body of knowledge over an extended period of time. Finally, as in every bureaucracy, the tendency is strong to analyze experience in a way that will confirm the wisdom of earlier bureaucratic decisions or support specific agency initiatives. For all three reasons fundamental questions about the Peace Corps experience remain to be answered.

People will differ on which research projects might deserve high priority, but among the most important is an assessment of the degree to which the Peace Corps has had an impact on host countries. Virtually no comprehensive effort has been undertaken to understand how the presence of the organization has affected a country, its level of economic and social development, and its attitudes toward the United States. Generally, assessments have been based upon uncritical analyses of anecdotal evidence. Although this evidence is overwhelmingly positive, the conclusions reached are frustratingly imprecise. Without minimizing the difficulties inherent in conducting country studies of this type, it does seem that the long-term presence of the Peace Corps in scores of countries should by now have provided sufficient evidence on which to base a series of soundly conceived assessments. In its youth the Peace Corps often found itself backed into a corner by its own rhetoric. One of the founders, Brent Ashabranner, lamented of the 1960s that "the rhetoric of the Peace Corps as a dramatic world force" had become a heavy burden.[70] When the skeptics asked for proof of such a grandiose assertion, the agency had to admit that as yet there was none. Eventually, the Peace Corps tired of that explanation and took another approach. It declared that the work of the agency was not susceptible to quantitative measures and needed to be accepted on faith. Surely, sufficient time has now elapsed and sufficient experience has been gained to permit another effort at serious assessment. It may well turn out that the early rhetoric was closer to the truth than its authors dared hope.

A second subject for research—and one that is closely associated with the first—might well be the extent to which Peace Corps has contributed to the science of social and economic development. In other words, how has the Peace Corps experience led to a new or different understanding of the development process and to the creation of new techniques for achieving it? Two such contributions are presented in chapter 10, although more needs to be done to confirm them. There are likely others whose existence can be discovered through a combination of quantitative and qualitative research techniques if only people will examine the record.

Another neglected aspect of the Peace Corps experience is the extent to which returned volunteers have influenced the United States. From the time when the first volunteers came home, people have speculated about how their presence would change American society. Yet little has been done other than to make estimates of career choices by former volunteers and to publish lists of notable returned volunteers, as the Peace Corps presently does.[71] As part of this same research agenda there needs to be an effort to determine how the experience has changed those who were part of it. Again, the anecdotal evidence overwhelmingly supports the belief that the volunteer experience is among the most formative an individual can have. Yet the answers to the 'what,' 'how,' and 'why' of the changes remain as elusive as ever.

The basic reason for conducting research along these lines is not simply to clarify what happened. The knowledge produced from filling in the historical record could also help shape the Peace Corps of the future. As more than thirty-five years of experience has shown, the agency needs to be responsive to changes in the world in which it works. The very existence of the Peace Corps came about as a creative response to a changing world. By the late 1960s further changes both at home and abroad required that the organization alter course or cease to exist. That ushered in New Directions—even though its arrival was neither welcomed by everyone nor free from rancor.

ACTION, widely acclaimed at its birth, was a mistake that needed to be corrected, and it was. The Peace Corps's response to the developments behind the Iron Curtain was another that was right, even if it came about over the strenuous objections of many traditionalists.

Change has always been the lifeblood of the Peace Corps, and there is every reason to expect that it will continue to be so. The Peace Corps Act is a flexible charter that establishes an overall mission but at the same time permits, even encourages, finding new ways to deal with new conditions as they arise. However, many of these new ways have required that the organization abandon the certainties of the past—an action often greeted with dismay and disagreement. One perceptive staff member from the 1970s criticized the tendency for an undue reverence for the past (including the bias in favor of the youthful generalist) as unintentionally constituting a barrier that causes "new ideas and challenges all too often [to be] treated as threats rather than seen as opportunities to expand the scope of the agency or to make it more effective."[72] The type of research being proposed here would make it easier to avoid these tendencies by replacing subjective reactions with objective analysis. Gearan, at the time of his confirmation, praised the "Peace Corps's constant sense of receptivity to new ideas," praise that has not always been warranted.[73] Its history is filled with accounts of battles fought over the prospect of change—the struggle over New Directions being just one of them. What Gerard Rice called The Bold Experiment continues, but its future can best be ensured if it learns to respond to conditions more quickly and with less contention and disruption than it has in the past. When the need for the next major change comes—and come it will—it is essential that the Peace Corps have a sound basis for deciding the issue and the courage to do what it did in 1969: chart a new course. The research program proposed in this section will help ensure that outcome.

Making a Difference   **10**

The idea "Making a Difference" reflects a concern that has driven the Peace Corps from the moment presidential candidate John F. Kennedy made his now-famous impromptu speech on that cold October morning at the University of Michigan. Alan Guskin, one of the students in attendance, remembered that Kennedy promised a means by which Guskin could "make a difference in helping to create a better and more peaceful world."[1] Twenty-five years later, the Peace Corps published a collection of reminiscent essays entitled *Making a Difference: The Peace Corps at Twenty-Five.* In 1996, as I was writing this paragraph, a Peace Corps alumni magazine arrived with two advertisements—one for a graduate program in intercultural relations, the other for an international student exchange program—that used the same theme: "Continue to make a difference."[2]

The question remains, however: Has the Peace Corps made a difference? An affirmative response means that the expenditure of public resources and the time and talent of many tens of thousands of people was justified; a negative answer reduces the entire effort to nothing more than the equivalent of a grand tour for a few privileged Americans.

The Peace Corps is only a small part of the development presence in the Third World, and its impact is difficult to isolate. When Peter McPherson, an administrator of USAID and a former volunteer, tried to measure Peace Corps's direct development impact, he concluded, "The very nature of the Peace Corps militates against effective and sustained measurement of progress—two-year tours, in-country jobs negotiated yearly with host governments, work with institutions that are disorganized, and, most important, the intangibility of the Peace Corps service to the disenfranchised and the disengaged."[3] It is not surprising that some supporters have responded to the difficulty of measuring success by simply declaring that such standards are irrelevant to the Peace Corps. Its mission, they claim, is not subject to quantification; its benefits are of the spirit; it is about bridging the gap between peoples; it is about peace and understanding. Such assertions have merit, but the difference the Peace Corps has made goes beyond them and deserves to be recognized.

The greatest difference can be seen in the lives of the volunteers and staff members who participated in the experience and, by extension, in the life of the country to which they returned. To acknowledge that the agency bestowed its greatest gifts on those who served in it and on the nation that supported it is not meant as a criticism of the organization or its volunteers and staff. Nor is it to lessen the value of the benefits provided the people of the developing world. It is simply to recognize what has become a universal truth in the Peace Corps world: Virtually all who have served believe that they received more from the experience than they gave. A survey of returned volunteers in 1970 reported that 92 percent agreed that it had been a valuable personal experience.[4]

Statements of the people who helped with this project indicate that the pattern continues. These former volunteers, now well into midlife, say: "My Peace Corps years (1972-76) were some of the most cherished years of my life." "My Peace Corps experience laid much of the foundation for what I do today." "I owe where I am today to my three years in the Peace Corps." "I use the PC experience as an anchor or turning point in my life." "My eyes were opened during those two years." "The Peace Corps experience breeds a sense of compassion and understanding which is simply not available through more conventional exposures with foreign cultures." "Peace Corps did give a lot of us a solid base from which to grow." "[We] feel that Peace Corps changed our lives completely. Neither one of us would be doing what we are today if not for that experience." "It was among the mountain folk where my real Peace Corps experience happened, where I truly began to understand life outside of American trappings, where my personal value system received a heavy dose of reality. . . . It was both dreadful and wonderful, empty yet satisfying, the most wretched of days and among the brightest and best of days."[5] Warren Wiggins, an early Peace Corps official, reported that a returned volunteer told him that it was "the best goddam experience a young man can have. Worth four years of college."[6]

An experience such as the Peace Corps offers is bound to bring change at the personal level. It challenges one's preconceived notions of the world and one's place in it. Few of the values one brings to the Peace Corps remain untouched afterwards. Some are destroyed, some altered, and some strengthened. The two fine Peace Corps writers whose works were mentioned earlier, Mike Tidwell and George Packer, lived in small African villages where the defining characteristics were poverty, cultural tradition, and the legacy of a colonial past. Each village had the same daily rhythms, the seasonal shifts, the constant struggle to eke out a living from an unforgiving landscape, the presence of disease and untimely death, and the eventual willingness of the local populace to accept a stranger as family. Yet the two men responded in different ways. Tidwell—for all of his frustrations—invariably found the glass half-full, whereas Packer found the glass half-empty. The same set of stimuli produced powerful yet different reactions in these two Americans.

For all of the differences in the way individuals were affected, there was one nearly universal similarity: The effect was profound and for the better. In fact, often a hint of guilt appears as volunteers describe how they benefited from their experience abroad. They worry that they received too much and gave too little. They feel they returned home better men and women whereas, despite all of their hard work, the Third World seemed to be unchanged. The contribution of any one of them was, in Steve Shaffer's felicitous phrase, only "one grain of sand." Individual volunteers find it difficult to accept the fact that the many grains of sand form the beach. Their own efforts seemed small, even inconsequential, in the face of such great and obvious need. In contrast, their own personal experience was immensely and immediately rewarding, and they found it difficult to accept that the trade-off was an equal one.

By making such a dramatic difference in the lives of so many volunteers, the Peace Corps also had an important impact on the United States. Gradually, as more and more volunteers returned home, their presence began to be felt in the nation's collective character. The change became particularly noticeable in certain governmental departments and agencies. The first of these to understand the value of the Peace Corps experience to its own special mission was, quite appropriately, USAID. As Peter McPherson remembered, the relationship between the two was in the beginning one of "constant bickering" and "a basic mistrust, or perhaps a misunderstanding, of each other's policies and purposes." This made it difficult for them to cooperate, and both missions suffered as a result.[7] By the 1970s, however, USAID had come to value greatly the grassroots perspective that former volunteers could bring to its own development work. A number of volunteers in the Philippines were hired by USAID immediately upon the completion of their service. One of them, a volunteer in the program that made bank loans available to small farmers, recalled twenty years later, "The relationships [with Filipinos] that I had established during Peace Corps [and] my language capability" were what USAID found attractive.[8]

As the importance of working at the delivery end of the development pipeline became more apparent, USAID realized that the Peace Corps was in effect training thousands of potential USAID staff members in this skill every year. By 1986 McPherson could boast of "five hundred former Peace Corps volunteers, myself included," on his agency's roster.[9] The special sensitivity toward other people and their culture that the Peace Corps volunteers exhibited had become an essential part of USAID as well.

The State Department also discovered that Peace Corps experience provided solid and valuable training for future diplomats. As one former volunteer and sometime critic of the American government, Paul Theroux, concluded, "When we began joining the State Department and working in the embassies, these institutions were the better for it and had a better-informed and less truculent tone."[10] The Peace Corps showed considerable pride (and the State Department perhaps some astonishment) when an American ambassador, Julia Chang Bloch, reported in 1990 that for "the first time in history . . . all the heads of all U.S. civilian agencies in a country [including the American ambassador herself] are former PCVs." She was speaking of Nepal, the quintessential Peace Corps country.[11]

For many years about 10 percent of each year's crop of fledgling diplomats at the State Department have been former Peace Corps volunteers and staff members. Like their counterparts at USAID (and at many private American and international institutions devoted to economic and social development), they bring with them a worldview that is tempered by a clear understanding of what life is like for the majority of the world's population and what it is that motivates these people. And one hopes that such an understanding has led to a more realistic and humane representation of American interests abroad, particularly in the Third World.

The Peace Corps contribution to the United States goes beyond its direct impact on the nation's international activities, although it is most easily demonstrated in that arena. The 150,000 former volunteers and staff members can be found in all walks of life. One can add to the six serving in the House of Representatives and the four in the Senate (in 1996) thousands of others who are employed as congressional aides and committee staff members and in civil service positions throughout the government. Still others are in elective office at the state and local levels; they are found throughout the academic world as teachers and administrators; they are doctors, nurses, bankers, lawyers, engineers, farmers, writers, musicians, and artists; they can be found in every nook and cranny of the country; and they range in age from the midtwenties to elder retirees. They are generally well educated, middle-class, and influential. And, perhaps most of all, they remain interested in making a difference. Their experience in the Peace Corps has taught them that solutions are rarely simple, that people the world over share certain common characteristics, and that the existence of cultural differences need not be a barrier to human understanding and cooperation. They bring a badly needed perspective to the discussion of America's place in the world and the legitimacy of the Third World's claim on a small portion of the nation's bounty. They are more willing to seek and accept change, more comfortable with making room for other views and voices, and committed to the proposition that the world can become a better place given a sufficient supply of those old Peace Corps ideals: understanding, patience, and perseverance.

A second way the Peace Corps has made a difference is in improving the way ordinary citizens of the Third World view Americans. For most of these people the image they had was the one reflected in American movies. Or perhaps the image arose from the occasional glimpse of an American tourist, government official, or military person. It was a one-dimensional picture that bore little resemblance to reality or to the way Americans wanted to be seen. A volunteer from Tanzania wrote that people in her rural village thought "white people came from countries paved with gold: where everyone has a job and a house lit with electricity, there are no fevers, people eat meat each day, and buildings are warm when it is cold and cold when it is hot."[12] Americans were assumed to be a breed apart, one that did not have to bear the normal burdens of life, one that dealt only with the joys of existence—not both the joys *and* sorrows. From the beginning the Peace Corps has believed it essential that the people of the Third World come to understand that Americans are in many ways similar to themselves, that they are not wedded to the luxuries of an affluent society, and that they can share the lifestyles of the world's poor.

The Philippines presented a somewhat unusual situation in that there were two contending views of Americans. One was the legacy of Taft's policy of attraction and of the thousands of American teachers, the Thomasites, who had worked for decades in the country. Many Filipinos, especially among the older population, remembered the Americans who had taught them, helped them govern themselves, and introduced modern technologies in medicine, sanitation, and engineering. A genuine gratitude for American assistance existed alongside an uncritical appraisal that often placed too high a value on anything American. As one volunteer discovered to her dismay, Filipinos seemed "obsessed with the notion that anything white or American is good. Even the least key ring, if imported from the states, is a prized possession."[13]

The other contending view of Americans was more prevalent among younger people, particularly those who were well educated, and was based on what they observed every day. The American business community remained largely aloof from the lives of ordinary Filipinos. The Americans lived in large, walled-off compounds (called villages in Manila) with armed guards constantly patrolling the perimeters, did their playing at the exclusive Polo Club, and only ventured into downtown Manila with great trepidation. A volunteer couple was befriended by a Manila-based American business family from their home state. After a weekend visit to the family the volunteers wrote home: "It's funny that for all the things we don't have, we are better adjusted and happier than they. . . . They haven't traveled, except to Baguio [the mountain resort city] and just don't have the opportunity to make friends that we do. They are too set apart from Filipinos, and the foreigners who people their neighborhood are largely engaged in bitter cutthroat competition—over business, entertaining, dress, child-raising, etc. It [is] dreadful."[14]

The official American community enjoyed a lifestyle similar to that of the business community, differing only in that the nature of their representational duties required frequent contact with their counterparts in the Philippine government. Neither the business nor the government communities gave the local people reason to feel a close bond or to assume that there could be a mutuality of interests between themselves and the Americans. And, unfortunately, certain segments of the American military presence actually gave Filipinos genuine reasons for wanting to keep their distance. Off base, American servicemen, even out of uniform, were instantly recognizable. Their frequent presence in the red-light districts, their boisterous behavior and rakish intemperance, and their insistence on acting American in the worst sense of the word were offensive to many Filipinos. Virtually every Peace Corps volunteer and staff member in the country experienced the occasional desire to deny any possible connection between themselves and a particularly raucous and embarrassing bunch of American servicemen. Moreover, it was not just overly sensitive Peace Corps volunteers who were aware of the damage being done to the American image. David Bain, the author of the exciting book about Emilio Aguinaldo's capture in 1901, found that the women with whom he had a professional relationship in Manila were reluctant to be seen in public with him. "When one sees a Filipina with an American man," he was told by a woman friend, "there can be only one conclusion drawn."[15]

Every Peace Corps program faced its own special set of image problems, and the Philippines presented neither the most difficult nor the easiest to overcome. But the Peace Corps quickly came to understand its unique ability to soften any negative images and to present another side of the American character. One Filipino entrepreneur told a volunteer when he said good-bye, "It's been a pleasure knowing you. You were the first American I ever worked with face to face. . . . Before I met you I didn't think very highly of Americans. I thought that they were all arrogant, egotistical imperialists. . . . But you have changed all that. . . . You and the other volunteers here are greatly appreciated."[16] An older volunteer wrote about his experience of finding doors that "had been closed to me as a tourist, journalist, diplomat, and scholar magically opened by [having] Peace Corps credentials. . . . Twenty years of the Peace Corps presence [in the Philippines] . . . had sown seeds of trust."[17]

Such sentiments were common throughout the Peace Corps world. Two volunteers traveling on vacation found themselves stranded in a small Malaysian town by storms and floods. Not being able to speak the language, having little local currency (they had expected only to pass through en route to the airport in Singapore), and having neither food nor lodging, they faced a difficult situation. Then a stranger discovered that they were Peace Corps volunteers. He explained that ten years earlier a volunteer had come to this same town, organized the construction and staffing of the region's first hospital, encouraged the man to continue his education, and won his and the town's eternal gratitude. For the Malaysian, helping the marooned volunteers was his way of paying back a bit of the debt he and the town owed to that fondly remembered volunteer.[18] Wherever one travels in the Third World, a Peace Corps connection brings about the same reaction: a smile of welcome and an automatic gift of the friendship and trust that has been earned through the years by volunteers.

The cumulative presence of thousands of Peace Corps volunteers in the Philippines has probably not erased entirely the unfortunate image created by some of the many more thousands of American business, government, and military personnel who have lived in the country. But, like the Thomasites before them, the volunteers have created a much more attractive American image, and that is the one that prevails in the provinces. Nowhere is this demonstrated more clearly than in the reception former volunteers receive when they return to the Philippines for a visit or in the warmth of the friendships that continue decades later. A volunteer from the mid-1970s recalls that "one of the best things that happened as a result of my PCV tour in the Philippines is my ongoing relationship with the Camilio Hilario family. . . . I have returned to the Philippines and stayed with the Hilarios three times. . . . I consider them my 'second family' and hope to see them again within the next few years."[19] Another volunteer couple from the same era returned after a number of years to find themselves "welcomed with many hugs and kisses." Later they were feted by the governor of the province, who was still supporting the agricultural project the volunteers had started during their service.[20] The bond volunteers have formed with the people of their host countries is strong and long-lasting, and the people of the Third World remember their volunteers with great fondness. These are the memories that have finally begun to dilute the ugly-American stereotype once common around the globe.

The most difficult question to answer is this: Did Peace Corps make a difference in economic and social development? With the exception of the mid-1960s, when its numbers peaked at about fifteen thousand, the organization has had between six thousand and nine thousand volunteers, trainees, and staff members in the field each year. Certainly not a large presence given the number of countries and people needing help. Its annual budget has fluctuated over the last thirty-five years from about $80 million to about $230 million, a sum that is nearly lost in the approximately $60 billion spent annually by a score of developed countries on Third World aid.[21] Add to this already complex situation the fact that volunteers often work within a host country bureaucracy and one can begin to sense the difficulty in trying to isolate the impact of the Peace Corps. Moreover, the Third World has been buffeted by a series of setbacks that has lessened the actual rise in living standards that otherwise might have occurred. Excessive population growth has continued to absorb a portion of the benefits of increased agricultural production and economic development. Civil wars and political strife have diverted huge amounts of Third World resources to unproductive ends. Corruption and entrenched power structures have siphoned off both foreign assistance and domestically generated income into private hands and offshore bank accounts. And, as always, natural disasters have periodically left in their wakes ruined crops, starving people, abandoned or lost homes, and displaced people searching for refuge.

Given the relatively small part the Peace Corps plays in the total development effort and the overwhelming character of the forces impinging on the Third World, it is little wonder that some people despair at ever being able to measure the Peace Corps contribution to development. Although endorsing the Peace Corps development efforts and encouraging it to do more, Peter McPherson asked rhetorically, "How can one quantify the short-term (let alone the long-term) effects on three farmers [helped by one volunteer to learn] how to raise more crops on their land? Or the development consequence of twelve mothers who understand that they must boil water before giving it to their babies to drink? Or the cost-benefit impact of immunizing twenty children?"[22] John Dellenback chose to downplay the importance of 'things accomplished' to avoid defending the assertion that the Peace Corps was effective as a development agency. He wrote that the "real magic was not in the physical things accomplished, however welcome and helpful they were. The real magic was in the influence of the service itself—both upon the served and the servers."[23] Each of these comments is completely valid—the benefits are hard to measure and the personal nature of Peace Corps service is important—but each is also unnecessarily modest in assessing the agency's effect on Third World development.

The problem many analysts encounter is that they do not know how to sum up the *individual* experiences of 150,000 volunteers, admittedly a difficult—if not impossible—task. But there is an alternative: Measure the impact of the *institutional* Peace Corps. Using this approach the Peace Corps can lay claim to valid achievements in what economists like to call the *macro* level of development. (By macro level they mean the general aspects of development such as those which concern Rostow and other economists. Macro stands in contrast to *micro* development, which deals with the specific aspects of the process such as changing the way individual farmers, entrepreneurs, and homemakers do their work.)

At the macro level the Peace Corps has made two important contributions: First, it has increased the body of knowledge that informs the development process and, second, it has created a cadre of development professionals working in the Third World. With respect to the first of these it is important to understand that turning concept into practice is much more difficult than developing the concept in the first place. And it is in the conversion of theory into practice that the Peace Corps has made its contribution. The real-life experience of tens of thousands of Peace Corps volunteers has shown that development only occurs when the lives of ordinary people are improved in terms of the basic needs of life, such as nutrition, health, and hope for the future. Without such an improvement, all of the steel mills, superhighways, hydroelectric dams, and high-tech medical centers that can be built are worth little. This is the lesson that the Peace Corps has taught the development community.

As McPherson said, "The Peace Corps approach has remained consistent—local, low-cost solutions to local problems, direct assistance to the neediest, and direct service in the field. That methodology . . . has dramatically affected the way in which development has been reevaluated and development strategy reformulated. It has come to be recognized as having elements of success lacking in earlier development philosophies."[24]

The Peace Corps was not the sole advocate of this grassroots approach. There were many others as well. Ernst Schumacher, as mentioned above, did much to spread the message in *Small Is Beautiful*, which quickly became the bible for many in the development field. His was a low-tech world that relied on finding solutions to common problems that were practical and affordable in the local context. Juan Flavier and the Philippine Rural Reconstruction Movement (PRRM) had been engaged in rural development of this sort for more than a decade before the arrival of Peace Corps and its New Directions. PRRM sent young men and women to live in the barrio and improve the lives of its residents by introducing development projects that were simple, economical, practical, and duplicable.[25] The movement traced its roots to the teachings of Dr. James Yen, a Chinese rural development specialist. When Yen was forced to flee China in the late 1940s, he continued his crusade for the improvement of rural living conditions in the Philippines and elsewhere. Yen believed that the four basic problems facing the rural masses were illiteracy, disease, poverty, and civic inertia. He devoted his long life to overcoming these barriers, as did the PRRM. The Peace Corps's contribution was to expand this approach and send thousands of volunteers into scores of countries.

In time the Peace Corps also came to realize that it was the custodian of accumulated wisdom. Beginning in the late 1970s it gathered materials covering nearly the entire range of Peace Corps activities in the field, organized them into a usable collection, and made them available to staff and volunteers. Initially, the material was used primarily by the Peace Corps, but in time its existence became more widely known, and other agencies, private donor organizations, and Third World governments began to benefit from it.[26]

An example of how this transfer of knowledge worked involved a New Directions program in the Philippines. Group 49, as the first of the fisheries volunteers in-country were known, arrived in mid-1972. Their primary program objective was to increase the production level of existing fishponds and to introduce the concepts of aquaculture to other farmers. The program's potential was indicated by the fact that modern fish-growing methodologies could produce more than two thousand pounds of fish per acre annually, whereas Philippine fish farmers were producing only three hundred pounds. The initial training went well, the government provided strong support, and solid results were produced almost at once. As one of the volunteers in the program wrote in 1973, "After working with cooperating fishpond operators for only two months, I have already seen some significant improvements through the introduction of very basic fertilization and other management techniques."[27] Group 49 and its successor projects learned how to take the work of academic and professional fisheries experts and convert it into practical advice for local farmers. These volunteers had unusually productive tours, and a number of them have gone on to become prominent in the field of aquaculture.

But the story does not end there. One Group 49 veteran, Marilyn Chakroff, was hired by Peace Corps to write a fisheries training manual for future fisheries programs based on the lessons she and her colleagues had learned. *Freshwater Fish Pond Culture and Management* made its way to the United Nations Food and Agriculture Organization in Rome. The FAO asked Chakroff to write several more papers for its use. In 1982 Chakroff, who ten years earlier had been a fledgling Peace Corps fisheries volunteer, was sent to Malaysia by the FAO to oversee fisheries extension work in Southeast Asia. In a decade the experiences of volunteers in the Philippines, supplemented by the experiences of fisheries volunteers in other countries, had become part of the body of knowledge that enabled the United Nations to address more effectively food and agricultural concerns in the Third World.

The other major Peace Corps contribution to macro-level economic and social development has been its role in providing the formative international development experience for a number of experts and professionals in the field. As discussed above, hundreds of former staff and volunteers have joined the USAID and State Department rolls. Others work for United Nations agencies; for universities conducting research in the Third World; for private philanthropic agencies such as CARE, Save the Children, and Oxfam; for the World Bank, the Asian Development Bank, and a host of other public and private institutions that cumulatively make up the international development community. Based on an informal survey of 250 former volunteers and staff members from the 1970s in the Philippines, at least eighteen are involved in international development work. If this proportion is even directionally correct, it suggests that there is a considerable force of perhaps seven thousand to ten thousand former volunteers who have dedicated their professional lives to completing the task they began in the Peace Corps.[28] As one of them—also an alumnus of Group 49 in the Philippines—said, "I learned [in the Peace Corps] the art of cultural sensitivity which enables me to perform my job [with the United Nations' FAO] in virtually any country. I feel I know when to speak and when not to. And my ability to deal with people at any level makes it much easier to provide the technical expertise which has become my trade. . . . We listen to each other, exchange ideas [and] solutions to problems, and take corrective action. I would not trade what I am doing now for anything else in the world. These are not boastful comments or words of arrogance, but rather the way I feel in undertaking my work. . . . I owe where I am today to my three years in the Peace Corps."[29]

Beyond these achievements at the macro level, there are literally tens of thousands of examples showing how the Peace Corps made a difference at the micro level. Volunteers have been the catalysts for changing the way people farm, the way they feed their children, the way they care for their health, the way they earn their living, and the way their governments deliver services. The difference can be as simple as causing "the office [to work] a little more efficiently," as one volunteer modestly claimed, or as meaningful as a crafts production and marketing project started in the 1970s that "is STILL going on in the Philippines [in 1993]," as another proudly reported.[30]

A sampling of the anecdotal evidence from a few years in one country would include the stories of the volunteers who developed a market in Manila for a highland barrio's cabbages, thus bringing galvanized iron roofs to people accustomed to making do with thatched roofs;[31] started a pig- and chicken-raising cooperative that tripled the income of its twenty-eight members;[32] helped save from extinction an exotic specie of eagle, originally called the monkey-eating eagle but now renamed the Philippine eagle;[33] and brought dramatic improvements in the awareness and practice of good health habits in one rural province.[34] The list could go on at some length and still not give adequate recognition to those whose work made a difference. The Peace Corps files in Washington contain hundreds, if not thousands, of reports collected over the years of individual volunteer achievements. Not surprisingly, given the fact that these reports were often used for advocacy purposes, they emphasize only the positive aspects of volunteer service. Lacking is an equally accurate description of the frustrations, failures, hardships, cultural barriers, health concerns, job problems, and periods of depression and loneliness. Yet all of the reports that came from the Philippines during the early 1970s are generally accurate with respect to volunteer accomplishments.

Did the Peace Corps make a difference? The answer must be a resounding yes. First, the Peace Corps experience changed those who were part of it, and they in turn have changed America. The country is different now than it would have been in the absence of the agency. This can be seen in the greater sense of interrelatedness of the world's peoples, in a more informed understanding of the reasons the United States cannot ignore the plight of the Third World; in the increase in tolerance and the acceptance of differences both at home and abroad. Through the Peace Corps the willingness of the people of the United States to help others in need has been affirmed and strengthened.

At the same time the American image in the Third World has been softened, humanized, and made more representative of the country at its best. Volunteers have shown by the way they lived that they respected the local culture and willingly made it part of their own lives. They dispelled the notion that Americans were some sort of people set apart, interested only in power, profits, and play.

Finally, the Peace Corps has made a difference in the way development is practiced and in the way that many in the Third World live their lives. One must be careful not to exaggerate these accomplishments, however, because the job is far from complete. Some progress has been made, but much more is needed. The Peace Corps has proved that it has a role to play, along with the legions of other public and private institutions active in the effort. And this role need not be limited to continuing its good works in the cross-cultural arena. The organization can also confidently assert its role as an agent of development, secure in the knowledge that it has, indeed, made a difference.

Notes

1 The End of the Beginning

1. Halberstam, *The Fifties*, x.
2. Alan Guskin, "Passing the Torch," in *Making a Difference,* ed. Viorst, 27.
3. See, e.g., Whyte, *Organization Man;* Packard, *Hidden Persuaders;* Wilson, *Man in the Gray Flannel Suit;* and Gans, *The Levittowners.*
4. Steigerwald, *The Sixties and the End of Modern America,* 6.
5. *Life,* 28 December 1959, 36.
6. See Wofford, *Of Kennedys and Kings,* 244-48.
7. Joseph H. Blatchford, interview with author, 30 November 1994. Blatchford reports that he was contacted in 1960 by the Nixon campaign to comment upon the idea of a Peace Corps–type program. See also Wofford, *Of Kennedys and Kings,* 249.
8. Wofford, *Of Kennedys and Kings,* 247.
9. Guskin, "Passing the Torch," 26.
10. Wofford, *Of Kennedys and Kings,* 250.
11. Ibid., 281.
12. Redmon, *Come as You Are,* 157.
13. Fuchs, *Those Peculiar Americans,* 5.
14. Lowther and Lucas, *Keeping Kennedy's Promise,* 6-7. Although I know of no research on this subject, my guess is that Shriver was the only Peace Corps director whose name was familiar to more than a few volunteers in the field in the entire history of the organization. Volunteers simply were not interested in what happened in Washington.
15. The story of the bureaucratic struggle for independence is told in Rice, *Bold Experiment,* 60-67; Wofford, *Of Kennedys and Kings,* 262-66; and Redmon, *Come as You Are,* 38-42.
16. "Peace Corps Wins Fight for Autonomy," *New York Times,* 4 May 1961, 1.
17. President Kennedy signed Executive Order 10924 on 1 March 1961, thus giving the organization authority and money to operate.
18. Rice, *Bold Experiment,* 74-89; Wofford, *Of Kennedys and Kings,* 266-68.
19. It was with no little satisfaction that I watched his fall from grace later in the decade. Passman was indicted in 1977 on charges of bribery, conspiracy, and income tax evasion following an investigation into his dealings with a Korean businessman. The Korean testified that he had paid Passman to intercede for him at the Department of Agriculture with respect to some lucrative contracts to sell American rice to the Korean government. In fairness it should be said that a jury in Passman's hometown— the trial had been moved to that locale because of Passman's alleged failing health—

found him not guilty of all charges. But, as a result of the preceding furor, he was by then gone from the national scene.

20. Rice, *Bold Experiment*, 84.

21. See Fuchs, *Those Peculiar Americans*, chap. 2, for a discussion of the problems that result from placing volunteers in nonjobs.

22. Ashabranner, *A Moment in History*, 377.

23. Peace Corps Act, sec. 5 (a) and sec. 6.

24. See Wofford, *Of Kennedys and Kings*, 252-62; Lowther and Lucas, *Keeping Kennedy's Promise*, 21-23.

25. See Wofford, *Of Kennedys and Kings*, 252-54; Rice, *Bold Experiment*, 39-43.

26. Fuchs, *Those Peculiar Americans*, 3.

27. See Redmon, *Come as You Are*, 135-55, for an entertaining account of what traveling with Shriver was like. Wofford, *Of Kennedys and Kings*, 268-74, provides an account of some of the real challenges facing Shriver as the Peace Corps tried to enlist host countries in the program.

28. Wofford, *Of Kennedys and Kings*, 271-74.

29. Amin, *Peace Corps in Cameroon*, chap. 2.

30. Rice, *Bold Experiment*, 157-67.

31. Wofford, *Of Kennedys and Kings*, 275.

32. Many of the volunteer success stories chosen for public relations purposes told of classroom teachers who started poultry projects, health clinics, school gardens, and community centers in their spare time.

33. Michelmore's unhappy experience and Peace Corps's excessive reaction to it is told in Redmon, *Come as You Are*, 118-28.

34. Rice, *Bold Experiment*, 85-88.

35. Manchester, *The Glory and the Dream*, 906-7.

36. Leuchtenburg, *Great Age of Change*, 158.

37. Rice, *Bold Experiment*, 162.

38. Lowther and Lucas, *Keeping Kennedy's Promise*, 8.

39. Wofford, *Of Kennedys and Kings*, 298-99.

40. Redmon, *Come as You Are*, 399-403; Lowther and Lucas, *Keeping Kennedy's Promise*, 8-9.

41. James McClure, "A Conservative Institution," in *Making a Difference*, ed. Viorst, 202.

42. Lowther and Lucas, *Keeping Kennedy's Promise*, 11.

43. The sad story of Johnson's rejection of his role in the founding of the Peace Corps and his rejection of Bill Moyers is told in Wofford, *Of Kennedys and Kings*, 334-35.

44. The story of the Peace Corps's woeful handling of the Bruce Murray episode is told in Schwarz, *What You Can Do for Your Country*, 101-11.

45. Blatchford, interview with author, 30 November 1994. Blatchford was director at the time. He reports that he worked through the weekend to keep his more aggressive administration colleagues from sending in the police to "bust some heads." In the end he persuaded the CRV to leave quietly, and the occupation was over.

46. Schwarz, *What You Can Do*, 137.

47. Fuchs, *Those Peculiar Americans*, chap. 2.

48. Lowther and Lucas, *Keeping Kennedy's Promise*, 54, 79.

49. Warren Wiggins, "The Benefits," in *Making a Difference*, ed. Viorst, 72. Wiggins was the deputy director of the Peace Corps in its early years and during that time often filled the role of acting Peace Corps director.

50. Charles Peters, as quoted in Redmon, *Come as You Are*, 205.

51. Kluge, *Edge of Paradise*, 19.

52. Dina Kageler, letter to author, 13 September 1993.

53. Lowther and Lucas, *Keeping Kennedy's Promise*, 9-10.

54. Jack Vaughn, "Now We Are Seven," *Saturday Review*, 6 January 1968, 21-23. The article points out that training has been improved, former volunteers have been hired as trainers and staff members, more attention has been paid to job development, and some of the program decision making has been decentralized.

55. Caroline Ramsay, "The Peace Corps Revisited," master's thesis, Goddard College, 1975, 10. A copy of the thesis is in the Peace Corps Archives, Washington.

56. See "Blatchford takes office" and "Eyeing changes in the Peace Corps" in *Peace Corps Volunteer*, June 1969, 2-5, for a brief account of his initial activities and plans. Copies are available in the Peace Corps Archives, Washington.

57. Leuchtenburg, *Great Age of Change*, 136-37.

58. See "ACCIÓN Speaks Louder Than Words," *Readers' Digest*, September 1962, for an account of Blatchford's role in founding the organization and examples of the work that ACCIÓN volunteers did. See also William Bulkeley, "Joe Blatchford: Man in the Middle," *Wall Street Journal*, 13 September 1971.

59. Blatchford, interview with author, 30 November 1994; Wofford, *Of Kennedys and Kings*, 243.

60. "Hopeful Head of the Peace Corps," *New York Times*, 15 January 1971, 22.

61. Blatchford, interview with author, 30 November 1994.

62. Schwarz, *What You Can Do*, 158.

63. Haldeman, *Diaries*, 181, 291.

64. Drew, "Reports: Washington," 7.

65. "Blatchford takes office," *Peace Corps Volunteer*, June 1969, 2.

66. See "Fredericksburg: Meeting of Minds—Banging of Heads," *Peace Corps Volunteer*, November 1969, 2-9, for a full account of the positive and negative responses voiced at the conference, comments ranging from those indicating a complete lack of trust in the new director to those expressing relief that the existing problems were at long last finally being addressed.

67. Blatchford, telephone conversation with author, 13 February 1995.

68. See Schwarz, *What You Can Do*, 160-62.

69. William Haddad, as quoted in Redmon, *Come as You Are*, 10.

70. Lowther and Lucas, *Keeping Kennedy's Promise*, 10.

71. Blatchford, letter to author, 15 November 1994. A report of the House of Representatives Committee on Foreign Affairs, 10 February 1973, used a similar phrase, "realistic and pragmatic ex-businessman," to describe a country director involved in implementing Blatchford's new program. See also Ronald G. Shafer, "Peace Corps Recruits Business Executives to Manage Programs," *Wall Street Journal*, 27 April 1970, 1.

72. Terrence Smith, "93 in Peace Corps Facing Dismissal," *New York Times*, 15 November 1971, 1.

73. See Redmon, *Come as You Are*, 129-31, for an account of how the policy was developed.

74. Perry Letson, "In, Up, and Out," *RPCV Writers and Readers*, March 1995, 13.

75. Frederick A. Kalhammer, "Peace Corps Direction," letter to editor, *Washington Post*, 29 September 1969.

76. Blatchford, interview with author, 30 November 1994.

77. Unnamed Peace Corps staff veteran quoted in Smith, "93 in Peace Corps Facing Dismissal."

78. Blatchford, interview with author, 30 November 1994. Quotation from "Frank Spokesman in Curious Company," *Kansas City Star*, 24 December 1969.

79. Drew, "Reports: Washington," 9.

80. The Shriver comment was recorded in Ramsay, 11; See Lowther and Lucas, *Keeping Kennedy's Promise*, 14, for their comments; Richey is in Mike McKinney, "Peace Corps Rebounding after Discouraging Years," *Louisville Courier-Journal*, 11 July 1971. See also Drew, "Reports: Washington," 7, who claimed that "all of this has been tried before" and implied that it could not work. See also Schwimmer and Warren, eds., *Anthropology and the Peace Corps*, 8.

81. The best complete statement of New Directions is contained in Joseph H. Blatchford, "The Peace Corps: Making It in the Seventies," *Foreign Affairs*, October 1970, 122-35.

82. Many years later Blatchford received a call from the foreign minister of an African country who was in Washington on an official visit. The foreign minister asked if he could come by to express his personal thanks to Blatchford for starting him out on the path that led to his present position. The foreign minister had been one of the first host country nationals hired under New Directions to fill key Peace Corps staff positions, and this had eventually led him to a career in his country's foreign service.

83. Congressman Wayne Hays of Ohio, as quoted in Robert S. Allen and John A. Goldsmith, "Peace Corps 'Import' Stirs Protest," *Philadelphia News*, 4 October 1969.

84. Peace Corps Act, sec. 10 (a) 1.

85. Wofford, *Of Kennedys and Kings*, 301, reports that of the returned volunteers in 1965 about half went on to graduate school. Most of the rest were working in education, government, business, and the professions.

86. Blatchford, "Making It in the Seventies," 131-32.

87. The first quotation is from Drew, "Reports: Washington," 8, and the second from Deborah Jones, "Superiority Complex," letter to the editor, *Peace Corps Volunteer*, May 1969.

88. Drew, "Reports: Washington," 8.

89. See, e.g., "The Peace Corps Matures," editorial, *Washington Star*, 1 November 1969; and Don Wolfensberger, "'Nixonized' Peace Corps," letter to the editor, *Evening Star* (Washington), 19 June 1970, A10.

90. The quotation comes from the citation accompanying the Golden Harvest Award which was given to the Peace Corps in the Philippines by the Department of Agriculture and Natural Resources in May 1974.

2 The Call of Service

1. See Jonas, *On Doing Good*, 3, for a discussion of how doing good has come to be associated with "an army of self-righteous busybodies intent on reshaping society in their own image" and of the difficulties in finding a replacement terminology that recaptures the original benevolent meaning of the phrase.

2. Not everyone would agree that the sixties started with Kennedy's death. Steigerwald, *The Sixties and the End of Modern America*, 1, for example, places its beginning as the date of Kennedy's inaugural address because it challenged the American people in a way that was very different from that to which they were accustomed. He ends the period with Nixon's resignation in 1974, although he probably would accept, as would I, the notion that the period has never completely ended.

3. Henry Hewes, "The Theatre," *Saturday Review*, 13 January 1968, 95.

4. Holis Alpert, "SR Goes to the Movies," *Saturday Review*, 8 July 1967, 39.

5. "Cinema," *Time*, 30 June 1967, 73.

6. See Steigerwald, *The Sixties and the End of Modern America*, 62-64, for a brief account of the rise and fall of the Black Panther movement in the late 1960s.

7. Schwarz, *What You Can Do*, 162.

8. Reeves, *Politics of the Peace Corps*, 157-58.

9. The quotation is from William Shakespeare's *Macbeth*, Act 5, Scene 5. A fuller quote reads, "Life's but a walking shadow, a poor player that struts and frets his hour upon the stage and then is heard no more. It is a tale told by an idiot, full of sound and fury, signifying nothing."

10. For many years PC/W was at 806 Connecticut Avenue, a short distance from the entrance to Lafayette Park and very close to the White House. The agency is now located in offices about a half mile away on K Street.

11. Kenneth MacLeish, "Help for Philippine Tribes in Trouble," *National Geographic*, August 1971, 220.

12. See Wofford, *Of Kennedys and Kings*, 279-80, for a discussion of the decision to keep the Peace Corps and the CIA widely separated.

13. See Redmon, *Come as You Are*, 135-55.

14. Catherine Johnson, letter to author, 16 July 1993.

15. "Grenades Kill Ten at Manila Rally," *New York Times*, 22 August 1971, 7.

16. Pattie Paxton Hewitt, memoir, ca. 1942, Schlesinger Library, Radcliffe College, Cambridge, Mass., File 86-M73, 3.

17. Mary Searles, letter to "Dear Friends," 15 September 1971, author's files.

3 To Hurl a Brick or Kiss His Hand

1. Leroy Hollenbeck, letter to author, 30 March 1994.

2. Guerrero Nakpil, *A Question of Identity*, 82.

3. Theodore Friend, "Philippine-American Tension in History," in *Crisis in the Philippines: The Marcos Era and Beyond*, ed. John Bresnan, 3.

4. See Karnow, *In Our Image*; Bain, *Sitting in Darkness*; Bonner, *Waltzing with a Dictator*; Constantino, *A History of the Philippines*; Gates, *Schoolbooks and Krags*; Lightfoot, *The Philippines: Nations of the Modern World*; Stanley, ed., *Reappraising an Empire*; Stanley, ed., *A Nation in the Making*; Steinberg, *The Philippines: A Singular and a Plural Place*. Also see relevant chapters in Leech, *In the Days of McKinley*; Manchester, *American Caesar*.

5. See Leech, *In the Days of McKinley*, 156-69, for a brief account of Roosevelt's tenure as an assistant secretary of the Navy and his decision to send Dewey's squadron to the Philippines.

6. Lightfoot, *The Philippines*, 111-12.

7. Leech, *In the Days of McKinley*, 285-89.

8. Philinda Rand Anglemyer, letter home, ca. 1902, file 86-74, folder 20, Schlesinger Library, Radcliffe College, Cambridge, Mass.

9. Gates, *Schoolbooks and Krags*, 188.

10. Glen A. May, "Private Pressler and Sergeant Vegara," in *A Nation in the Making*, ed. Stanley, 35-48, 56.

11. Bain, *Sitting in Darkness*, 87.

12. Anglemyer, folder 20. A slightly different version of the song is contained in Karnow, *In Our Image*, 155.

13. See Bain, *Sitting in Darkness*, for a highly readable and entertaining account of Aguinaldo's capture by Funston, esp. chap. 14.

14. Constantino, *A History of the Philippines*, 230.

15. May, "Private Pressler and Sergeant Vegara," 52-60.

16. Constantino, *A History of the Philippines*, 229.

17. Leech, *In the Days of McKinley*, 345.

18. Karnow, *In Our Image*, 170, 174.

19. Leech, *In the Days of McKinley*, 345.

20. Patti Paxton Hewitt, memoir, ca. 1942, Schlesinger Library, Radcliffe College, Cambridge, Mass. file 86-M73, 1.

21. See Pecson and Racelis, eds., *Tales of the American Teachers in the Philippines*, 8, for a chart that tracks the gradual decline of American teachers in the Philippine school system as the number of Filipino teachers rose.

22. Julian Encarnación, "From the Days of the Lakans to the Coming of the Transport Thomas," ibid., 13, puts the number at 540. Hewitt, one of the teachers aboard the *Thomas*, counted 598.

23. The *Thomas* arrived in Manila on 13 August 1901. It was an army transport ship that ferried troops—and the occasional load of teachers—from the American West to the Philippines. Small groups of teachers had arrived earlier in 1901—aboard the USTS *Sheridan* in June and the USTS *Buford* on 1 August. Philinda Rand sailed aboard the latter.

24. Around the turn of the century, many women found the courage to break free. Among Rand's classmates at Radcliffe College who did this was Alice Spencer Geddes, who went off to do good in the Appalachian region of Kentucky. The college she founded there continues to provide a liberal arts education for Appalachian students and now bears its founder's married name: Alice Lloyd College. The woman's story is told in Searles, *A College for Appalachia: Alice Lloyd on Caney Creek*.

25. Anglemyer, "Summary written by PRA," ca. 1945, folder 20.

26. Anglemyer, "My dear Kathie," 16 February 1902, folder 17.

27. Guerrero Nakpil, *A Question of Identity*, 145.

28. The legislation, known as the Jones Act, was signed into law by President Wilson in August 1916.

29. Karnow, *In Our Image*, 174, 32.

30. Steinberg, *The Philippines*, 70.

31. Constantino, *A History of the Philippines*, 292.

32. Wolfert, *American Guerrilla in the Philippines*, 76-77.

33. Manchester, *American Caesar*, 271.

34. Steinberg, *The Philippines*, 107.

35. See Manchester, *American Caesar*, 413-20, for a full account of the tragedy that befell Manila and its citizens in the early months of 1945.

36. Guerrero Nakpil, *A Question of Identity*, 204-5.

37. Alan B. Brainerd, letter to author, 17 June 1993.

38. Guerrero Nakpil, *A Question of Identity*, 206.

39. See Karnow, *In Our Image*, 336-55, for a good summary of the Huk rebellion and the American role in putting it down.

40. Bresnan, ed., *Crisis in the Philippines*, 4.

41. Guerrero Nakpil, *A Question of Identity*, 54.

42. Michael McQuestion, "Dear Prospective Volunteer," in *Volunteer Life Styles*. A copy is in the Philippines files, Peace Corps Archives, Washington.

4 New Directions in the Philippines

1. Richard W. Soderberg, letter to author, 11 January 1993.

2. Michael Baffery, letter to author, 6 July 1993.

3. Arthur Goodfriend, *The Dimmed Ideal: The Peace Corps/Philippines after 20 Years*, 25 September 1981, Peace Corps Archives, Washington, 27.

4. David Riesman, foreword, in Fuchs, *Those Peculiar Americans*, xvii.

5. Fuchs, ibid., 3, 217-18.

6. Ibid., 219.

7. Ibid., 218-19.

8. It was with great sadness that we closed the training center in 1973 when it became obvious that it was no longer suitable for training volunteers in noneducation programs and too costly to maintain for occasional use as a language training site.

9. See Lightfoot, *The Philippines*, chap. 15, esp. 144-47, for a good summary of the economic situation in the Philippines following the end of World War II.

10. Rostow, *Process of Economic Growth*, 298-99n.

11. Wilfred Malenbaum, "Book Reviews," *Annals of the American Academy of Political and Social Science* 333 (January 1961): 164.

12. Critics in later years have not been kind to Rostow's economic theories. They find fault with his sweeping generalizations, his use of scanty data, his ability to overlook contradictory evidence, and his failure to take political and cultural factors into account. One of the most comprehensive examinations of the way Rostow's theories worked out in the Philippines is Boyce, *The Philippines: The Political Economy of Growth and Impoverishment in the Marcos Era*. Rostow's reputation as an economic historian has also suffered, perhaps unfairly, because of his prominent role as a Vietnam War hawk during the Kennedy and Johnson administrations. On the latter point see the numerous references to Rostow in Halberstam, *The Best and the Brightest*.

13. See, for example, Boyce, *The Philippines*, chap. 3, for an extensive account of the Green Revolution in the Philippines and the controversy that now exists in some circles concerning the merits of miracle rice.

14. See Lester R. Brown, "Peace Corps Faculty Paper No. 7," in *The Green Revolution: The Role of the Volunteer as a Manpower Link*, for an excellent description of the new variety of rice and a technical explanation of how it achieved its improved productivity.

15. The composition of the Peace Corps program in the Philippines in 1973 is included in J. Herrera, "35 Peace Corps Volunteers Arrive Today to Assist in Masagana 99 Rice Drive," *Business Day* (Manila), 6 August 1973, 24.

16. The project to save the monkey-eating eagle is discussed in some depth in *National Geographic*, June 1981, 847-56. See also "MSU, UM Alums End Peace Corps Study of Monkey-Eating Eagles in Philippines," *Great Falls Tribune* (Montana), 21 December 1975, 3.

17. "Peace Corps Changing Task," editorial, *Bulletin Today* (Manila), 6 August 1973, 6.

18. "Peace Corps Volunteers Share 30 Years of Illinois Farm Know-How with Farmers in the Philippines," in *ACTION NEWS* (publicity release), ca. 1973, Peace Corps Archives, Washington.

19. Lloyd J. Johnson, "To Whom It May Concern," in Barry Devine, untitled collection of volunteer letters, 1 September 1973, Peace Corps Archives, Washington.

20. "Former Ohio Poultry Farmer, Atlanta Market Reporter Helps Filipinos Increase Livestock, Poultry Production," in *ACTION NEWS* (publicity release), ca. 1973, Peace Corps Archives, Washington.

21. "Former Marquette Mayor, Now a Peace Corps Volunteer, Helps Filipino Farmers Get a Better Price for Produce," in *ACTION NEWS* (publicity release), ca. 1973, Peace Corps Archives, Washington.

22. "New Plymouth, Idaho, Farm Couple Serve as Peace Corps Volunteers in the Philippines," in *ACTION NEWS* (publicity release), ca. 1973, Peace Corps Archives, Washington.

23. Pamela Tripp Melby, memorandum to Craig Gill, 18 January 1996, copy in author's possession.

24. Donald Hess, letter to author, 5 January 1995.

25. See Lowther and Lucas, *Keeping Kennedy's Promise*, 11, 27, 28, 35, 47, 50, 63, 72, chap. 6, 121-24.

26. Rice, *Bold Experiment*, 164.

27. Blatchford, "New Policies: Untie Some Apron Strings," *Peace Corps Volunteer*, June 1969, 7-8. Peace Corps Archives, Washington.

28. The budget crisis of 1971 and early 1972 was the most serious of the many budget crises to affect the agency in its first three decades. Congress had moved to cut the funds available for the fiscal year then more than six months old, meaning that the Peace Corps administration had few options other than to bring volunteers home and close programs. Because volunteers in the Philippines and other Southeast Asian countries were so far from the United States and the cost of plane tickets so much more than the savings that could be realized by eliminating volunteer living allowances, these programs were not in danger. The same could not be said for programs in the rest of the world. See, e.g., Skelton, *Volunteering in Ethiopia*, chap. 16. Skelton makes frequent mention of the uncertainty and harm caused in Ethiopia by the constant rumor that the whole program would be canceled and the volunteers sent home. This subject is dealt with more completely in chap. 8.

29. Peace Corps Act, sec. 5(a), and sec. 6.

30. Fuchs, *Those Peculiar Americans*, 228-31.

31. Blatchford, interview with author, 30 November 1994.

32. See, e.g., Lowther and Lucas, *Keeping Kennedy's Promise*, 137.

33. Searles, letter to Phil Waddington, 29 December 1972, Peace Corps Archives, Washington.

34. Lowther and Lucas, *Keeping Kennedy's Promise*, 99; Fuchs, *Those Peculiar Americans*, 131.

35. Charles Peters, "Tilting at Windmills," *Washington Monthly*, December 1995, 27.

36. See Amin, *Peace Corps in Cameroon*, chap. 4, for an excellent description of the early Peace Corps approach to training. The quotations are from p. 86.

37. Rice, *Bold Experiment*, 165.

38. Donald Hess, letter to author, 5 January 1995.

39. Searles, letter to Waddington, 29 December 1972.

40. See, e.g., Pascarella and Terenzini, *How College Affects Students*, 604, where they conclude, "The environmental factors that maximize . . . educational attainment include a peer culture in which students develop close on-campus friendships, participate frequently in college-sponsored activities, and perceive their college to be highly concerned about the individual student, as well as a college emphasis on supportive services (including advising, orientation . . . [and] survival skills)."

41. Blatchford, "New Policies: Untie Some Apron Strings," 8.

42. Blatchford, "The Peace Corps: Making It in the Seventies," 129.

43. President Marcos made a brief visit to a reception hosted by the Philippine Amateur Athletic Foundation, with whom fifteen volunteer physical education specialists worked, and the secretary of the foundation, Col. Arsenio de Borja, introduced me to him.

44. "Philippine Army on Alert for Elections Tomorrow," *New York Times*, 7 November 1971, 36.

45. Sue Jones, "To All Possible Trainees," in Devine, untitled letters.

46. Day, *The Philippines*, 16.

47. See Karnow, *In Our Image*, chap. 13, and Bonner, *Waltzing with a Dictator*, 107-37, for good summaries of the events leading up to the declaration of martial law and the role of the United States in it.

48. Bonner, *Waltzing*, 127, 109-11.

49. Christopher Newhall, "Hi," in *Volunteer Life Styles*, 5.

50. Dana J. Lefstad, "To Prospective Philippine Volunteers," in Devine, unpublished letters.

51. Abner O. Andrew, "United States Peace Corps Volunteer," in Devine.

52. Alan B. Brainerd, letter to author, 17 June 1993.

53. The telegram was sent 5 December 1972, signed by Dominador Racho. Copy in author's files.

54. See Sullivan, *Obbligato, 1939-1979*, for an entertaining account of Sullivan's foreign service career, including his initial expectation that he would initiate diplomatic relations with the North Vietnamese from his home base in Manila.

55. See Bonner, *Walzing*, 63-66, for a brief account of Nixon's 1969 visit to Manila.

56. Fuchs, *Those Peculiar Americans*, 224.

57. Johnson, "To Whom It May Concern," in Devine.

58. Rona Roberts, letter to author, 2 March 1993. The arrival of this letter, two decades after we last met, triggered a series of events that eventually led to the writing of this book.

59. Johnson, "To Whom It May Concern," in Devine.

60. "U.S. Peace Corps, AID Experts Honored by R.P.," *Stars and Stripes*, 5 May 1974, 1.

61. Packer, *Village of Waiting*, 313-15.

5 When Cultures Collide

1. Rosalina Morales, *An Introduction to Filipino Thought and Action*, ca. 1970, Peace Corps/Philippines files, Peace Corps Archives, Washington, 203.04.

2. Juan Flavier, "How Long-Winded Can You Get?" in *My Friends in the Barrios* (Quezon City: New Day, 1974), 164. His economic and social development theories are explored more fully in chap. 6.

3. Morales, *Filipino Thought*, 203.07.

4. Flavier, "Select Instead of Elect," in *My Friends in the Barrios*, 181-82.

5. Flavier, "Unwritten Law," ibid., 81.

6. Patricia Auflick, letter home, 26 February 1974.

7. Carmen Guerrero Nakpil, *A Question of Identity: Selected Essays* (Manila: Vessel Books, 1973), 69, 71. See also Alfredo Roces and Grace Roces, *Culture Shock!* (Singapore: Times Books International, 1986), 203.

8. Morales, *Filipino Thought*, 203.10.

9. Wilma Casaclang, as quoted in Karl Schoenberger, "Living Off Expatriate Labor," *Los Angeles Times*, 1 August 1994, 1.

10. Flavier, *Doctor to the Barrios*, 129.

11. Flavier, "The Price of Affluence," in *My Friends in the Barrios*, 69-70.

12. Tidwell, *Ponds of Kalambayi*, 83-91; Packer, *Village of Waiting*, 225-28.

13. Byron Lee, letter to author, 10 October 1993; and Byron Lee, "Maka Hiya." The phrase *maka hiya* is usually translated 'without shame,' a concept indicating a very serious breach of accepted standards of conduct.

14. Morales, *Filipino Thought*, 203.12.

15. Roces and Roces, *Culture Shock!* 205.

16. Sister Sylvia McClain to "Dear Stell, Alan, Pat, Barb," 14 December 1971.

17. Flavier, *Doctor to the Barrios*, 93.

18. Patricia Auflick to Mr. and Mrs. J. A. Moore, June 1974.

19. Guerrero Nakpil, *A Question of Identity*, 51.

20. See F. Landa Jocano, "Rethinking Smooth Interpersonal Relations," *Philippine Sociological Review* 14 (October 1966): 282-91, for an interesting but ultimately unconvincing rebuttal to the idea that SIR is a key factor to understanding Filipino society.

21. Roces and Roces, *Culture Shock!* 225.

22. Joe and Pat Richter, "Christmas," *FARMS International Newsletter*, December 1993.

23. Rona Roberts to Mr. and Mrs. L. V. Roberts, 23 May 1975, 4.

24. "Letter from Sister Sylvia McClain to the community," July 1973. The original letter was addressed to "Dear Sister Thomas Aquinas and Sisters" and was copied by one of the recipients and shared with the entire community.

25. Patricia Auflick, letters home.

26. Auflick, letter to author, 31 August 1993.

27. The Philippine Rabbit is one of the many private bus companies that use a motley collection of decrepid, ancient, diesel-smoke-belching converted trucks to convey passengers, freight, and the occasional crate of chickens to the provinces. The Philippine Rabbit Line serves the mountainous region north of Manila.

28. Shaffer, *One Grain of Sand*, 90-91.

29. Abner Andrews, "My Experience Living in a Foreign Country," in Devine, 1 September 1973.

6 The Challenges of Everyday Life

1. Marilyn S. Chakroff, letter to author, 4 January 1994, 3-4.

2. See George Packer, *The Village of Waiting*, chap. 3, for his assessment of his role as an English teacher.

3. John Coyne, as quoted on back cover of Skelton's *Volunteering in Ethiopia*.

4. The Philippines officially counts 7,107 islands, about 2,000 of which are inhabited.

5. Alvin Hower, "Hello everybody," December 1969, Christmas newsletter from Hower in the Philippines to family and friends in the United States. Hower provided a copy from his personal files.

6. Sister Sylvia McClain to "Dear Sisters," 18 October 1970.

7. Rudyard Kipling, "Mandalay," from his *Barrack-Room Ballads*, 1892.

8. Dina Kageler, letter to author, 27 June 1993, 1.

9. In 1995 the Peace Corps estimated that 40 percent of its volunteers worldwide live and work in metropolitan areas.

10. Patricia A. Auflick to Mr. and Mrs. J. A. Moore, 13 September 1973.

11. Rona Roberts to Mr. and Mrs. L. V. Roberts, 2 October 1973.

12. Tidwell, *Ponds of Kalambayi*, 118.

13. Shaffer, *One Grain of Sand*, 57.

14. Ibid., 81.

15. Jens Peters, *Philippines: A Travel Survival Kit*, 87.

16. Rona Roberts to Mr. and Mrs. L. V. Roberts, 4 September 1974.

17. Rona Roberts to Mr. and Mrs. L. V. Roberts, 26 June 1975.

18. Anonymous, as quoted in H. L. Mencken, *A New Dictionary of Quotations*, 322.

19. Paul and Helen Peterson, in Devine.

20. Thomas Lovett, "Life on the Winding Road," in Devine.

21. Joe and Pat Richter, 3.

22. Patricia Auflick to Mr. and Mrs. J. A. Moore, 3 December 1973.

23. Flavier, *My Friends in the Barrios*, 42-43.

24. See Flavier, *Doctor to the Barrios*, 157-69; *My Friends in the Barrios*, 41-66; and *Back to the Barrios*, 14-35, for firsthand accounts of the difficulties encountered by those working to introduce family planning concepts in the Philippines.

25. Vaughn and Lorenne Rundquist, letter to author, 5 August 1993, 1.

26. Dina Kageler, letter to author, 27 June 1993.

27. Angela Wallace, in *Volunteer Life Styles*, 22.

28. Roces and Roces, *Culture Shock!* 212.

29. See Guerrero Nakpil, "Men Are People," in *A Question of Identity*, 114-20, for an amusing, yet accurate, portrayal of Filipino men.

30. Patricia Auflick to Mr. and Mrs. J. A. Moore, 11 September 1973.

31. Auflick to Mr. and Mrs. J. A. Moore, 27 April 1974.

32. Preface, *Peace Corps/Philippines Medical Handbook*, 1 June 1973, Peace Corps/Philippines files, Peace Corps Archives, Washington.

33. During the course of Peace Corps's thirty-five years of existence 225 volunteers have died while in service.

34. The Women of '53 to P. David Searles, 6 December 1972.

35. Rona Roberts, letters home.

36. Fuchs, *Those Peculiar Americans*, 6.

37. Tidwell, *Ponds of Kalambayi*, 27-31.

38. Quoted from a Philippines Peace Corps newsletter, ca. 1970, provided by former PC/P volunteer Alvin Hower.

39. Patricia Auflick, "Happy Birthday, Bing," 31 March 1974.

40. Unsigned postcard, ca. 1974, in author's files.

41. Skelton, *Volunteering in Ethiopia*, 327.

42. Maureen Waters, "To New Volunteers," in *Volunteer Life Styles*, 4.

43. Mark A. Van Steenwyk, "Some Personal Observations on Being a Peace Corps Volunteer," August 1976. Copy enclosed in Van Steenwyk, letter to author, 1 November 1994.

7 New Directions at Work

1. Leroy Hollenbeck, letter to author, 30 March 1994.

2. Ron George, letter to author, undated, 1993.

3. Frank Tuma, "As I start this letter," in Devine.

4. Raney, *Peace Corps's Third Goal*, 13.

5. Bill Moyers, "At Home in the World," in *To Touch the World*, ed. John Coyne et al., 153.

6. Christopher Newhall, "Hi," in *Volunteer Life Styles*, 9.

7. Tony Hart, "Over 30 Years Ago," in *Volunteer Life Styles*, 18, 17.

8. The complete set of materials is available in the Philippines section of the Peace Corps Archives, Washington.

9. Hart, "Over 30 Years Ago," 16.

10. Moyers, "At Home in the World," 167.

11. House of Representatives Committee on Foreign Affairs, *The Peace Corps in the 1970s*, 10.

12. Ibid., 25, 31.

13. Ibid., 29.

14. Terry Deppner, "Dear Prospective PCVs," in Devine.

15. House of Representatives Committee on Foreign Affairs, *The Peace Corps in West Africa*, 7.

16. Skelton, *Volunteering in Ethiopia*, 264-68.

17. Newhall, "Hi," 10.

18. Rona Roberts, letter to author, 2 March 1993.

19. Maureen Waters, "To New Volunteers," in *Volunteer Life Styles*, 3.

20. Kathrin Kudner, "Annual Report," 4 October 1974, 3. A copy of this report is in the Philippines files at the Peace Corps Archives, Washington.

21. Ernst Schumacher popularized the concept of appropriate technology in his book *Small Is Beautiful*.

22. See Boyce, *The Philippines*, chap. 5, for a discussion of the loss of employment opportunities for the rural poor—an unintended consequence of the Green Revolution—as a result of the use of herbicides.

23. See Flavier, *Doctor to the Barrios*, 133, for the three-fourths of deaths estimate.

24. Boyce, *The Philippines*, 52.

25. Flavier, *Doctor to the Barrios*, 44-45.

26. Boyce, *The Philippines*, 8-9 (emphasis in the original).

27. Blatchford, "The Peace Corps: Making It in the Seventies," *Foreign Affairs*, October 1970, 125.

28. House Committee on Foreign Affairs, *Peace Corps in the 1970s*, 23.

29. Rona Roberts, letter to author, 2 March 1993.

30. Rebecca Okie, "To Prospective Volunteers," in *Volunteer Life Styles*, 21.

31. Lester R. Brown, "Peace Corps Faculty Paper No. 7," in *The Green Revolution: The Role of the Volunteer as a Manpower Link*, 5.

32. Barry North, "Upon Arrival," in *Volunteer Life Styles*, 31, 32.

33. Michael McQuestion, "Dear Prospective Volunteer," in *Volunteer Life Styles*, 24.

34. House Committee on Foreign Affairs, *Peace Corps in the 1970s*, 4.

35. Dina Kageler, letter to author, 27 June 1993. Kageler was christened Vivian, but was renamed Dina by the T'boli. She continues to use her T'boli name.

36. Hart, "Over 30 Years Ago," 18.

37. See Schwarz, *What You Can Do*, inside front cover, for this estimate.

38. Ibid., 16.

39. Greg Flakus, "Having Spent 16 Months Here," in *Volunteer Life Styles*, 14.

40. McQuestion, "Dear Prospective Volunteer," 25.

41. Dennis Walters, "Dear Barry," in Devine.

42. Mark A. Van Steenwyk, "Some Personal Observations on Being A Peace Corps Volunteer," August 1976, copy in author's files.

8 Life along the Potomac

1. Fuchs, *Those Peculiar Americans*, 218-21.

2. House of Representatives Committee on Foreign Affairs, *The Peace Corps in West Africa*, xx.

3. See Peace Corps, *Congressional Budget Presentation, Fiscal Year 1996* (Washington: Peace Corps, 1995), 8, for authorizations and appropriations for the Peace Corps for the years 1962-1995.

4. Congressman Hamilton Fish Jr., "Weekly Report from Washington," *Tri-Town News* (Sidney, N.Y.), 7 July 1971.

5. Nixon's speech is reported in Robert B. Semple Jr., "Nixon Proposes Agency to Enlist Service of Youth," *New York Times*, 15 January 1971, 1.

6. "Congressman Myers Reports from Washington," *Saturday Spectator* (Terre Haute, Ind.), 12 June 1971. The vote actually was against a motion that would have killed Nixon's reorganization plan since the reorganization did not require congressional approval. Congress had only the right to veto it.

7. Lowther and Lucas, *Keeping Kennedy's Promise*, 17.

8. Shriver and Mankiewicz, as quoted in Nathan A. Haverstock and Richard C. Schroeder, "In the Name of Efficiency," *Baltimore Sun*, 27 June 1971. Williams, as quoted in Sen. Stuart Symington, "Centralization Regretted," *Sun-Gazette* (Fulton, Mo.), 2 July 1971. "Action Agency Employees to Oppose Blatchford," *Evening Star* (Washington), 29 July 1971, A3.

9. "New Volunteer Agency Made Official by Nixon," *New York Times*, 2 July 1971.

10. Shriver, as quoted in Schwarz, *What You Can Do*, 162.

11. John Dellenback, "The Future," in *Making a Difference*, ed. Viorst, 211.

12. Blatchford left ACTION in December 1972 having tendered his resignation shortly after the election when Nixon requested *pro forma* resignations from all of his appointees. At the time it was said that Blatchford left to explore the possibilities for elective office in California. In recent interviews with the author he has explained that another reason for leaving was a growing uneasiness about the direction Nixon's second term would take.

13. Linda Rose, "Here's Whatever Happened to Vista [*sic*]," *Norwalk Hour* (Norwalk, Conn.), 11 August 1971. This article also contains a brief summary of Balzano's background and education.

14. Charles Colson was later convicted and sent to jail for his part in the Watergate affair. Balzano was interviewed repeatedly by Watergate investigators but was never charged with any wrongdoing.

15. See Schwarz, *What You Can Do*, 179-87, for a summary of the struggle between Sam Brown and Peace Corps director Carolyn Payton. In doing so, however, remember that Schwarz's account used mostly Washington-based sources and therefore quite likely exaggerates the negative impact it had on the *real* Peace Corps, i.e., the Peace Corps in the field.

16. Senator Symington, "Centralization Regretted," *Sun-Gazette* (Fulton, Mo.), 2 July 1971.

17. The federal fiscal year ran from July 1 until June 30 of the following year until 1976, at which time it was changed to the present system of October 1 until September 30. The situation in which the Peace Corps found itself as a result of the foreign aid dispute is summarized sympathetically in Thomas Oliphant, "Peace Corps being forced to halt recruiting or to leave nations," *Boston Globe*, 28 December 1971, 40.

18. Carl T. Rowan, "The Peace Corps May Be an Innocent Victim," *Evening Star* (Washington), 14 January 1972.

19. Charles E. Claffey, "Slashes Feared as Peace Corps Awaits Funding," *Boston Globe*, 6 February 1972.

20. These headlines represent a small sampling of the many such headlines contained in *ACTION News Digest*, no. 2 (1972): 95-189. The *ACTION News Digest* provided a quarterly survey of newspaper clippings from around the country. The author was provided a copy of a number of issues for the 1969-73 period by Blatchford.

21. Bill Mauldin, "Poor Peace Corps," *New Republic*, 19 February 1972, 7.

22. Terrence Smith, "Nixon Assures Peace Corps of Funds," *New York Times*, 10 March 1972.

23. William Steif, "ACTION Budget a Choice Spot for Some Chopping," *Press-Scimitar* (Memphis), 6 November 1972.

24. Blatchford, interview with author, 30 November 1994.

25. Haldeman, *Diaries*, 181, 291.

26. Blatchford, as reported in Nick Timmesh, "We May Find Ray of Hope in Viet Tragedy," *Evening Tribune* (San Diego), 22 June 1971.

27. See Skelton, *Volunteering in Ethiopia*, 259-64 and 275, for an example of the upset caused in Ethiopia when the volunteers learned that their programs were being threatened by the budget crisis of 1971-72.

28. Searles, speech given at Department of Agriculture and Natural Resources, Quezon City, Philippines, 14 May 1974. Copy in the author's files.

29. An example of this situation is the tragic dilemma that so many erstwhile Vietnam War hawks found themselves in when they began to realize the error of their original positions. When Governor George Romney, e.g., then a candidate for his party's nomination for president, attempted to explain his abandonment of hawkish views, he was laughed out of the race.

30. "Peace Corps Tries to Broaden Base," *Spokesman-Review* (Spokane), 9 October 1969. Don Wolfensberger, "Nixonized Peace Corps," *Evening Star* (Washington), 19 June 1970.

31. The quotations are from a sampling of the hundreds of Peace Corps press releases from the early 1970s contained in the Peace Corps Archives, Washington.

32. "Recommendations of the Committee of the National Academy of Science," Attachment A of memorandum from Acting Deputy Associate Director to Regional Directors, 24 December 1974. Peace Corps Archives, Washington.

33. NANEAP country desk officers to Searles, 5 March 1975, Peace Corps Archives, Washington.

34. Craig Storti, memo to Peace Corps staff, 11 February 1976, Peace Corps Archives, Washington.

35. Dellenback, "The Future," in *Making a Difference*, ed. Viorst, 215.

9 Twenty Years Later

1. Carol Bellamy, letter to the Hon. Jesse Helms, 1 March 1995. The letter, which accompanied the 1996 budget presentation to the Senate, stated that the Peace Corps served in ninety-four countries.

2. Joan Timoney, "A Voice on the Hill," *Peace Corps Times*, winter 1995, 35.

3. In 1995 six former volunteers were serving in the House: Sam Farr (Calif.), Tony P. Hall (Ohio), Thomas Petri (Wisc.), Christopher Shays (Conn.), Mike Ward (Ky.), and James T. Walsh (N.Y.). In a conversation with the author on 13 May 1995,

Congressman Ward of Kentucky described the efforts he and his House colleagues made to change McConnell's plan.

4. Ruppe (1981-88) was followed by Paul Coverdell (1989-91), Elaine L. Chao (1991-92), Carol Bellamy (1993-95), and Mark Gearan (1995–).

5. Carol Bellamy, statement before Subcommittee of Foreign Operations, Committee on Appropriations, House of Representatives, 7 March 1995, 4-5.

6. *Health and Nutrition,* 1994 Peace Corps recruiting pamphlet.

7. See "New Publications from ICE," *Peace Corps Times,* fall 1994, 28-32, for a brief description of the Peace Corps approach to technical support, a list of new titles, and an announcement of the "library in a shoebox."

8. *New York Times Index* for 1962-64, 1972-74, and 1992-94.

9. See *Time,* 29 June 1995; *New York Times,* 22 June 1995, B18.

10. Charles Dambach, president of the National Peace Corps Association, described his organization's effort to influence the selection of President Clinton's second Peace Corps director during a conversation with the author in Washington, 15 June 1995. As it turned out, the administration ignored the suggestions of the NPCA and nominated Mark Gearan. See also "Clinton to Pick Peace Corps Writer to Head Agency?" *RPCV Writers and Readers,* May 1995, for an article speculating that Clinton would nominate Harris Wofford to head the Peace Corps.

11. Jason DeParle, "The Man inside Bill Clinton's Foreign Policy," *New York Times Sunday Magazine,* 20 August 1995, 46.

12. *Peace Corps Fact Sheet* (Washington: Peace Corps Press Office, 1 June 1995).

13. See "A Closer Look at What Peace Corps Volunteers Are Made Of," *Peace Corps Times,* winter 1995, for a breakdown by age of volunteers in the mid-1990s. Twelve percent of the approximately eight thousand volunteers and trainees are forty or older.

14. The breakdown by program area comes from the Peace Corps's *Congressional Budget Presentation, Fiscal Year 1996* (Washington: Peace Corps, 1995), 12-15.

15. John Coyne, "It's a Family Affair," *Peace Corps Times,* winter 1995, 11-12.

16. Barbara Baklini Pabotoy, conversation with author, 23 March 1994.

17. Blatchford, conversation with author, 27 November 1994.

18. Boutrous Boutrous-Ghali, "A New Departure on Development," *Foreign Policy* (spring 1995): 44.

19. James E. Hug, "Health Care: A Planetary View," *America,* 11 December 1993, 8.

20. James O. Jackson, "Off the Screen," *Time,* 17 July 1995, 56.

21. Paul Lewis, "A New World Bank: Consultants to Third World Investors," *New York Times,* 27 April 1995, quoting World Bank president James D. Wolfensohn.

22. See Boyce, *The Philippines,* 2, for data showing the comparative growth and infant mortality rates between 1962 and 1986 for several Asian countries including the Philippines.

23. Barbara Crossette, "The 'Third World' Is Dead, but Spirits Linger," *New York Times,* 13 November 1994, quoting the 1994 report of the United Nations Human Development Index.

24. Federico Mayor, "What Happened to Development?" *UNESCO Courier,* September 1994, 15.

25. M. Peter McPherson, "As a Development Agency," in *Making a Difference,* ed. Viorst, 101.

26. Boyce, *The Philippines,* 9.

27. Among the countries the Peace Corps no longer serves but which had large programs in the 1970s are Korea, Malaysia, Thailand, Iran, Oman, Columbia, Brazil, Peru, and Venezuela.

28. "Peace Corps Cutting Missions," *Messenger-Inquirer* (Owensboro, Ky.), 3 June 1996, 3A.

29. *Congressional Budget Presentation, Fiscal Year 1996*, 3, 21, 143.

30. Thomas L. Friedman, "World Bank at 50 Vows to Do Better," *New York Times*, 24 July 1994, 4, quoting World Bank president Lewis Preston.

31. See, e.g., "World Bank Set to Make Micro-Loans," *Toronto Star*, 17 July 1995.

32. *Congressional Budget Presentation, Fiscal Year 1996*, 5.

33. Bruce Watson, "The New Peace Corps Steppes Out—in Kazakhstan," *Smithsonian* (August 1994): 28.

34. Bellamy, statement, 5, quoting President Nursultan Nazarbayev of Kazakhstan.

35. See Schwarz, *What You Can Do*, 275-86, for a summary of the controversy surrounding the Peace Corps decision to enter former Soviet Bloc countries.

36. The quotations come from the Peace Corps Act, Title 1, sec. 1.

37. Bellamy, statement, 3. Watson provides a good description of the difficulties the Peace Corps had in opening up behind the Iron Curtain in "The New Peace Corps Steppes Out."

38. Fuchs, *Those Peculiar Americans*, 4, 6.

39. John Coyne, "The Perils and Pleasures of Volunteer Training, *Peace Corps Times*, fall 1994, 12.

40. Andrew Lilienthal, as quoted in John Coyne, "It's a Family Affair," *Peace Corps Times*, winter 1995, 12.

41. Watson, "The New Peace Corps Steppes Out," 28.

42. Ibid., 30.

43. Barbara Pabotoy, conversation with author, 3 March 1994.

44. James Scott, as quoted in Coyne, "It's a Family Affair," 12.

45. See Schwarz, *What You Can Do*, chap. 12, for an account of the AIDS problem in the Peace Corps.

46. Suzanne Grelson, as quoted in Jim Smith, "Peace Corps Demise Predicted," *Springfield Daily News* (Mass.), 13 July 1971.

47. J. William Fulbright, as quoted in Willard Edwards, "Peace Corps Stands Turn 180 Degrees," *Chicago Tribune*, 21 September 1971.

48. United Press International, news release UPI-125, 7 April 1972.

49. Ralph Novak, "Does Peace Corps Still Exist?" *Trenton Evening Times*, 27 March 1972.

50. Ibid.

51. See Bonner, *Waltzing with a Dictator*, chap. 7, "Embracing the Conjugal Dictators," and Karnow, *In Our Image*, chap. 13, "Conjugal Autocracy," for an unflattering but accurate portrayal of Imelda Marcos.

52. Steinberg, *The Philippines*, 134. See also Karnow, *In Our Image*, 386, for World Bank data suggesting that the percentage of people living below the poverty line in cities increased from 24 to 40 percent between 1974 and 1980.

53. Boyce, *The Philippines*, 155.

54. See Bonner, *Waltzing*, chaps. 16 and 17, and Karnow, *In Our Image*, chaps. 14 and 15, for detailed accounts of Marcos's fall and the American role in it.

55. Steinberg, *The Philippines*, 166-67.

56. Boyce, *The Philippines*, 277, n. 45, lists four American banks as the ones with "the greatest exposure" in the Philippines debt crisis of the mid-1980s.

57. Joaquin Bernas, as quoted in Steinberg, *The Philippines*, 177.

58. A videotape of the ceremony can be found in the Peace Corps Archives, Washington.

59. Tracy Walmer, "Philippine Kidnap Spawns Questions," *USA Today*, 5 July 1990. See also Walmer, "Manila Says Peace Corps Pullout 'Rather Hasty,'" *USA Today*, 29 June 1990.

60. Eugenia Jamias, letter to author, 3 August 1993.

61. See, e.g., "Pulling Out the Peace Corps," *Newsweek*, 9 July 1990. See also Steven Erlanger, "Under Threat, Peace Corps Is Leaving Philippines," *New York Times*, 28 June 1990.

62. Bill McAllister, "Peace Corps Is Withdrawing Workers from Philippines," *Washington Post*, 28 June 1990.

63. "Ramos Rampant," *Economist*, 20 May 1995, 36.

64. *Congressional Budget Presentation, Fiscal Year 1996*, 98.

65. "Typhoon Hits Main Island in Philippines Killing 35," *New York Times*, 4 November 1995, 8. Two days later, as the results came in from the hinterlands, Associated Press reported the death toll had risen sharply. See Romy Tangbawan, "Philippines Storm Toll Rises to 500," *Messenger-Inquirer* (Owensboro, Ky.), 6 November 1995, 6A.

66. As reported on *Background Report*, Radio Australia, 27 August 1995. Ramos outlined his plans during a state visit to Australia.

67. See, e.g., Bob Drogin, "Dr. Condom Gets Scant Protection from Critics," *Los Angeles Times*, 11 May 1995, A10; and "Philippine Health Chief, Preaching Safe Sex, Stirs Wrath of Church," *New York Times*, 4 August 1993, A6.

68. Charles Dambach, "Hot on the Hill," *Three/One/Sixty-One*, winter 1995, 12.

69. Mark Gearan, as quoted in *Three/One/Sixty-One*, fall 1995, 2.

70. Ashabranner, *A Moment in History*, 173.

71. A recent list of "notable" Peace Corps alumni, dated 5 May 1995, contains fewer than 100 names and undoubtedly understates the number of former volunteers deserving notice by a factor of ten or twenty, if not more.

72. Francis Luzzatto, "The Vocation," in *Making a Difference*, ed. Viorst, 155.

73. Gearan, as quoted in *Three/One/Sixty-One*, fall 1995, 2.

10 Making a Difference

1. Alan Guskin, "Passing the Torch," in *Making a Difference*, ed. Viorst, 28.

2. *World View* 8 (spring 1995): 52, back cover.

3. M. Peter McPherson, "As a Development Agency," in *Making a Difference*, ed. Viorst, 100.

4. "Less Zeal Found for Peace Corps," *New York Times*, 4 April 1970, 1.

5. Excerpts taken from letters written to the author in 1993 and 1994 by Mark Pitzen, Rona Roberts, Leroy Hollenbeck, Steven K. Lahey, Ron George, John F. Rohe, Karl F. Jensen, Marilyn Chakroff, and Dina Kageler.

6. Warren W. Wiggins, "The Benefits," in *Making a Difference*, ed. Viorst, 76.

7. McPherson, "As a Development Agency," 104.

8. Jensen, letter to author, 7 July 1993.

9. McPherson, "As a Development Agency," 105.

10. Paul Theroux, "Reminiscence: Malawi," in *Making a Difference*, ed. Viorst,

85. In this article Theroux vents some of his anger toward the Peace Corps and the American government, but in the end he concludes that the Peace Corps has been a good thing.

11. "Déjà (PC) Vu," *Front Lines,* March 1990.

12. Susan K. Lowerre, "To Spend the Night Laughing," in *Going Up Country,* ed. John Coyne, 131.

13. Rona Roberts to "Dear Mom, Dad and Jonathan," 10 July 1973.

14. Rona Roberts to "Dear Mom and Dad," 14 May 1975.

15. Bain, *Sitting in Darkness,* 143.

16. Shaffer, *One Grain of Sand,* 211.

17. Arthur Goodfriend, "The Dimmed Ideal: The Peace Corps/Philippines after 20 Years," 9-10. A copy of this unpublished paper is in the Peace Corps Archives, Washington. The paper is an exceedingly critical appraisal of the Peace Corps program in the Philippines from 1979 to 1981. I do not know if its criticisms are valid.

18. Chakroff, conversation with the author, 15 May 1995.

19. Mark Pitzen, letter to author, 5 July 1993.

20. Lowell Lambert, "A Philippine Vacation," ca. 1981. A copy of this unpublished memoir was provided by its author.

21. The estimate for the worldwide total of annual financial aid to the Third World is based on data from the Organization for Economic Cooperation and Development.

22. McPherson, "As a Development Agency," 101.

23. John Dellenback, "The Future," in *Making a Difference,* ed. Viorst, 212.

24. McPherson, "As a Development Agency," 106.

25. Flavier, *Doctor to the Barrios,* 10.

26. See Francis Luzzatto, "The Vocation," in *Making a Difference,* ed. Viorst, 155, for a description of the effort at the Peace Corps to build a library of useful information.

27. Paul D. Peterson to Barry Devine, 24 January 1973, in untitled collection of volunteer letters, Peace Corps Archives, Washington.

28. Based on my limited survey, 7 percent of the volunteers became development professionals. If this were to hold true for the 150,000 Peace Corps veterans, it would mean a force of 10,500 development professionals, a group larger than the Peace Corps itself in the 1990s.

29. Leroy Hollenbeck, letter to author, 30 March 1994.

30. Dennis Walters, "Dear Barry," in Devine; Dottie Anderson, letter to author, 7 July 1993.

31. See "Indianapolis Peace Corps Volunteer Boosts Vegetable Production in Remote Philippine Village," ACTION press release, April 1972, Peace Corps Archives, Washington.

32. See "Peace Corps Volunteer from South Bend, Ind., Ends Three Years Service in Philippines, Joins International Rice Research Institute Staff," ACTION press release, November 1975, Peace Corps Archives, Washington.

33. Three successive "generations" were assigned to the monkey-eating eagle project during the 1970s. See "Rundquist's Complete Tour with Peace Corps," *Phillips Country News* (Montana), 25 December 1975; and "MSU, UM Alums End Peace Corps Study of Monkey-Eating Eagles in Philippines," *Great Falls Tribune* (Montana), 21 December 1975. See also Robert S. Kennedy, "Saving the Philippine Eagle," *National Geographic,* June 1981, 847-56.

34. See "Peace Corps Volunteer from Franklin Square Assists Philippines as Rural Health Worker," and "Wisconsin Peace Corps Volunteer Serves as Health Education Educator in the Philippines," both ACTION press releases, December 1975, Peace Corps Archives, Washington.

Bibliography

Amin, Julius. *The Peace Corps in Cameroon*. Kent, Ohio: Kent State University Press, 1992.

Ashabranner, Brent. *A Moment in History: The First Ten Years of the Peace Corps*. New York: Doubleday, 1971.

Bain, David Haward. *Sitting in Darkness: Americans in the Philippines*. Boston: Houghton Mifflin, 1984.

Beetle, Mel, and Brian Furby et al., eds. *Volunteer Life Styles*. Manila: Peace Corps/Philippines, 1975. (Copy available in Peace Corps Archives, Washington, D.C.)

Benjamin, Medea. *The Peace Corps and More: 120 Ways to Work, Study, and Travel in the Third World*. San Francisco: Global Exchange, 1993.

Blatchford, Joseph H. "Whatever Happened to the Peace Corps?" Speech. Business Club. California, May(?) 1969.

———. "New Policies: Untie Some Apron Strings," *Peace Corps Volunteer*, June 1969, 7-8. Peace Corps Archives, Washington, D.C.

———. "The Peace Corps in the 1970s." Address. Peace Corps Conference. Fredricksburg, Va., 29 August 1969.

———. "New Directions: Partnership in Development." Address. Tufts University. Boston, 20 October 1969.

———. Address. Boston University. Boston, 21 October 1969.

———. "In Pursuit of Lasting Peace." Address. Washington University. St. Louis, 29 October 1969.

———. Statement before the Subcommittee on Legislation and Military Operations of the House Committee on Government Operations. Washington, D.C., 29 April 1971.

———. "From a Noble Experiment . . . to a Continuing Obligation." Press release. Washington, D.C., fall 1971.

———. "The Peace Corps: Making It in the Seventies." *Foreign Affairs*, October 1970, 122-35.

Bonner, Raymond. *Waltzing with a Dictator: The Marcoses and the Making of American Policy*. New York: Times Books/Random House, 1987.

Boyce, James K. *The Philippines: The Political Economy of Growth and Impoverishment in the Marcos Era*. Honolulu: University of Hawaii Press, 1993.

Brainard, Cecilia Manguerra. *Philippine Woman in America.* Quezon City, Philippines: New Day, 1991.

Bremner, Robert H. *American Philanthropy.* Chicago: University of Chicago Press, 1960.

Bresnan, John, ed. *Crisis in the Philippines: The Marcos Era and Beyond.* Princeton: Princeton University Press, 1986.

Brown, Lester R. *The Green Revolution: The Role of the Volunteer as a Manpower Link.* Washington, D.C.: Peace Corps Office of Program Development, 1970.

Carey, Robert G. *The Peace Corps.* New York: Praeger, 1970.

Chakroff, Marilyn. *Freshwater Fish Pond Culture and Management.* Washington, D.C.: Peace Corps and Volunteers in Technical Assistance, 1976.

Coles, Robert. *The Call of Service: A Witness to Idealism.* Boston: Houghton Mifflin, 1993.

Constantino, Renato. *A History of the Philippines: From the Spanish Colonization to the Second World War.* New York: Monthly Review Press, 1975.

Costanzo, Richard. "Cross-cultural Adjustment among Peace Corps Volunteers." Ph.D. diss., 1981, University of Chicago.

Coyne, John, ed. *Going Up Country: Travel Essays by Peace Corps Writers.* New York: Scribner, 1994.

Coyne, John, et al., eds. *To Touch the World: The Peace Corps Experience.* Washington, D.C.: Peace Corps, 1995.

Day, Beth. *The Philippines: Shattered Showcase of Democracy in Asia.* New York: M. Evans, 1974.

Devine, Barry, ed. Untitled Collection of Letters. Manila: PeaceCorps/Philippines, September 1973. [Copy available in Peace Corps Archives, Washington, D.C.]

Drew, Elizabeth B. "Reports: Washington." *Atlantic,* July 1970, 6-9.

Flavier, Juan M. *Back to the Barrios.* Quezon City, Philippines: New Day, 1978.

———. *My Friends in the Barrios.* Quezon City, Philippines: New Day, 1974.

———. *Doctor to the Barrios.* Quezon City, Philippines: New Day, 1970.

Fuchs, Lawrence H. *Those Peculiar Americans: The Peace Corps and American National Character.* New York: Meredith Press, 1967.

Gans, Herbert. *The Levittowners: Ways, Life, and Politics in a New Suburban Community.* New York: Pantheon, 1967.

Gates, John Morgan. *Schoolbooks and Krags: The United States Army in the Philippines, 1898-1902.* Westport, Conn.: Greenwood Press, 1973.

Guerrero Nakpil, Carmen. *A Question of Identity: Selected Essays.* Manila: Vessel Books, 1973.

Halberstam, David. *The Best and the Brightest.* New York: Random House, 1969.

———. *The Fifties.* New York: Villard, 1993.

Haldeman, H.R. *The Haldeman Diaries: Inside the Nixon White House.* New York: Putnam, 1994.

Hapgood, David and Meridan Bennett. *Agents of Change: A Close Look at the Peace Corps.* Boston: Little, Brown, n.d.

Hebl, Sharon, ed. *Peace Corps Roller Coaster: The Letters of Dan and Lisa Hebl.* Eau Claire, Wisc.: Heins, 1994.

Jonas, Gerald. *On Doing Good.* New York: Scribner, 1971.

Karnow, Stanley. *In Our Image: America's Empire in the Philippines.* New York: Ballantine Books/Random House, 1989.

Kennedy, Geraldine, ed. *From the Center of the Earth: Stories out of the Peace Corps.* Santa Monica: Clover Park Press, 1991.

Kennedy, Robert S. "Saving the Philippine Eagle." *National Geographic,* June 1981, 847-56.

Kittler, Glenn D. *The Peace Corps.* New York: Paperback Library, 1963.

Kluge, P.F. *The Edge of Paradise: America in Micronesia.* New York: Random House, 1991.

Lacoff, Cheryl Klein, ed. *Who's Who in the Peace Corps.* Greenwich, Conn.: Reference Press International, 1993.

Lavinal, Françoise. "Le Peace Corps: Une Histoire Critique d'une Utopie." Ph.D. diss., Institute Universitaire de Technologie Paul Sabatier, 1996.

Leech, Margaret. *In the Days of McKinley.* New York: Harper and Brothers, 1959.

Leuchtenburg, William E. *The Great Age of Change.* Vol. 12 of The *Life* History of the United States. New York: Time, 1964.

Lightfoot, Keith. *The Philippines.* Nations of the Modern World. New York: Praeger, 1973.

Lowther, Kevin and C. Payne Lucas. *Keeping Kennedy's Promise.* Boulder, Colo.: Westview Press, 1978.

Manchester, William. *American Caesar: Douglas MacArthur, 1880-1964.* Boston: Little, Brown, 1978.

———. *The Glory and the Dream: A Narrative History of America, 1932-1972.* Boston: Little, Brown, 1974; reprint, New York: Bantam Books, 1990.

Mencken, H.L. *A New Dictionary of Quotations.* New York: Alfred A. Knopf, 1942.

Packard, Vance. *The Hidden Persuaders.* New York: Pocket Books, 1981.

Packer, George. *The Village of Waiting.* New York: Vintage Books, 1988.

Pascarella, Ernest T., and Patrick T. Terenzini. *How College Affects Students.* San Francisco: Jossey-Bass, 1991.

Pecson, Geronima T., and Maria Racelis, eds. *Tales of the American Teachers in the Philippines.* Manila: Carmelo and Bauermann, 1959.

Peters, Jens. *Philippines: A Travel Survival Kit.* Oakland, Calif.: Lonely Planet, 1994.

Raney, Jane. *Peace Corps's Third Goal.* Bellingham: Center for Pacific Northwest Studies, Western Washington University, 1988.

Ramos, Teresita V. and Josie Clausen. *Filipino Word Book*. Honolulu: Bess Press, 1993.

Redmon, Coates. *Come As You Are: The Peace Corps Story*. San Diego: Harcourt Brace Jovanovich, 1986.

Reeves, T. Zane. *The Politics of the Peace Corps and VISTA*. Tuscaloosa: University of Alabama Press, 1988.

Rice, Gerard T. *The Bold Experiment: JFK's Peace Corps*. Notre Dame: University of Notre Dame Press, 1985.

———. *Twenty Years of the Peace Corps*. Washington, D.C.: Peace Corps, 1981.

Roces, Alfredo and Grace. *Culture Shock!* Singapore: Times Books International, 1986.

Rostow, W.W. *The Process of Economic Growth*. 2d ed. New York: W.W. Norton, 1962.

Roszak, Theodore. *The Making of the Counter Culture*. New York: Pantheon, 1970.

Schumacher, Ernst F. *Small Is Beautiful*. New York: Harper, 1973.

Schwarz, Karen. *What You Can Do for Your Country: Inside the Peace Corps: A Thirty-Year History*. New York: Anchor/Doubleday, 1991.

Schwimmer, Brian E., and D. Michael Warren, eds. *Anthropology and the Peace Corps: Case Studies in Career Preparation*. Ames: Iowa State University Press, 1993.

Searles, P. David. *A College for Appalachia: Alice Lloyd on Caney Creek*. Lexington: University Press of Kentucky, 1995.

Shaffer, Steve M. *One Grain of Sand: A Peace Corps/Philippines Experience*. Orlando, Fla.: Gasat, 1988.

Skelton, James W., Jr. *Volunteering in Ethiopia: A Peace Corps Odyssey*. Denver: Beaumont Books, 1991.

Skinner, Michelle Cruz. *Balikbayan: A Filipino Homecoming*. Honolulu: Bess Press, 1988.

Stanley, Peter W. *A Nation in the Making: The Philippines and the United States, 1899-1921*. Cambridge: Harvard University Press, 1974.

———, ed. *Reappraising an Empire: New Perspectives on Philippine-American History*. Cambridge: Harvard University Press, 1984.

Steigerwald, David. *The Sixties and the End of Modern America*. St. Martin's Series in U.S. History. New York: St. Martin's Press, 1995.

Steinberg, David Joel. *The Philippines: A Singular and a Plural Place*. Boulder, Colo.: Westview Press, 1994.

Sullivan, George E. *The Story of the Peace Corps*. New York: Fleet, 1964.

Sullivan, William H. *Obbligato, 1939-1979: Notes on a Foreign Service Career*. New York: W.W. Norton, 1984.

Thomsen, Moritz. *The Saddest Pleasure: A Journey on Two Rivers*. Seattle: Gray Wolf Press, 1990.

———. *The Farm on the River of Emeralds*. New York: Houghton Mifflin, 1978.

————. *Living Poor: A Peace Corps Chronicle.* Seattle: University of Washington Press, 1969.

Thomson, James C., Jr., Peter W. Stanley, and Curtis Perry, eds. *Sentimental Imperialists: The American Experience in East Asia.* New York: Harper and Row, 1981.

Tidwell, Mike. *The Ponds of Kalambayi: An African Sojourn.* New York: Lyons and Burford, 1990.

Tolley, Howard, Jr. "Five Years of the Nixon Peace Corps." *National Affairs,* November 1974, 96-98.

U.S. House of Representatives Committee on Foreign Affairs. *The Peace Corps in the 1970s: New Directions vs. Tradition.* 93d Congress, 1st sess. Washington, D.C.: Government Printing Office, 1973.

————. *The Peace Corps in West Africa.* 94th Congress, 1st sess. Washington, D.C.: Government Printing Office, 1975.

Viorst, Milton, ed. *Making a Difference: The Peace Corps at Twenty-Five.* New York: Weidenfeld and Nicolson, 1986.

Weitsman, Madeline. *The Peace Corps: Know Your Government.* New York: Chelsea House, 1989.

Whyte, William H., Jr. *The Organization Man.* New York: Simon and Schuster, 1956.

Wilson, Sloan. *The Man in the Gray Flannel Suit.* New York: Simon and Schuster, 1955.

Wofford, Harris. *Of Kennedys and Kings: Making Sense of the Sixties.* Pittsburgh: University of Pittsburgh Press, 1980.

Wolfert, Ira. *American Guerrilla in the Philippines.* New York: Simon and Schuster, 1945.

Index